Into the World

Note on illustrations: This book contains original artworks by Leila Lees not previously published, these works are uncaptioned and are dispersed throughout the book. It also references a number of classic artworks. These works are captioned.

Tipi Press,
an imprint of Lasavia Publishing Ltd.
Auckland, New Zealand

www.lasaviapublishing.com

Copyright ©Leila Lees, 2019

This book is copyright including original images by Leila Lees. Apart from any fair dealing for the purpose of private study, research, criticism or reviews, as permitted under the Copyright Act, no part of this book, excluding non-original referenced artworks, may be reproduced by any process without the permission of the publishers.

designed by Daniela Gast

ISBN: 978-0-9951165-4-2

Into the World

a Handbook for Mystical and Shamanic Practice

Leila Lees

in memory of Piripai

*My mother groaned! My father wept.
Into the dangerous world I leapt,*

                      William Blake

Contents

Introduction

18

Getting Started

22	dedication
22	integrating sacred and ordinary
23	taking space
23	simple rituals (activity)
24	journaling
25	reflection (activity)

Ethics

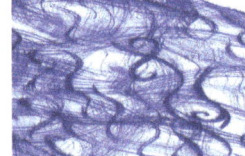

28	living ethics
30	borrowing indigenous spiritual concepts
30	in your journal (activity)

the Medicine Sphere

34	from medicine wheel to medicine sphere
34	the cardinal directions
37	the in-between directions
38	the centre, the above and the below
39	walking the medicine sphere in the tropics
41	origin
42	creating a medicine sphere (activity)
43	visualising the sphere
44	the mystery
44	seven steps (activity)
45	letting go (activity)

the Co-Creative Circle

48	invoking spirit
49	intention
50	co-creativity in society and community
51	medicine and gesture
53	our gift
54	the talking stick
55	in your journal (activity)

Land

58	protocol
60	intention in land healing
63	essence of landscape
64	spirit guardians
65	the etheric body of the earth
65	memory of water
67	impact of people and the language of landscape
69	wounds, gifts and mirrors
70	finding your power place (activity)
70	in your journal (activity)

Nature Connection

74	observation, research and journaling
76	seeing with the heart (activity)
76	guardianship
77	sensory meditation (activity)
78	discomfort, fear and hazards
79	gratitude
80	Prayer of gratitude (activity)
82	walking
84	walking meditation and gatha (activity)
84	in your journal (activity)

Chickweed

86   description
87   essence

the Shamanic Journey and Visioning

90   imaginative consciousness
91   preparing for journeying
92   notes on terminology
92   difficulties and dangers in journeying

the Power Animal

97   finding your power animal (shamanic journey)
98   the power animal and individuality
98   separation from and connection with the animal kingdom
101   power animal as medicine
102   the weka: a cool thief
103   field trip: a visit to the zoo (activity)

Ritual

108   conducting rituals
109   the magic salt cellar – Scandinavian folk tale
110   sacred and ordinary
110   lighting a candle (activity)
111   creating a sacred place (activity)

Awakening Our Inner Selves

114	authenticity
114	compulsion to serve
115	nourishment
116	in your journal (activity)
117	structure and space
118	roles
118	flicking-out
119	fear
119	crisis
120	lightness of heart
120	power and the energy beyond thought
121	in your journal (activity)

Cleaver

124	description
125	essence
125	prayer
128	prayer to the great spirit
129	the element of air
129	the brain
131	letting go
131	the shadow of cleavers and intention

Clearing

134	entities
135	attending to the physical
136	clearing, merging and absorbing energy
138	technique
139	finding your own clearing processes
139	physical cleansing in our body
140	shadow projections and soul loss
140	in your journal (activity)

Body Dreaming

144 training exercise (activity)
145 body dreaming on others in a professional context
145 stories

Symbolic Language

149 revelatory receiving
150 deepening your understanding of symbols
152 a walk in the forest
153 in your journal (activity)

Comfrey

156 background
156 description
157 essence

the Teacher and the Realms of the Upper World

160 the upper world
160 finding your spiritual teacher (shamanic journey)
162 the spiritual teacher
163 the trickster as teacher
164 places of learning (shamanic journey)

Wisdom and Knowledge

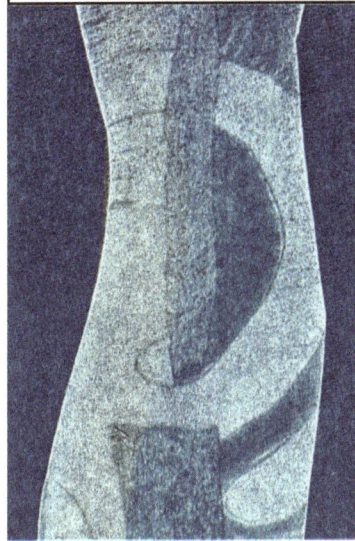

168	learning
169	integrating extraordinary experiences
169	in your journal (activity)
170	nga kete o te wananga – the three baskets of knowledge
173	the three wisdoms
173	the first wisdom
173	the second wisdom
174	the third wisdom
175	belief systems and patterns
176	temperance
177	questions to ponder
178	contemplation (activity)
179	observational meditation (activity)

Bittercress

183	description
183	essence

the Warrior

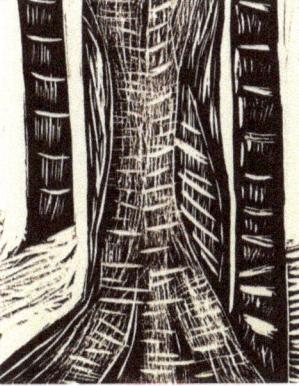

184	the warrior spirit guide
185	finding your warrior (shamanic journey)
186	blame and projection
187	petty tyrants
190	metanoia
190	death and the unknown (shamanic journey)
192	standing meditation (activity)
193	presence of action
194	a samurai warrior's creed

Dandelion

198	description
199	essence
200	the sun
200	the seed

the Beneath

204	connecting with our spiritual ancestors (shamanic journey)
205	the wise one (shamanic journey)
206	Finn McCool and the Salmon of Knowledge
208	the underworld
209	earth beings
210	journal extract
212	the element of earth
213	talking to the earth (activity)
213	in your journal (activity)
215	earth prayer

Scotch Thistle

218	background
218	description
219	essence

Ancestral Work

- 222 whakapapa
- 224 my ancestral journey
- 225 ancestry imprinted on land
- 227 in your journal (activity)
- 228 the ancestral ally and the place of the ancestors (shamanic journey)
- 229 ancestral patterning
- 231 work on ancestral patterning
- 230 heirlooms
- 232 sharing stories (activity)
- 232 forgiveness (activity)

Origin

- 237 early morning observation
- 238 spiritual work and science
- 239 the creation of the universe
- 241 the rope of mankind
- 242 ethnic groups and belonging
- 244 morphic resonance
- 245 connecting to the circle of elders (shamanic journey)
- 245 free writing
- 246 in this world

- 249 Appendix Lasavia Vibrational Remedies
- 253 Annotated Bibliography
- 261 Index

Acknowledgements

This book would not have been possible without the support and input of others. I am especially grateful to my editor, Rowan Sylva, for the amount of work he put in, his critical questioning and his support. My gratitude and love to my partner, Mike, for the lively discussions, his patience, encouragement and sense of humour. My appreciation to Deah Swift who has stood by my side through thick and thin, offering practical and emotional support. Thanks to Daniela Gast for her passion, wonderful eye for design and for bringing forward my illustrations. Thanks to Odette Wards for her eagle eye. Thanks to Alexis Neal for opening me up to printmaking. Thanks to Chalice Malcom for encouraging me to provide original material for the Lasavia course, from which this book would eventually emerge. Thanks to Leanne Tamaki for her generosity in contributing her writing on Nga Kite o te Wananga. Further thanks to Rhiannon Boelens, Charissa Snijders, Meggan Young and Steffi Kurz. Thanks to the numerous other students, colleagues and groups who have shared in my exploration.

Introduction

We learn because we desire to understand our experiences. That is the fundamental dynamic of my life, and, as it seems to me that everything is constantly evolving, so I have become the eternal student of life. I wrote and rewrote *Into the World* over years of teaching shamanic practices, and exploring spiritual experience, alchemy, plant medicine and nature. I worked on *Into the World* because I needed a structure to support people's understanding in matters of spirituality, wisdom and heart.

My experiences, and by extension the content of this book, have a paradoxical component. I feel ill at ease with cultural borrowing, and yet it was through studying shamanism and reading books about indigenous practices that enabled me to find the interweave between the spiritual and nature which I loved. I am dismayed by new age spiritualism – which I sometimes feel is ungrounding and ego boosting – yet it is the category I am often put into by others. I feel uncomfortable around guru worship and yet I have a leadership role in a spiritual organisation. I was brought up an atheist and feel deeply uneasy around religions and yet I often experienced uplifting and deep shifts in consciousness when I was around those dedicated to the spirit and to God and was drawn to the mystical aspects of the great religions. In coming to terms with my gift I have been ever a reluctant participant, preferring to place others before me, and practise my work in secret. Thus, for me to publish this book, is also a step into the world.

All my training and absorption of knowledge, whether I willed it or not, drew me to the role of the healer, work that is fundamentally a service to people and the environment. My path wound circuitously through study and the practices of colour healing, homeopathy, massage, Chinese medicine, herbalism, energy healing, auric reading, gestalt therapy, shamanic counselling, soul retrieval, plant medicine and flower essence work. The healer was a role that I resisted and rejected where I could because of the stigma of the healer. But all I was really doing was resisting my own gift.

Vibrational medicines gave me a structure that I could teach with. It is through their development that this book emerged. The gesture of the wild weeds that are interspersed throughout this book is quintessential to this teaching. These weeds are important as they are persistent. Often, we reject them or they simply become invisible to us in their commonality. I see this as a metaphor for the societal denial of the invisible world beyond the physical.

I wanted people to notice the ordinary and see how the sacred is fused within it. I was tired of the 'specialness' associated with spiritual experiences. I felt these experiences were part of an ongoing evolution and our job was to integrate them and understand them where we could. I started to respect ritual and guardianship of knowledge in the spirit plane. As I worked deeper, I saw the need to teach ethical foundation and at the core to see ourselves as part of the world and be aware of how we impact the energetic fabric of the world. My intention is that this book creates a framework to enable the reader to explore the energy behind the physical and to realise öthe sacred within the ordinary.

Getting Started

Dedication

Any form of training takes dedication and discipline, and spiritual practice is no different. It's the everyday simple practices that matter. This book approaches how we come into our authentic self and aims to help the reader express their inner nature. This may mean change. Often because of dramatic, even traumatic, shifts and changes in our external world, we hold onto things that are familiar, even if they do not serve us. To allow positive change to occur we need to be willing to walk into unknown territory. If we simply keep walking, then gradually the changing landscape becomes familiar. Another way of looking at this is to trust the process itself. We often lose our points of reference when we venture into unknown territory and this is where dedication is helpful. It can be a reminder of our inner desire, as we tend to desire yet resist transformational experiences. A dedication can be a letter written to ourselves where we write down our intention, what we love and remind ourselves what is important in our lives. This simple practice can become that inner reference point and can help realign ourselves when the going gets tough.

Integrating the Sacred with the Ordinary

In creating our own spiritual practice, it is important that we carry what we learn with us. A person may attend a workshop on spiritual practices. They take time out of their lives and experience a spaciousness, a connection they haven't felt before. Yet when they go back into their lives there is no room for what they have experienced to enter and be part of their everyday lives. This form of compartmentalizing spiritual work and putting it outside of everyday life is like shutting out a piece of yourself from living with you. This may be because there is a fear that spirit might disrupt the ordered world. I see the world as what we evolve with, we are finding out how to live and grow in all our relationships. Integrating the sacred and ordinary experiences into everyday life is important. It takes time and conscious effort.

Taking Space

We live in a demanding and often distracting environment, there is so much jostling for our attention that we may lose our purpose or be overwhelmed so that we find it hard to centre ourselves. As we go about our day, take space to consciously slow down, connect to a tree through observation, or try extending our senses. In these moments where I pause, I often experience a feeling of timelessness, like I have been lifted outside time's linear movement. A way of remembering to do this is to choose a reminder signal in your life. You may decide that your signal could be hearing a song thrush, or seeing a kingfisher, these act as reminders to pause and connect.

Simple Rituals

If we start out with a desire to be more present in our life, we can assist this by bringing in rituals. The key to these rituals is simplicity. It might be that we carry an object with us that we can connect to when needed. A simple ritual can support transitions between one activity and another. Drinking a cup of tea in a way that we are participating in a conscious way with the material world might be a ritual. When we wake up, we may light a candle, have a moment of quiet, or speak our intentions, for the day, out loud. Lighting the candle is a ritual that creates an inner focus. Speaking our intention generates dedication. Blowing it out ends the ritual. Simple yet powerful, this practice starts us experiencing the place that choice has in our lives.

Journaling

> I had discovered that the journal was my most powerful ally in crafting the kind of life I wanted. I was building a scaffolding of choices and attitudes, forging affinities, discovering what colours, places, times of the day I could truly call mine.
>
> Hannah Hinchman, American artist and writer

Journaling can help integrate an experience while helping you explore your practice through reflective questioning. Journaling may combine nature observation, personal insight, as well as dreams and visions. This kaleidoscopic reflection of life may show up our patterns and aid us in becoming open to new opportunities. Inner exploration is an adventure and how we perceive this is worthy of being recorded. Journaling, moreover, will aid you in bringing that inner observation to the everyday world. I encourage you to begin by observing the commonplace, the plants and animals around you and the seasons and the moon cycles. By journaling, we may see the patterns around us and how we impact and are impacted by our landscape.

A journal is a private exploration and therefore does not need to be shared with others unless it feels right. Sometimes when we have an experience that is hard to understand we try to understand it by placing it into our limited belief patterning. Rather than do this I would encourage you to write it down. You are not forcing it to be anything other than the experience. As you write a thought, a feeling may arise and you can jot it down on the side. Some people write down the experience as it is on one side of the page and then note down their feelings to that experience on the opposite page. All of this helps us to integrate and acknowledge events, ordinary and extraordinary. Some experiences may only begin to make sense later.

There are many good books on nature journaling, artistic journaling or adventure journaling, and if you are new to it, a good first step is to go to the library and see how others do it.

> How big the world is, how big and how wonderful. It comes to me as ridiculously presumptuous that I should dare to carry my little personality half across it.
>
> Gertrude Bell, writer, traveller and archaeologist (1868–1926)

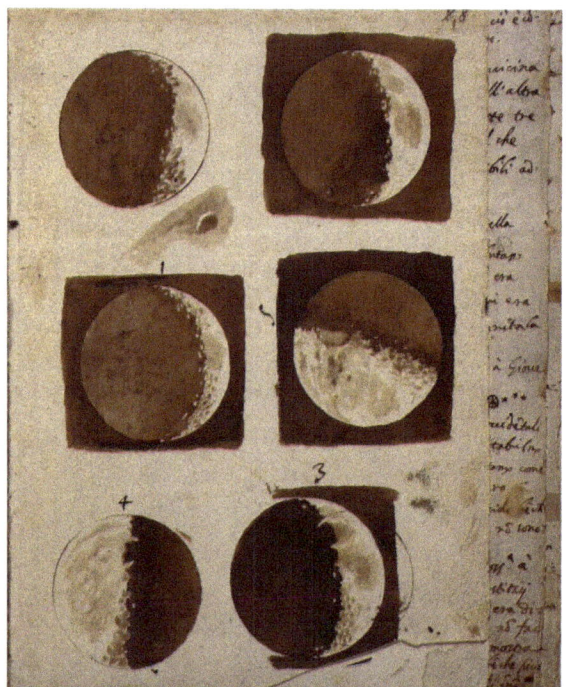

Reflection

> If you can look back over a long life and see that you have owned your choices, then there is little ground for resentment. Bitterness comes to those who look back with regret on the choices imposed upon them. The greatest creative challenge is the struggle to be the architect of your own life. It was through travel that I became a writer, and it was through the wonder of being a writer that I learned to be patient, not to compromise and give my destiny time to find me. And it all began with those first journals, and that promise to 'risk discomfort for understanding.'
>
> Wade Davis, Canadian-Colombian anthropologist

Reflection is the ability to be alone and look at how we are doing in relationship to the many people, things to attend to and situations that arise in our lives. Sometimes reflection is strenuous as it's about a consciousness as to who we are and the shadows that show up in our responses to our lives. Journaling supports reflection as we write down our thoughts and then see them from a different perspective. We can be in dialogue with ourselves, uncovering ways that we perceive, and even conditioning, sorting out what feels true to us and what might be imposed by others. The following reflection practice is something you can do at the end of the day. Find somewhere comfortable you can sit without interruption and play your day backwards in your mind. Start with the things you did a few minutes ago and keep moving backwards until you get to the point at which you awoke. Allow yourself to be neutral, you are watching through your mind's eye. You may wish to sense in your body, you may wish to take note of how your body reacts to replaying certain events.

Reflection is about how. How am I when I meet with such and such? How am I when I do this action or that action? How could I be? How is my life being disrupted? How do I let my life be disrupted? How can I be with the natural demands of my life? Are those demands normal or am I creating a demanding monster by fulfilling those needs? Ultimately, reflection brings forward one of the most important aspects of how we run our lives – where do we choose to place our energies.

Galileo's drawings of the moon, c. 1609

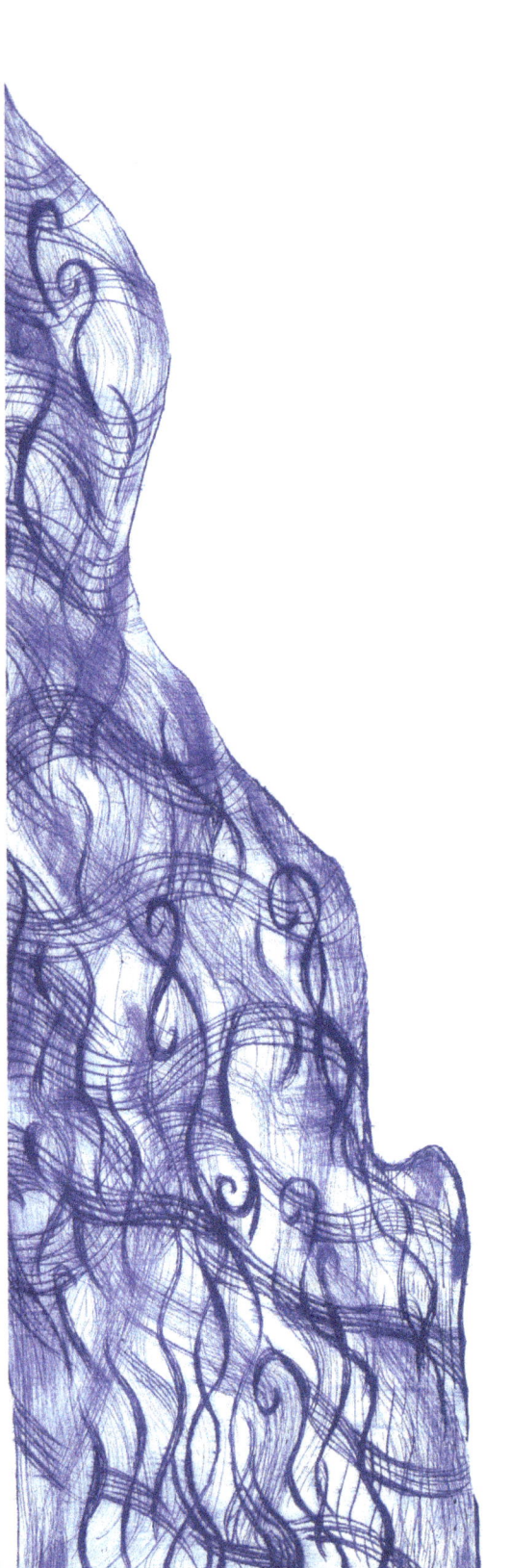

Ethics

Living Ethics

I have always been thoughtful around rules that govern our behaviour. I have seen the impact of righteousness on a group, ostracising and splitting people from family, friends and community. I witnessed how righteousness could warp the notion of ethics by shaming and focusing on one demeanour, blowing it out of proportion, whilst others were unable to act ethically in the face of the righteous. In those moments I wondered where was the heart, the understanding of the whole, the creation of space for self-reflection. It was from these kinds of experiences within groups that I started to realise the importance of growing and keeping alive an inner ethical foundation rather than look externally for guidance. When people gather together for the purpose of spiritual work, patterns of defensive behaviour arise simply because change is taking place. To me, ethics is about relationships, the heart, and how we respond through the heart.

I have discovered over the years that the most usual way people learn about shamanic practices and alchemy is in short weekend workshops. I used to think that if people had attended lots of these workshops they would be well trained in shamanic work. But I discovered that when they are *in circle* they are ill practised in respectful process. They are in fact beginners. Ethics is not something separate from what we practise, but it is within the work itself. If people are coming and going to different circles they are not

> I cannot but have reverence for all that is called life... That is the beginning and foundation of morality. Once a man has experienced it and continues to do so – and he who has once experienced it will continue to do so – he is ethical. He carries his morality within him and can never lose it, for it continues to develop within him.
>
> Albert Schweitzer, French-German theologian (1875–1965)

> Ethics, apprehended by a loving heart, contribute to a sense of harmony and trust through right relationships and sensitivity to appropriate boundaries.
>
> Kabir Helminski, author and translator of Islamic, Sufi wisdom

having to work together with the same people over a few months. Working together in respectful practice over time enables a greater reflection of our own challenges and shadows.

An ethical foundation can be understood like a walking stick that can support us when we are only beginning to open up to our moral sensitivity. When our moral sensitivity is strong, we no longer need it. Simple processes like questioning our assumptions, giving positive feedback and reflecting on our reactions, help to strengthen our moral sensitivity.

When we form a group we share a purpose. We learn the most when we are able to work co-creatively with a group. In brief, this means that we gather with some purpose and we give space to each other through *being with* each other. I put the emphasis on *being with* because it is a process of deep listening and empathy. Groups are difficult for many people for a variety of reasons. Many participants have been wounded by people who have some kind of power within a group, these wounds have happened through family, through cults and through spiritual groups and therapy groups.

Facilitating effectively with patterns of pain and vulnerability takes skill and requires an innate ethical foundation. It also requires a continued personal journey of reflection and spiritual practice. Kylea Taylor, in her book *Ethics of Caring* writes 'The degree of our willingness to delve into the dark truth of our own motivations, desires and fears will determine our ability to be caring, flexible and ethical.' This is true, I see within myself and others that my mistakes, assumptions and misaligned reactions are always triggered by my own survival patterns or anxieties. The ability to reflect healthily upon our mistakes is an important practice in growing our work within an ethical framework.

Borrowing Indigenous Spiritual Concepts

In developing my spiritual practice, as well as finding a language to express my spiritual understandings, I have borrowed widely from different cultures, writers and religions. In using these concepts, I am conscious that I am reshaping them into tools for my own work. Reading widely and borrowing terms and concepts enriches our practice and understanding. However, it is important that we do not claim to own those concepts, we are conscious of the cultures from which we are borrowing and we borrow only with the utmost respect.

Borrowing is particularly problematic when we are borrowing from colonised indigenous cultures which may have been subject to genocidal colonial policies, and who may view the use of their concepts as appropriation. My relationship with Māori spiritual concepts is a long one beginning in my earliest childhood. I have gradually grown more comfortable with my use of some Māori concepts, but as a pakeha coming to terms with the history of colonisation is a lifelong journey. In North America, the United States army forced hundreds of tribal groups off their land. Most of them starved to death on barren reservations. Their spiritual beliefs were once a cause of their persecution. I do use some North American indigenous concepts, most notably the medicine wheel and shamanic journeying. I do so in full respect and with an awareness of the open wounds of colonisation.

in Your Journal

In your journal write down five values that are important to you. Under each value write down what this means to you. Research what other people write about these values. Start to engage in an inner dialogue around these values and your actions. How do your actions and your values connect? Think of this as an ongoing exploration.

Explore how you feel about making mistakes and the value of mistakes. Look at the roles you have in your life. Do some roles have certain ethical practices? How do these roles and ethical practices overlap in your life? Take time to reflect and write. Share your ideas and reflections with others.

Start to write down the mistakes you make in your life. In this process, the mistakes may not actually always be the mistakes that you think they are. Any wobbles or feelings of mistakes can actually be the most interesting and educational moments. By journaling them you are picking up on the edge of your growth and gathering insight about your own values and ethics.

an Old Woman and an Old Man Conversing While Holding on to Their Walking Sticks, c. 1630, etching, Rembrandt

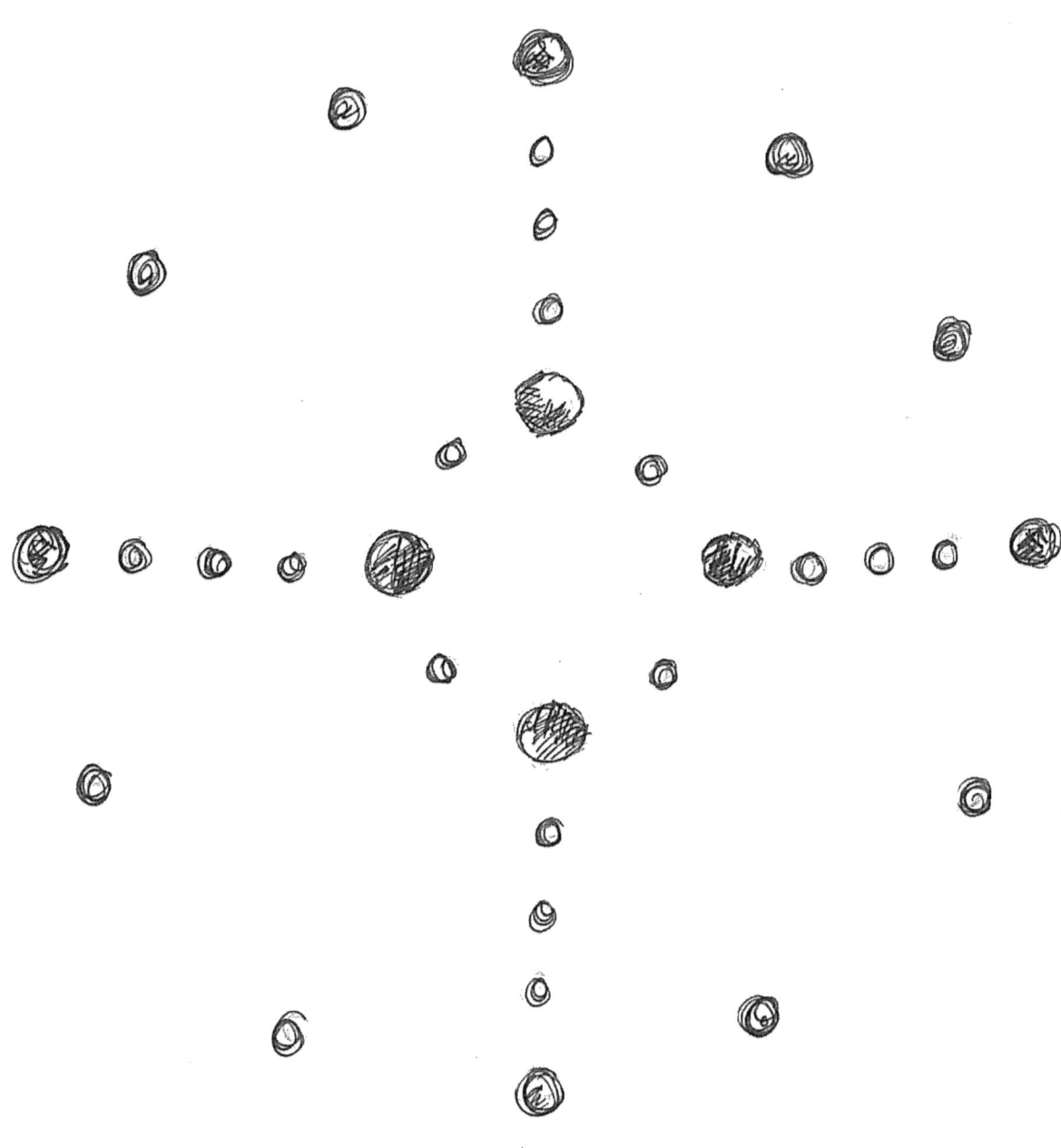

The Medicine Sphere

from Medicine Wheel to Medicine Sphere

The phrase *medicine sphere* emerged from teaching a workshop on the medicine wheel. A medicine wheel is usually formed by a circle of stones. These stones represent the four directions – East, North, West and South. The in-between directions may also be delineated, creating a circle or wheel. This circle represents the natural cycles of life and in particular the path of the sun as it moves from morning to day, to evening and to night. In engaging in the medicine wheel, we work with the cycles. This means in walking the medicine wheel we walk in a sunwise direction. In the southern hemisphere we walk anti-clockwise going from east to north and in the northern hemisphere we go clockwise from east to south. Alternatively, you may simply place things down in a circle and traverse through the imaginal mind. The concept of the sphere comes from adding three more directions: the centre, the above, and the below.

The term medicine sphere brings the attention to the above and the below, but it also allows me to distance myself from, the medicine wheel, an indigenous North American spiritual concept on which much has been written. The medicine sphere as discussed below is an interweave of indigenous lore and my own original thought and practice. I would, therefore, like to give my gratitude to the generosity of wisdom from the indigenous traditions that I have here borrowed.

Cardinal Directions

People often desire to categorise what lies in each direction, but I consider it better to experience the medicine sphere as a series of pathways. To begin, look at the simple things that you see and experience in each direction.

I face the east. I feel the warmth of the sun, there is dew on the plants so everything is sparkling. Sometimes the way the sun reflects through the dew has a rainbow effect. Everything is clear, I become particularly aware of the butterflies and I am reminded of emergence.

I face the north in the midday sun, there is a height of expansion. The cicadas are singing at full volume. There is little shadow. I experience an opening. This opening comes in the form of surrender. At the same time, I feel life bursting forth. The bees are humming. The chamomile attracts my attention, particularly the yellow heads with the small white petals falling back.

In the west, the shadows are elongating. It is evening. The tui and bellbirds are the last birds of the day to sing. They usher in the night as they usher in the day. As the sun sets, we naturally enter into a reflective time, a going-within space. The ruru (owl) will enter here and nourish us. The cricket will sing through the darkness. The first stars appear.

As we turn to the south, the night is at its depth. In darkness we see with the inner eye. The night has the unknown and the unseen. Our listening, our sense of smell and touch, become more acute. There is an experience of stillness and timelessness. Here, I am aware of the mountains in the South Island, the large wild oceans south towards Antarctica. I see the stars and I become aware of the movement of the universe.

I turn east and pause. I feel centred. I have traversed and experienced a cycle. I am at the beginning again, but I am not, because I am at a different place within myself. This illustrates the spiral nature of the medicine sphere.

I can express a pathway around the medicine sphere through gesture. To the east, I move my hands outwards in an open posture. As I move towards the north, I extend the arms, lifting the breastbone, an open posture. In the west, I bring forward a reflective posture, a prayer. In the south, a stillness.

The next time I move around I might find the particular direction I am most drawn to. There may be a symbol that I am shown, or a story reflected to me. It might show me an aspect of service or a new way of looking.

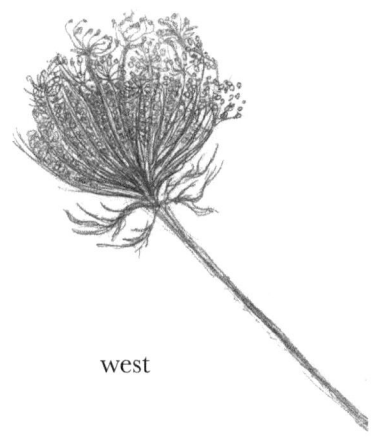

west

north

south

east

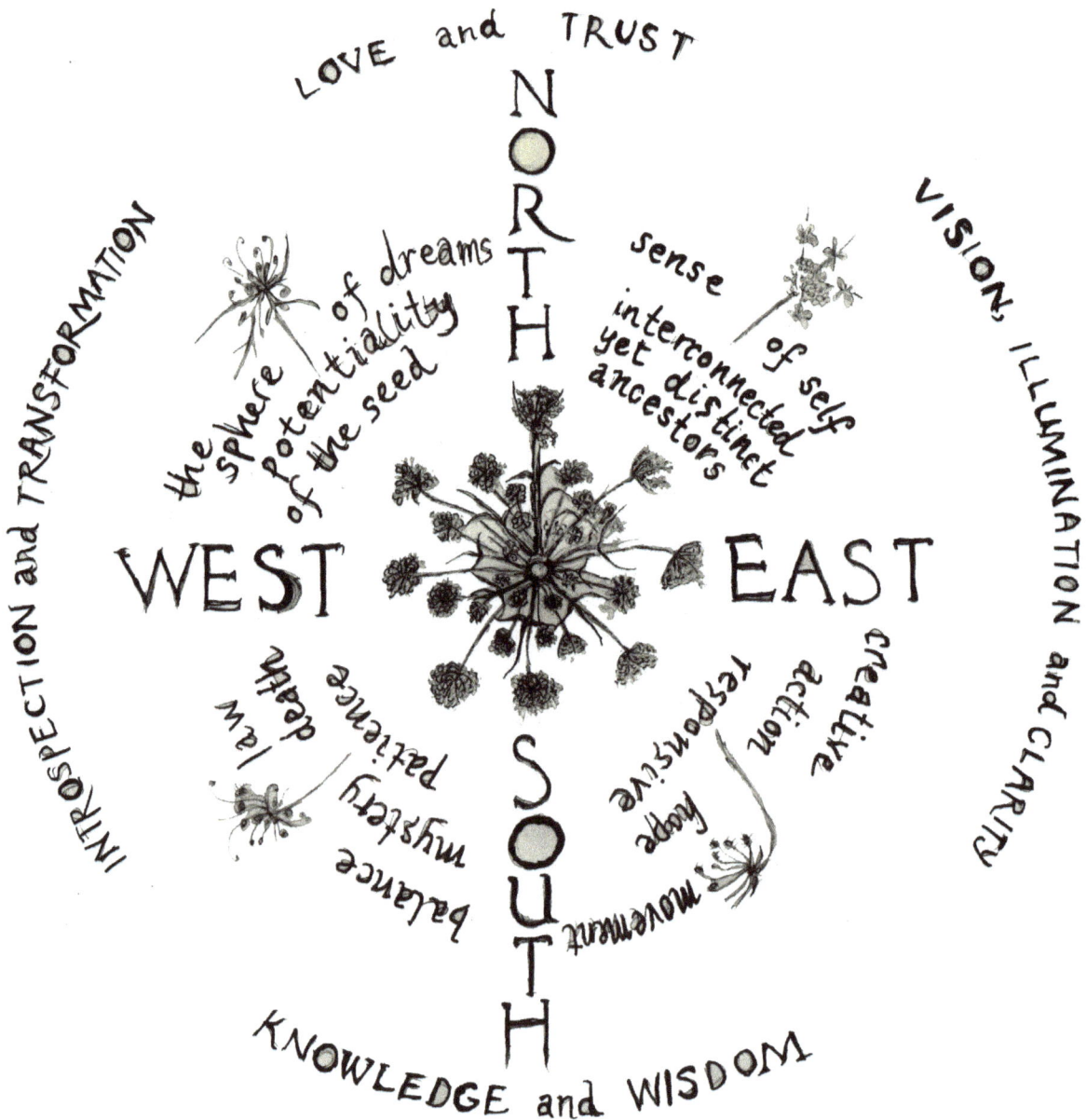

the In-Between Directions

The in-between directions, the northeast, the northwest, the southwest and the southeast signify the transitory phases between the cardinal directions. It is through these transitional phases that we move deeper into the medicine sphere. I visualize these as layers of cyclic labyrinthine pathways or as doorways to the betwixt and between. More simply they can be imagined as quadrants of a sphere. Each segment has depth and height. As we journey through the directions we can also journey across the dimensions of the upper and lower parts of the sphere. In each aspect of the medicine sphere are the shadow and the light, spirit and matter.

We are moving sunwise. In the southern hemisphere, we are moving from east to north. Starting at the east, a place of vision, illumination and clarity, we move to the northeast, where we experience ourselves as distinct from all that is around us. We are sensitive to our place within the inter-connective web of life. I also experience an acute awareness of my socialization, how I am brought up to see things, and connect with others. The northeast is a gateway to the ancestors and the history of place.

We move to the north. The north is about trust and love. This may be where we experience uncertainty. Here we can examine past experiences that cause us to hesitate.

The northwest quadrant is where I see the seed forming. Here is potentiality through dream. As we aspire to express our gift, we also begin to shed what is an encumbrance to that expression. The northwest is the sphere of the dream world.

The west is the sphere of transformation and introspection; finding our essential power through nourishment and humility. We examine our strengths and weaknesses. This is the place of structure and discipline. We express and communicate with the divine through understanding the nature of ritual. We find balance.

As we come into form we move through constriction. This is the southwest quadrant. This is the place of understanding the relationship between form and spirit. This is the sphere of universal law. An old understanding resides here about the reciprocal balancing between worlds, the balance between the ordinary and the extraordinary worlds. Through listening, patience and ritual, the shaman takes the responsibility to bring harmony and balance between the spirit and ordinary worlds. Here is patience, mystery, death and receptivity.

The south, the sphere of knowledge and wisdom, conveys a state of harmony and wholeness. True wisdom always remains whole and intact. In the southeast quadrant there is movement and energy. We had constriction, now the energy begins to move towards expansion. This is the state of creativity, in which the seed is dispersed.

Recently when working with the medicine sphere in my garden, I saw a baby praying mantis resting on some yarrow leaves, positioned directly to the southeast of me. The praying mantis encapsulates the divine and the essence of the creator. By being present in our physical surrounds, and being present in the connective fabric of the universe, we are invited to partake in the well of creativity. In this quadrant the shaman observes persistent thoughts, that take them away from being quiet or observing. Here we commit to action.

the Centre, the Above and the Below

The centre is everything and nothing. It is the void, the place of mystery. The centre is about being with what is. To be with what is is to surrender the desire to be different to who you are at that moment. The centre encompasses the whole.

This centre is a place of otherworldly dimensions. It is a place of potential. The centre is analogous to the Māori concept of te kore, central to notions of mana, tapu and mauri. To understand these concepts a bit more deeply and how it applies to the centre is to see mana as power, essence, and potentiality, but having not yet taken form. For things to take form requires restrictions and discipline – tapu. The mauri is the energy behind each of the things in the world. Each thing and set of things have its own mauri. The mauri of things needs to be respected.

The centre encompasses the above, the below and the middle. The above is all that is above you, the air you breathe, the creative force of the universe. The above encompasses the stars, the moon and sun; the realms of wind, of rain and sunshine. It is the upper realm, where resides etheric bodies of spiritual teaching, energy beyond thought and the consciousness of existence.

The below is all that is below you. There is the darkness, the shadow and the universal mirror. Old earth wisdom resides here, instinct and the power of the subconscious mind. In walking through illusion, we walk through darkness. In darkness we develop the consciousness of separate form, the knowledge and understanding of will and our ability to choose. Beings reside in the lower word who are extinct from the world of light.

The middle is the sphere of now. To be with the middle world is to work with balance and harmony. It is the place where we are conscious of the physical world. Here resides the knowledge of kinship, the connectedness of things and their connection to source. This is the sphere of the physical world and the energy behind it. When I work with the middle sphere, I consciously become aware of space.

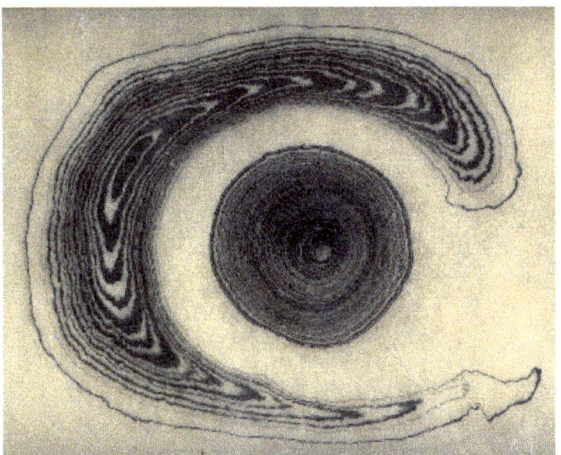

Walking the Medicine Sphere in the Tropics

The celestial sun path is very important to working with the medicine sphere. When we walk the medicine sphere, we walk sunwise facing the equator in the northern hemisphere, the sun appears to move from left to right, i.e. clockwise. In the southern hemisphere it appears to move from right to left, i.e. anticlockwise. But what if we are in tropical zones close to the equator?

I encountered this problem when I taught the medicine sphere in Singapore. I had a mixed group of people, some were born and grew up in the UK and Europe and some were born in Singapore and Malaysia. The sun's pathway becomes internal and it takes consciousness to internally shift into another hemisphere. The northern hemisphere people, even though they were in Singapore, tended to naturally move clockwise around the directions. The concept of the medicine sphere was new to them and their movements reflected their innate internalisation of the sun's path. Those born in Singapore or Malaysia, and myself were unsure which way to go and whether it was important or not.

What actually happens on the equator is that during the equinoxes the sun rises directly in the east and sets in the west and its zenith is directly overhead. So that the shadows of the sun disappear in its zenith entirely. But on solstices there is a 23-degree shift, caused by the Earth's tilt on its axis, which gives us

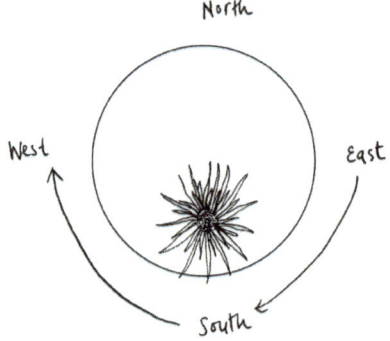

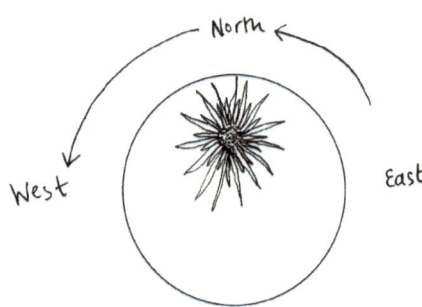

the seasons. On the 21st of December the sun rises 23 degrees south of east and sets 23 degrees south of west, the line of the tropic of Capricorn. On June the 21st the sun rises 23 degrees north of east and sets north of west, the line of the tropic of Cancer. Good practice in the tropics therefore could be to walk clockwise when it's summer in the southern hemisphere from June to September, then switch to anticlockwise when it is summer in the northern hemisphere. Seasons in the equator are usually about the dry season and the rainy season as the tilt of the earth moves between the tropical belts.

The key to creating a medicine sphere in the tropics, and indeed anywhere, is intuitive connection. Explore for yourself what is in each direction. Check deeply what occurs for you when you move clockwise or anticlockwise. From my perspective, it is about personal experience and connection to the natural world. Therefore, for me to deepen my understanding of working with the medicine sphere in the tropics is to connect and take time with the land, with the old stories that are within the land and the people. Presenting nature connection in Singapore felt like I was bringing forward an almost alien concept. Yet it is through nature connection that we align and work with the medicine sphere.

Stonehenge, watercolour on paper, William James Müller (1812 - 1845)

Origin

The term medicine wheel originated in the naming of the Bighorn Medicine Wheel in Wyoming, where a large ray of white limestone stones emanates from a central core of stones. This medicine wheel was used in sacred ceremony and as a meeting place for many of America's indigenous nations. Though the Medicine Wheel exists in the ancestral lands of the Crow Nation, Crow elders state that the wheel had been present when they first arrived in the region.

The use of stone circles as sacred meeting places, places of ritual and conscious reflection, is common to many cultures and peoples. Stone circles often have stones specifically in the cardinal directions with a centre standing stone. When I visited the Boscawen-Un Circle in Cornwall I observed that the stones are regularly spaced out and the west stone is quite remarkable as it's rich in quartz. Taking time to be there I experienced a sense of peace exuding from this circle, as I went on with the rest of my day in Cornwall time seemed to flow in a way that allowed unexpected events and synchronicity to occur in a natural way. This lasted a number of days.

The imprint of sacred stone circles, and the importance of the directions can be seen in stories like *East of The Sun and West of The Moon*, where the heroine journeys with a bear to bring the balance between the worlds, freeing a person from enchantment. Often in such stories there is a particular direction that the hero walks in. There are journeys to the upper world and journeys to the lower world. The protagonist seeks what might have been stolen and thereby redresses the balance, or they seek a cure, wisdom or gift.

A medicine sphere creates a sacred energy from which teachings arise. It balances the sacred within the ordinary. This enhances our ability to sense the mystic union and gives us the power to reflect that into the physical world. The medicine sphere aids us in communicating with the natural rhythms of land, of the heavens, the seasons, the phases of the moon. It aids us in discovering our relationship to tree, plant and animal. As we position the directions, we acknowledge the natural cycles.

Creating a Medicine Sphere

Gather eight stones from your environment. Start by going for a walk and keep a look out for stones. Let the stones speak to you. Look at which ones you are drawn to. It's worthwhile researching and finding out more about the minerals and stones in your area. When you are drawn to a stone, sit with it a moment. By simply being quiet with a stone is to perceive how it is to relate to something inanimate and distinct from us. Consciousness is an awareness of something external to us and also within us, consciousness is analogous to intelligence. If we accept the idea that consciousness permeates through the universe rather than existing as an exclusively human or animal attribute then we are free to suppose the consciousness of a stone. When you sit with a stone maybe consider this idea and allow yourself to sense what that feels like. This practice starts to bring an awareness that our environment has intelligence. When you take it away to create your medicine sphere, give thanks. You may like to leave a small natural token in respect of this stone.

When you have gathered your stones, find a place outside where you can work undisturbed. I often start by facing east but this is not necessary. Sense what direction you wish to begin to create your medicine sphere. Be present to your feelings and then choose a stone to represent this direction. Go slowly around the medicine sphere, placing stones in the four directions, followed by the four in-between directions.

By creating this circle of stones, you have created a centre. You have defined a sacred space. Step inside. Notice how it feels inside and how it feels outside. Reflect on what is happening in your life. When I first did this, I experienced the centre as if I was going into the earth. When I stepped outside of the circle, I felt that I was on top of the earth. I started exploring what this curious sensation represented for me. I looked at external and internal relationships and saw how I had created a structure to deepening enquiry into the underworld.

Consider carefully how you delineate space. Where do you put the stone that delineates the size or space of the medicine sphere you are creating? Immediately you are faced with a reflection simply in how much space you create, whether you feel 'hemmed in' or uncomfortable. By changing and working the medicine sphere you can experience shifts in the nervous system and these can create differences in the way you perceive your life.

Look at your surroundings in relative terms to the centre. How does the centre feel? What is in the centre? In your mind's eye go through your home. How is space in your room delineated? What rooms are in each direction? Look at the home within the circle. See the rooms as circles in that they are based within a particular direction. Look at the land, look at the sense of the island or continent you are on. What is to the east, the west, the north and the south.

In your journal write down any thoughts and reflections that have arisen from this work. When you are writing think about what directions felt easeful and what directions felt uncomfortable. Write down any images that arose or associations you had with each direction.

Visualising the Sphere

One way to understand the medicine sphere is to think of it as a map. It is a map of the essential nature and interconnectedness of things. I see the map as alive and evolving. As a map, the medicine sphere allows us to place spiritual energetic concepts within a spatial understanding. I have always found maps interesting. When I go to a new place I begin to map, looking at the landscape and observing landmarks to create a narrative so that I may remember my way back. If you ask directions from someone and they draw a map they will always put in their landmarks – we are involved in the mapping, and so it is with a medicine sphere.

Each of the directions within the medicine sphere can also be visualised as a sphere or a globe. Thus, the medicine sphere may be visualized as spheres within a sphere. The medicine sphere is a structure that works like an energetic blueprint of our world. Conceptually, though this is difficult to visualise, the medicine sphere encapsulates all that exists (the whole). *The whole* refers to the connectedness of all things, even the minutiae of our lives. The medicine sphere encompasses the whole. In each direction is the whole. In each small part is the whole. Because the medicine sphere contains the whole, it holds balance. This enables us to delve deeper into an issue, knowing that we are held in the bigger picture. It can show us our day, an insight into a project, a way forward in our relationship and checks our alignment to our purpose, always in context to a larger intelligence. The medicine sphere is mystical yet is also grounded through its representation of our physical world.

Begin by conceptualising the medicine sphere as a globe. All the myriad things – birds, trees, mountains, stars are within that globe. Imagine you are the centre. Above you are the heavens, light, stars, sky, sun, and moon. Below you is earth, beneath which is as an underworld, darkness and light within darkness. Both below and above encompasses universes within universes, the creation of our world. There is a sense of timelessness. Within the globe is a cyclic, pulsing movement; these are the seasons, the cycle of the moon, day and night. Visualise the myriad things interconnecting like a web.

Step outside of the sphere. Imagine a spiral running from the centre of the sphere outward. Within the spiral are the macrocosm and the microcosm. It denotes eternity. It is limitless and infinite in its unfolding. It is a symbol of life. The spiral is at the beginning and end of our life. Within us is the consciousness of the whole (the interconnectedness of everything). Imagine the medicine sphere is within you. Now imagine it is outside of you and within you simultaneously.

> All things are implicated with one another, and the bond is holy: and there is hardly anything unconnected with any other thing.
>
> Marcus Aurelius, Roman Emperor (121–180)

Mystery

When we invoke the medicine sphere, we invoke a spiritual metaphor for the physical world. Yet central to that invocation is our relationship to the mystery, the energy beyond thought. It is hard to find words to convey the experience of a communion with the mystery. The mystery pervades all things, it is tangible and intangible. To allow a relationship with the mystery is to surrender knowing.

Our separation from the spiritual through form (the physical body) is the paradox required for our evolutionary journey. In the state of separation is the knowledge and experience of unity. The medicine sphere has within it the spirit that moves through all things. It contains the spirit before it enters form. It contains the shadow cast by the light so that through the shadow we might uncover and see ourselves.

Seven Steps

This is an exercise to connect with nature and find a way to explore an issue or deepen an enquiry. You might even find an answer. To begin, go outside, have your journal with you, and connect by creating a simple medicine wheel. Greet and honour the directions. Give thanks – deep gratitude. Put forward the issue you would like to explore. Turn slowly sunwise sensing what direction you need to go. When you find that direction start to walk in that direction. If something attracts your attention or a place makes you feel like you need to stop, then stop. Pause, look and write. What do you see? What comes up in relationship to your question? Keep walking and stop again. The seventh time you stop, turn three times around and then really look. Is there a way forward for you in relationship to your question? Write up and reflect on what happened. Note your feelings and look for the humour and symbolic possibilities of what you experienced.

Letting Go

This exercise is an awareness exercise. It brings our awareness to the creation of a sacred circle, and the experience of letting go what may no longer be serving us.

Gather nine stones. Create a medicine wheel using eight of the stones you have gathered. Make it big enough to sit comfortably inside. Stand in the centre of this circle and using your senses feel what it is like in each direction. Step outside of the circle and sense what that feels like. Step back in and give thanks for all the things that you feel gratitude for. Take your time.

Sit in the centre of your circle and hold your ninth stone. Think about what it is that you would like to let go of. Let the stone, that you are holding, represent that thing or situation or behaviour that you would like to let go of. As you hold the stone describe what it is that you are doing or holding that is no longer serving you. You might want to write this down.

How does it feel if you were to let it go? Put it outside of your circle and experience the feeling that arises inside of you when it is outside the circle. Bring it back into the circle. Experience what it is like to hold on to that. This exercise aids you understanding the way you relate to this aspect of your life. Write down the feelings that come up for you. To clear the stone, you can put it in water. You can take it to the ocean, or just find a place in nature to place it. In your mind just ask that what you have imbued in the stone be released.

At the end of this work release all the stones one by one. You may want to keep them as your stones for further work or you may give them back to nature. When you place them back in their natural environment, give thanks for their service. The stones have been imbued with the energy of your sacred work.

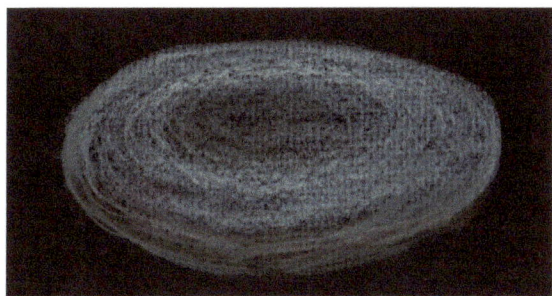

Walk alone, walk alone
Even if nobody follows you
Walk alone,
Even if nobody listens to you
Walk alone

Don't give up.
Walk alone.

Keep flowing.
Walk alone.

Rabindranath Tagore,
Bengali polymath (1861–1941)

The Co-Creative Circle

the Co-Creative Circle

It can symbolise wholeness, unity and the cyclic process of renewal. A co-creative circle is a gathering of people working with a common purpose within a medicine sphere. By gathering together within the structure of the medicine sphere we build a sacred place of learning. The focus is not on a teacher but towards the centre of the circle and within oneself.

Every circle is unique because we are individually unique. When we come together, we bring that difference forward. Each circle is influenced by time and by place. This also brings its unique flavour to the work. Each circle also differs in the purpose that brings the group together. A circle needs to invite in all those that come. Everyone has a place in the circle and a contribution to make. Working together to prepare the space enables each individual to bring forward their contribution.

Invoking Spirit

The central requisite to the co-creative circle is the invocation of spirit, the spirit that moves through all things, the unconditional energy of the universe. We may invoke this by speaking our intention. We may sing, drum, light a candle, give prayers, or simply be in a state of quiet. By bringing our attention to the centre of the medicine sphere we acknowledge the sacred and the energy within and behind all things.

When we invite this connection to spirit, ordinary items may seem imbued with magic. Their intrinsic value becomes accentuated. This is the result of each person being more present to spirit. Afterwards, when we finish, we should close the circle. It is like opening a door to a sacred space, when we are finished, we close that door to help integrate anything that may have happened. We should share food, wash our hands, possibly make a joke and greet the ordinary.

...that behind the cotton wool is hidden a pattern; that we - I mean all human beings - are connected with this, that the whole world is a work of art. Hamlet or a Beethoven quartet is the truth about this vast mass that we call the world. But there is no Shakespeare, there is no Beethoven; certainly and empahatically there is no God; we are the words; we are the music, we are the thing itself.

Virginia Woolf - *Sketch of the Past - Moments of Being*

Intention

The purpose of invocation is partly to bring awareness to intention. On entering the circle, we offer up our intention in being there. Intention is the foundation of focus. It generates action. To intend is to activate a process. When you offer up an intention you cannot know the outcome of that process. Offering up intention should be understood within the context of reciprocity between the individual will and the divine will. When we have an intention, we have a responsibility in how we participate with the consequences of that intention. If we allow receptivity from something unknown then the outcome may be beyond what we imagined. When we offer up an intention, we enter into a relationship with the divine in which we offer something forward and allow ourselves to receive. To observe what we might be invoking through the intention may strike us with fear, fear of what we may manifest. It is during receiving that people are most likely to disrupt the process because it is at this point that they experience a feeling of unworthiness.

In darkness, intention is like a flare that is released upwards. Yet when people are submerged in trauma, they are unable to grasp their intention. Intention requires will, individuality, and desire. If prayer is a petition it is underpinned by an intention to receive something. With this comes an expectation to receive, to experience trust or faith. When we offer up our intention into the circle we are met by spirit and gifted back that intention. The intention has mana for it is given a space. Often, we throw out intentions half-heartedly without a sense of real focus, or gifting the intention the space it requires.

At the heart of the intention is the power of each one of us to be a creator. In contemplating this concept, you may be afraid of the destroyer. Creativity and destruction are potently connected. A totara tree, for example, is cut down to create a waka. If wisdom, time and a real connection to the forest and its spirit are considered then there is a sacred relationship between the tree and the person. In this case, the tree sacrifices itself and a spirit relationship is established between the creator and what is being created. Where, on the other hand, the creative process is driven by somebody that is unable to connect to the life force of things, then the relationship exercises power over, rather than *power with*. The life is taken to create.

Co-Creativity in Society and Community

Power with is the essence of a co-creative relationship. This requires that you meet with and respect what and whom you are working with. As creators, it is important to be part of a community. A healthy culture upholds the intrinsic values, of humility and authenticity. It acknowledges the mirror-like nature of the universe. These are the precepts of the sacred circle.

Believing that other people, plants, animals and landscapes have an intrinsic value should help to shape the society we live in, bringing greater harmony. When, on the other hand, people project their extrinsic values onto the world around them, society becomes a place of judgement and anxiety. Often extrinsic values are based on a perception of status and reaction to how others perceive us.

In a co-creative circle, where people listen and respect each other, we may see the reflection of our innate gifts and slowly begin to recognize and value them through expression and action. It is often others who show us our attributes and this is the value of working co-creatively. Self-esteem, self-worth, and self-image are intrinsically connected to community and culture. In a truly healthy culture the word *self-esteem* would be obsolete.

People often experience being an outsider in their own society. It takes courage to step out onto a different unknown path and to allow our innermost selves to lead us into places beyond our cultural patterning, such as constrictive gender roles.

Sobonfu Somè, African author, teacher and activist (died 2017), writes that 'The goal of the community is to make sure that each member of the community is heard and is properly giving the gifts that they have brought to this world.' Sobonfu Somè reminds us that the essence of a community should lie in creating the foundation for a healthy culture. We must look at the structures that work for us as a community. The co-creative circle, with its innate respect for all life could be a structure that helps to mend wounds in our culture.

Medicine and Gesture

Gesture refers to the essential quality of a plant, animal or mineral. Medicine in this context refers to the potential of the gesture to impact something else, usually in a healing context. By connecting to the gesture of a plant, animal or thing we can enable a shift to occur in a healing way. The gesture of a landscape, for example, may generate a harmonious experience that enables us to integrate a difficult teaching. This is the medicine of the landscape. When we observe a particular plant, the smell, the taste, how it feels on our skin, we observe its gesture. The information that our senses give us indicates what its physical and energetic medicine might be.

As I write, there is a Chinese paper wasp to my west. When I see the wasp, I am first aware that it exists regardless of my relationship to it. I observe it. Observation is the first step to understanding gesture. It has a tapered waist and is black with vivid yellow stripes. When it flies it tends to hover over different flowers and leaves before it lands. When it flies, its long legs dangle down. Sometimes it lands and cleans its abdomen with its hind legs. Its legs are a burnished gold colour. It looks elegant. A wasp will rest and preen in contrast to a bee which is always moving from flower to flower.

The gesture arises from the way a wasp goes about its life. Paper wasps love and require warmth. In spring and summer, it is only the females that I am likely to see. During the winter the young males and females hibernate, clinging to the underside of the abandoned nest. In the spring the females, whether fertilised or not, help construct the new nest and the males die. The fertilised queens deposit eggs into the new cells and then assist the unfertilised workers in gathering honeydew to feed to the larvae, which are attached to the cells. As the larvae develop the adults feed them protein-rich food such as macerated cicadas and caterpillars. When the larvae are fully grown, they spin a silken cover over the entrance of the cell and pupate. The adults that emerge are all females. At the end of the season the queen lays unfertilised eggs, which turn into males.

I look at the energy between the wasp and myself. This attendance will touch into my family and cultural conditioning. Then I look at the attributes of the west. The symbolic significance of wasp in the west is to do with initiation. The west is the transition from the day into night, looking at our shadows and watching for what we are afraid of. The wasp keeps us aware as they sting when we are clumsy and not looking out. A sting can push us into action that is better aligned to ourselves. The gesture of the wasp that stands out for me, is the way it goes about its business in an unhurried way. The wasp's medicine for me is to examine how I attend to myself within community.

Our Gift

Our gift refers to the concept that each person has within them a unique essence. Their job throughout their life is to express this essence. Genius, daemon, personal medicine and sacred dream are all words that describe this concept.

I have borrowed the word 'gift' from Sobonfu Somè. In *Women's Wisdom from the Heart of Africa*, she describes how in the Dagara tradition each child is understood to come into the world with a particular gift that no one else has. This gift is considered so important for the survival of the community that the elders will go out of their way to find out who is coming. Through a ritual, in which the baby answers critical questions while the mother is in a trance, the elders will ask who the child is, why they are coming and how can the tribe best support the child to hold the gift in integrity and to bring this into the world. They then name the child to match the gift.

The term 'daemon' comes from the classical philosopher Plato who wrote 'When all the souls had chosen their lives, they went before Lachesis. And she sent with each, as the guardian of his life and the fulfiller of his choice, the daemon that he had chosen.' The term was popularised by author Philip Pullman in his *Dark Materials* trilogy, in which each person is assigned a personal magical guardian that takes the form of an animal. When the characters are children their daemons can change form but when they come of age each daemon takes on its true shape. Our gift is connected to our personality. The German writer and thinker Johann Goethe (1749–1832) wrote 'The highest treasure of the earth is surely the personality.' The journey that we embark on when we work with the medicine sphere can be understood as a journey that strengthens rather than changes our personality. It is not a journey of depersonalization. Recognising our gift can give us a greater understanding and perspective about the things we have chosen to do and the events that have happened to us in our lives.

the Talking Stick

> A bird doesn't sing because it has an answer, it sings because it has a song.
>
> Maya Angelou, American poet, singer and civil rights activist (1928–2014)

Through sharing our stories, we create community and through acceptance of our fundamental differences we begin to create a healthier culture. In dream circles, a person shares their dream and everybody else reflects back what they got from the dream. It deepens the dream for the person who is sharing, but it also allows each person who feeds back to connect and learn. When we share in circle, we find aspects of ourselves in what other people are sharing and it deepens our own connection to ourselves and to others.

The most important tool in facilitating the co-creative circle is the talking stick. The talking stick, as I use it, originated from indigenous North American culture. It held the sacred power of words and when one held it, the other members of the circle remained silent and listened. It was created in a sacred manner and had an eagle feather attached to it for courage, wisdom and truthful speech. It had colours to represent the four directions and rabbit fur to remind the speaker to come to the heart for softness and warmth. It had turquoise to remember the Great Spirit hears the message from the heart and a shell to symbolise the constant changes that constitute life.

When using the stick in circle, take a moment to hold the stick before speaking. Indicate when you have finished by putting the stick down in the centre. Participants may stand up and walk around the circle before picking up the stick and again after speaking. Rather than passing it around the circle hand to hand, offer it back to the centre as an invitation to whomever would like to speak next. When we speak from the heart, we may feel vulnerable. Rather than closing off, or reverting to patterns of defence and protection, I recommend staying with the feeling. The talking stick offers a space to find yourself with others. When holding the talking stick, I feel the alignment to the circle and to spirit. This enables me to experience a pathway in my expression.

We should be present when in circle and bring our curiosity, our knowing and our not knowing. We bring our uniqueness. Rather than following a leader we should recognise that leadership resides in each of us. The circle means we can integrate the sacred. A circle means that we are all equal.

THE CO-CREATIVE CIRCLE

in Your Journal

Free write about Tribe. What does this word mean to you? Do the same with the word community, family and group. Reflect on your writings. What did the word invoke in you? What memories came up? What differences and commonalities arose? Write down the kind of groups you have been in and the roles you take in these groups. Is there a common thread around your role? How would you like to be different in a group?

Playing at Work, 1872, oil on canvas, Charles Edward Perugini

Land

Land

Kotare, the kingfisher, has a landing place on the fence. I see it on the old totara post, a keen and watchful sentry. I lean up against the fence exploring its landing post's quality, checking the view. I see sloping hills, beaches, bays, rocky outcrops, blue peninsulas, cattle, the rough paddocks of Mimiwhangata, and a wild Northland coastline. This landscape holds the language of its past, the human dominance, the lines of fences and tracks, rampant Kikuyu grass, cattle congregating near the waterways, further back, the hollows and ridges of pa sites. My focus shifts to the north, to the silhouettes of old puriri trees on a hill. I love their stark outlines, their hugging twisting trunks, accidental hollows and odd holes, lopsided wounded perfections that have allowed some inner grace to meet the elements that sculpt them. This coastal landscape is exposed to north-easterly gales, there is little reforestation and so it is stark and open to the elements. I climb over the fence and weave my way amongst flax and kanuka flattened by the wind. The kikuyu is long and enfolds over itself.

Protocol

Protocol in land healing starts with your approach and your intention. Assume that there is a powerful intelligence that you are working with, and that this intelligence is already aware of your intention. Think carefully about what part of the land you are drawn to and even where you should leave your car. When you come onto the land, pause and go quiet. Imagine that you are visiting somebody. You are entering their house and so what you want to do is be respectful to how that person is living. You knock on the door and they invite you in. That's how it should be. In this way you will be welcomed in. I have seen situations regarding spiritual work with land where people create an illusion of power and energy; often, they haven't understood deeper aspects of the land, aspects that have the potential to gift back immeasurably. Land work is about creating a relationship.

Begin with greeting. A greeting is a sign of welcome or recognition. In greeting we acknowledge each other. The following is a simple greeting that I use when I consciously connect to land.

I open myself to connect with you
I allow space and time for you to come forward to meet me
I acknowledge I do not know you so that I am able to listen and see with new ears and eyes.
I am here, I am not needing to be anywhere else

Take the time to greet and thank the guardian of the land, the trees, the animals, the birds and recognise that we are part of everything. When we connect there is a two-way movement, a dance. Two people slowly allow their fingers to connect, it becomes an intensity of connection and focus. There is consciousness in the etheric body and it pulls away at our barriers and protections. The slowest most respectful connection may feel the most vulnerable. To see is to be seen.

When we work with land we must arrive in a state of listening. What we perceive physically and energetically is often a reflection of ourselves. By taking time we can see past this. If I come and stay in a new place, I take time to thank the guardian of the land, the trees, the animals, the birds and recognise that I am integral to landscape. Landscape is not orientated around me. Landscape is its own entity. As I participate in landscape, I may see reflections for my own benefit. Objects may become personal symbols for my journey. Yet it's always important to bring it back to the whole and be aware of my imprint and that guardianship is part of a greater totality.

In a new place, I look at how the landscape responds to the elements and what has the most impact, whether it be elements, humans or animals. I note where the predominant wind comes from by observing how the trees will 'create a back to the wind, like someone turning away and opening their umbrella. I look for what might give me the essence of the place, the type of vegetation, the contours, the soil or the rocks and boulders.

I smell and taste the minerals in the rocks. I lie back and look up at the sky. If there is a hawk, I imagine I am flying with it. I feel the lift of the wind. I see the hill formations, the valleys and the plains. I see the plant world, the skin of the earth, I look at what trees attract my attention, and where they are positioned. I work with trees often in land healing. As well as creating healthy ecosystems they help the land energetically. I observe the waterways, their clarity and their flow.

As a healer, I have often worked with people who are sensitive to the energies of land. Often their sensitivities arise out of a wound, particularly if they experienced powerlessness when witnessing environmental destruction. I have seen these people move into energy work with land and the energies of land without any real thoughtful protocol or meditative observation. They may work out of their fear or their wound and will be either ineffective or disruptive.

The following imaginative scenarios are analogous to what happens when we attempt to clear energy from land, that may not even need to be cleared, without taking the time to properly understand our own wounds and gifts.

Scenario 1:

You're at home and a complete stranger walks into your house without knocking on the door or even being aware there might be a door. He doesn't see you. It's like you're invisible. You try to attract his attention.

'Hey what are you doing here?' you say.

He can't hear you or see you. He starts removing things, pushing stuff out of the way. He has a few tools with him and starts to break up the floorboards because he's interested in seeing what's underneath.

Scenario 2:

A stranger walks into your house. He actually trips over the doorstep. He sees you for a moment and gets a fright, then closes his eyes. He blocks his ears and hums loudly. He then opens his eyes and starts talking to your ornate dining table you inherited from your mother in law. He tells the table he understands that he has a very special role here then suddenly lifts up the table. He is in a hurry and goes out the door. It's quite a heavy burden but he's up for the job. It's difficult getting it through the door but he manages it by taking the door off the hinges. You wonder what he is doing. You try to pull him back. He begins to be afraid. He sees you as a force that he needs to battle with. He uses more force so you let him and the table go.

Intention in Land Healing

The first thing to consider, before you work energetically with land, is your own emotional state and your personal intention. Think about how you approach, and what you might be assuming about, the land. I was once asked to clear a building site that had problems such as delays and physical disruptions. The intention of the person who had asked me to do the clearing was that I would clear any blockages to the advancement of his building. My intention would be to receive the energies and observe the land that I may be shown its essence, and from here to see why the disruptions had been happening. I communicated this to him. Often disruption is a way to get our notice. Sometimes I have had to assist the land in accommodating a new building. In those cases, I shared that intention with the land and worked to convey information to the person building. In some situations, the overall healing work could only occur by working with the people who had the land to alter their plans and intentions so that they worked with the energy and the essence of the land.

We cannot change how some houses and buildings are built even though they are at variance to the environment. These buildings are a good example of a complete disconnect to the environment. Be thoughtful how you personally react to them. Try to be with the dissonance rather than be stuck in your reaction. This helps to make the small adjustments that will ultimately help ease the land around it.

We may arrive with unconscious intention, or we may have clear intentions. Clear intentions might be I intend to build a home, or I need to clear this home of any old imprints of the previous owner so I may begin anew. It may be that our intention is to create harmony. If you perceive the land as being in disharmony, first reflect back to yourself. Acknowledge your own sense of disharmony and then look at the land and observe each aspect that feels out of the natural rhythm. Check within yourself to see how you perceive harmony. To have an intention to bring harmony you need to check whether the essence of the land is in alignment with that.

When our intention is clear, we may ask that things that are not in alignment with that intention be shown up so that they may be released. Suppose there was a crooked business owner who conducted a lot of hidden transactions and bribery. This will transfer an energy to the building. When it is sold and the new owner wants everything to be clear and aboveboard you can bring that in as a new intention. The focus of that intention will show up the secretive energy. By aligning the new intention with the land, you can allow the land to assist you in releasing the old energies.

When we step into guardianship and are working with land you might want to go a bit deeper with your practice of intention. Land often reflects the power we have to manifest what we desire. Intention is connected to our ability to manifest and so we must pay particular attention to it. Consider where your intention emerges from. This may appear as an acknowledgement to your family or your ancestors, the spirits that stand behind you. It may be simply love or desire for a home, a place to create from.

The alignment of intention with the earth and the consequences of manifestation are expressed through ritual. A ritual is about creating a structure to best meet the force that you are wanting to work with. This could be about meeting the vision, or the new home or allowing the future to come closer. When we meet the vision or the force through ritual, we get close to making something manifest, it shifts from the imagination into something that is part of your life. In creating ritual, you are using physical objects, and these material parts have a role in symbolising the parts of the vision you are working with. A ritual may be very simple, using elements that you feel in alignment with. A ritual should act as an interface between the energetic/etheric world and the physical. Think of the ritual as a living speaking tool to convey the power of your intention.

The power of manifestation through intention may be opened through this visualization. Imagine an energy in the navel that is connected to your gifts. Imagine this energy rising from your navel to your heart. Allow your intention to flow around your heart. Taste it as if your heart is filled with taste buds. Swirl the intention around. Savour it. Let the intention flow into the pineal gland, the centre of energy. Feel the energy activate in your third eye, then your crown. Then sense it flow down the spine and into earth. The energy goes past the back of the heart, down the base of the spine to the sacrum. Sense the connection with place, move your intention to a dedication. Offer the dedication up.

Piripai Beach, New Zealand

Essence of Landscape

Each landscape has its own gesture and essence. The heart relates to earth, to land, and to landscape. The heart is the organ with which we connect to the Essence of Landscape and it is through our emotions, and our sensory body that we perceive that essence.

Land essence arises from its physical form. A gently inclining valley, for instance, will have a different essence to an exposed cliff. The surrounding elements also contribute to the generation of essence. An obsidian mountain located on the edge of a continent will be different in essence to an obsidian island in the Pacific. Comparison is helpful when meditating on elements. We might examine the quality of clay compared to pumice, or the nature of a sluggish creek to a fast-flowing river.

If I were to try to describe the essence of my garden, I would first look at its physical features and its position at the bottom of a valley. Through this observation of place, I allow myself to enter into a dreamlike state of receptivity where I extend my senses. In this place of meditative awareness, I perceive the garden as a timeless place, followed by a sense of rhythm, as if it, the garden, is breathing. Through this particular connection I find myself in a different place. I perceive the essential quality of the garden as a sanctuary and a gateway to other worlds.

Spirit Guardians

Spirit guardians are aligned to the essential nature of their landscape. When you connect to the essence of a place you may connect to a being that was acknowledged by the people that once inhabited the land. This is the spirit guardian. When you connect to the spirit guardian of a place, you reopen the etheric pathways of communication, pathways that may have been closed for some time. It is important to acknowledge this. Be thoughtful as to how you approach a spirit guardian because we are not as able as our forebears to be in constant communication with these beings and because our world is very different from the way it was. Greeting and sensitive listening is necessary. Be aware of the alignment of your service. You are in a co-creative relationship and the etheric pathway you use to communicate with this being must be respectful and true to yourself.

Some spirit guardians act as go-betweens between humans and elementals (magical beings of place). The taniwha is one such spirit guardian and will serve and be connected to certain tribes as well as to a land, river or ocean. They can be powerful forces and may be dangerous if they have been dishonoured, discarded or cheated by humans. If through your work you have woken a disgruntled guardian, disruption may take place. To communicate well in this instance, you need to set up a strong structure that enables your ability to cross through the worlds safely and allow the being to come correctly into your world. A medicine sphere is a structure that can work well here and you can set this medicine sphere up with the intention of this communication and acknowledgement. Simple deep acknowledgement and listening will set free pain that has occurred through human disregard. When connecting to a spirit guardian make it clear to the guardian how much time and space you are offering to be there.

Spirit guardians reside in all areas of land. They may show up as taniwha or other magical beings. Some seem like birds, others like an old man or a woman. Sometimes you may simply become aware of a presence, perhaps just a sense of reflection or something tall and giant like. Take the time to sense the energy that is being presented to you. These beings are of the land and are usually willing to work with you. Working with spirit guardians takes practise. Don't be in too much of a hurry to start shifting energy. Your observation, your intention does a huge amount.

Sense how the energy is or the stories that are imprinted in the land. As you observe you may see what to do. It might be singing or sounding and watching something shift that way. Enter in a way where not only are you observing in the physical but you are observing on the other planes of emotional imprinting and history of energy and place. By starting the observation in the physical world, you are honing your skill as to how the physical and the energy world reflect each other. Real balance occurs on both the energy plane and on the physical plane. Take the time to observe the flow of energy. There is often a lull before the actual completion of work. This is when most people will cut off, thinking they have finished, but if you wait a bit longer you will sense the energy build up again. That is the point of completion.

the Etheric Body of the Earth

The land has an etheric body, just as we do and is covered in many energy lines, nodes and centres. Once when I was working with a particular earth energy line, I had a vision in which I vividly saw the complexity of the earth's energy and energy lines. It was mind-blowing. I'll never forget the sensation. Every line and centre was pulsating with different intelligences and life. The world was covered in energetic veins. I saw in that moment how each of us was inextricably connected to those lines. The experience was overwhelming; how could I know what I was doing when there was that amount of complexity and connectivity? Yet the small things we do in relationship to the earth's energy have a real impact.

If you think of the lines over the earth like meridian lines, then there are main lines and there are smaller lines. Each line has a different function or carries a different energy. Energy and information move through the planet intelligently along these lines. The stars and the moon impact them. Some lines expand at full moon. If you stay and work with an earth energy line you can observe this happening.

In ancient times people sang these lines, communicated with them and kept them vibrant. They considered it important for the health of the earth. Through the human consciousness there was a connectivity that supported the renewal of energy through the etheric and physical bodies of the earth. With this consciousness, humans could energetically work on their own body, while the earth's body would also benefit. When its etheric, energetic body is not cleansed the earth suffers. It suffers a stagnation of energy. This stagnation, or sinking of energy, blocks its natural renewing processes. The etheric and the physical must meld and work together.

When there are blockages in the communication between the etheric and physical bodies, you are alive but you may feel dead. Depression is often related to blockages between the etheric and physical and you can sense depressed areas on the earth. It is like a connection is broken. The centre in the body to work with in this case is the pituitary gland, particularly the pineal gland that connects to the third eye. It is through the pituitary gland that the etheric body can be connected to the physical and how we are able to *sing lines*. The energy centres on the earth act to connect the etheric to the physical. Other energy centres connect the various different energies.

Our planet is unwell. It is challenging to face this and to find how to work with this. I had a very sobering experience one night when I connected with whales and I saw how whales also took a role in connecting to the meridian lines of our planet through the oceans. I saw that there are now so few that this is no longer happening. Simply to acknowledge the earth's lines, to sense our own etheric bodies in connection with the earth, is a stepping stone to restoring health.

Memory of Water

When I was asked by the owner of the timber yard to do some land healing, I was challenged because it was built on an old waterway. In healing and releasing the blocked energies, I had to first remember the water. I took time to remember the water. I saw it so clearly. It was a beautiful clear stream and it flowed down into the wetlands. None of this existed in the present, and yet I had to remember. I saw the forest as it was and I stayed with the insight. You can change energy by remembering, being present to what has passed and what is now. I held the memory of what had passed and I saw what was present. What was present was unpleasant. I wanted to rail at the recent history of forest burn-offs, farming practices and destructive buildings, all the while focusing on the memory of this water. In the present, I had a physical situation where the water was blocked and causing a stagnant energy in the timber yard. I couldn't physically unblock the water but water has an etheric body and it's that etheric body I worked with. I visualised it beginning to flow freely. I sensed the energy shifting through the whole timber yard. I am still left, of course, with the knowledge that the natural beauty of the stream has been lost forever, but the energies of that water have found their way to the sea.

Cook Strait, New Zealand, 1884, oil on canvas, Nicholas Chevalier

Summer Showers, c. 1865 - 1870, oil on canvas, Martin Johnson Heade

Impact of People and the Language of Landscape

I grew up surrounded by wild landscape. I started off next to bush and stream and then when aged nine, shifted to Piripai. Piripai was a very wild, mostly forgotten beach close to where the Whakatane river runs out to the sea. I spent a good deal of time wandering the sand dunes and learnt that it was a place teeming with life. When I was fourteen, a developer built a housing subdivision there. This highly sensitive natural world was utterly destroyed. Whole sand dunes were shifted to create small oddly shaped sections. Tar-seal roads were built, footpaths, even street lights were positioned neatly along the sides of these new roads. Within a few months the natural wilderness at my doorstep was gone. It was a shock. Few had a personal relationship with a tree that is now buried under a load of sand, but I did. I knew that landscape so well I can map it in my mind's eye. Huge machines pushed over small forests of kanuka that held the tenuous life in the hollows. Today people who live there do not know that it was called Piripai. It is only known as Coastlands – the name the developer gave it.

I learnt the language of Piripai. The language was in the way the wind sculpted the dunes and the power of the river and the plants that grew there. The language was also found in the past, the burial grounds, the farming and the introduction of boxthorn and macrocarpa trees. To discover the language of landscape we must first observe it. Start by looking, then soften your gaze. Allow yourself to let your body sense. From physical observation move to sensing the energy of the place. Your body can act as a divining rod. In some field trips with students we have divined a line and lain on it, sensing the quality of the line through our bodies. In general, you observe any discomfort, constriction or expansion in relationship to any particular part of the land. You may choose to close your eyes and sense in your mind's eye any images that arise. These can be very specific. Be aware that the dream world may accentuate things. Allow yourself time to be with the images rather than jumping to interpretation. When you start seeing visions and stories in land, the first thing to do is to stay very present. The first principle is power listening. Stay with what you observe. This may be all that is required. What is shown is also a mirror. Look within yourself.

When reading the language of landscape take time to observe how people are in relationship to the land. If it is a place that people visit often, see how somebody's intention can impact the energy of land. Is there a focal point where people focus their attention, or their view? The land will respond to that intensity of focus. Humans are very destination orientated. This impacts the land. Humans create pathways with their minds and so other humans find it hard to deviate from those pathways. Sheep form trails in the same way.

People congregate in places and intermingle their personality and their community with the landscape. Landscape impacts us and we impact land through our mind. We also change it physically to suit our requirements. The places where we connect affect our orientation to the world around us. By examining our relationship with land, we see what our relationship is to natural resources, the marking of boundaries and our personal emotional response to land. People create cultural identities based on their relationship to land. The projection of identity can be so powerful that newcomers may project on that land what they are familiar and identify with. This is the colonisation of land. The relationship is one of domination.

Wounds, Gifts and Mirrors

When we think about how short our lives are, the scale of environmental change is brought sharply into context. I have, in my lifetime, seen the most extraordinary forest ecosystem annihilated. The huge Horohoro Forest had a rich diverse bird population including kokako. This forest was deliberately destroyed in the 1980s, first poisoned with 245T (the active ingredient in Agent Orange) and then burnt to make way for pine plantation. Many landscapes that I identified with and loved no longer exist. The change is dramatic and the loss is intense. When you are faced with irretrievable loss you are faced with despair. Environmental despair can be debilitating and many people suffer from it. American environmentalist and author Richard Heinberg argues that information about the state of the world wounds us and that to live in the modern world is to be confronted with this information daily. This impacts our ability to be present.

It's important in land healing to face the pain that we may carry because that pain comes between us and our connection to land. Pain manifests in the way people remove themselves from nature. This separation is either physical or energetic. I have often noticed when bringing groups to observe and sit in nature that they can experience a great deal of emotion and discomfort. Some people suffer from environmental despair to the degree that they believe they are a burden to the earth and that there is no space for them to be here.

In healing land, we need to attend to healing our personal relationship to it. In doing so we confront an insidious survival pattern – denial. Denial may be inherited from our forebears but may also arise from our collective group-mind. Many believe denial is necessary for the survival of society.

The first step to healing ourselves is to express our grief to the land itself. There was some pretty ugly development on Waiheke a few years ago. It was right on the beach and it impacted several people in the group I was teaching. They avoided going there and tended to avert their eyes when they did. They felt angry at the landowners, even the workers. They also experienced helplessness. We needed to grieve. Grieving allows us back into connection and be able to face the landscape as it exists today. It also acknowledges the loss and allows us to remember.

Once when I was working in the Kaipara region, I walked down a track to a wharf. Right by the wharf, sinking into the estuary were piles of rubbish, old televisions, plastic and tires. It needed serious cleaning up. I was doing energy healing in relationship to the nearby hill. In connecting to this land I made a promise to ring the council because I knew that the physical situation was what needed attendance. Just when I was about to leave, a council officer came down the track. He looked at me and looked at the rubbish and organized for its removal. I couldn't quite believe the swift synchronicity, no phone call required.

Finding your Power Place in Your Journal

A power place may be a personal sacred space where you feel part of the place and experience a sense of belonging. It might be a place where you experience transformation or a sense of moving into other worlds and realms where you may find kinship and learning. It may have cultural significance. It may literally raise the hairs on your skin. It may be gentle and subtle. One place for me was Boscawen-un in Cornwall. Here I was able to access a grace and a gentle manifesting support while I was in the area. Since being there I can access that same sense by imaginative journeying.

The power place may be an area, even an earth line that connects different places. Within the power place there will be certain elements that are stronger than others. My power place is where the river meets the sea. It has sets of juxtaposed elements, dune and rock, river and ocean, mud flats and tumultuous waves. It is a place of transition, where two forces meet.

Centre yourself by bringing your attention to your breath and your senses. When you are in a relaxed state, walk slowly through your house and bring awareness to any emotions or feelings that you have in your body. Don't analyse these feelings just bring your awareness to them. When you have done this, centre yourself again. Write down in your journal what you noticed, or simply what happened.

In your journal create a map of your area. Make your home the centre of your map and start drawing some of the important landmarks around you. Note, the directions, the waterways, your favourite places, and trees. Write down what you know about your area. You may want to do some research. What direction is the prevailing wind? What are the predominate plant species? What animals predominate? How much local history do you know? Who was here before you? What was the landscape like? How did the people look after the land? Who built the house you are living in?

Write down how you relate to your local environment. What is your intention for the place you are living in? What is your relationship with the house and natural environment where you are living? Take time to describe this. Are you transitory? How does that impact your relationship with the space you inhabit? How would you like this environment to support you?

LAND

Friday September 10th
Mohakatino River the river flooded monday today it's warm and sunny. The river brown and muddy. Sudden cloud cover the wind comes up - cold.

sheep
remnant kahikatea
rimu kowhai
cabbage trees
Mohakatino River
Waikitikiti Stream
Daves' Place
pussy willow
fallen gum trees

opo taka
walking to Lake Rotoaira early morning the black swan and young swans gathering. The place of kainga

Motuopuhi Island.
Lake Rotoaira

Looking towards the east and seeing the hills that now I know → hold the lake of Rotopounamu that is like a crater lake and is protected by Pihanga. There is no water that comes out from Rotopounamu & there are streams that go into it.

this beautiful green heart lake
the podocarps around it
the huge beech trees
rimu. I saw the black robin firstly on the west side and then the east side swimming in the green green of it it was the most beautiful green.

Lake Rotopounamu

Pihanga

filled up with nature and joy.
mist, rain, playfulness.
the heart, the feminine, the protection and the warmth of the water.

Nature Connection

Nature Connection

> To draw flight I think one has to begin, in imagination, to sense the air as a bird's wing can feel it.
>
> John Busby, influential wildlife artist
> (1928–2015)

Nature connection refers to an active participation with nature and a conscious connection through sensory awareness. It is profound and exciting yet also playful, inspiring and may help to integrate things we are experiencing but struggle to understand. Plants, animals and minerals held in a dynamic interconnection contain extraordinary intelligence. Nature connection resides in the act of doing, of being outside whatever the weather.

Observation, Research and Journaling

A purpose of cultivating nature awareness is to reawaken our childlike curiosity. This might mean getting down on your hands and knees to watch the grasshoppers or to try to see the cricket singing in the cracks of the earth. It might be that you practise stalking a rabbit, seeing its alert stance with its ears upright when the evening sun is making them glow. It may mean grinning while you notice the young tui learning to sing, or identifying a hedgehog scat full of beetle exoskeletons.

Nature awareness requires you to stop, look, listen, smell, taste and feel. It deepens your connection to nature through your senses and being present to your surroundings. Jon Young, founder of The Kamana Wilderness Awareness School, calls this extension of senses 'owl eyes'. You start by looking ahead of you, then slowly bring forward and extend the other senses. This takes practise, and I often break my observation with sketches and writing descriptions. Author and illustrator Danny Gregory best describes this kind of sketching. 'It didn't matter what the drawing was like… what mattered was the slow, careful gaze.' It's worthwhile getting out of the way of yourself and enjoy simply seeing.

As a child, I read every book about nature I could lay my hands on. I read all of Gerald Durrell's (British naturalist 1925–1995) and as a consequence spent a good deal of time studying insects in the sand, the communities of slaters and the large burrowing sand scarab beetles. I spent hours walking along the beach so I could get to the lagoons and see bitterns. I read about people who spent their lifetime studying puffins and others who followed whales. I read books on birds and plants and even one about the study of a single spider in the attic of an old English house. All of the old naturalists drew, observed and kept nature journals, they noted the weather, and what had happened in the area. Through this journaling they got a picture of the ecosystems they studied. Their specialisations usually arose through their curiosity and a passionate love of, leading to obsession with, a few specific animals or plants.

Living on Waiheke and travelling on the ferry gives me time to observe. There's poetry in a wharf, places of gathering, waiting, and departing. Even the gulls seem to use it in this way. In the spring, blue penguins nest in the rocks. They gather in the evening with much noise and fussing. I always take the time to look down into the water. Once I had the privilege of seeing an octopus. More often there's a large dark stingray resting in the shallows.

Nature journaling can become a habit. Start to listen to the birds. See if you can discern their song. Watch where in the canopy they most spend their time. How do they fly? Write down your observations in your journal. Allow your curiosity to foster your learning. Follow up with research and look out for good field guides. At the time of writing, I just made a note of what time the tui first called. They are often the first bird to call on Waiheke and the transition to dawn is my favourite part of the day. Nature contains patterns. The diurnal and lunar patterns are part of the sense of harmony that we experience in nature. Note taking, star watching, and moon watching helps us to become aware of these patterns. I notice the lunar cycle never feels the same. Each month has its own particular quality, influenced by the moon. I tend to adjust any intentions or actions I wish to complete to coincide with the moon's cycle.

Seeing with the Heart

To see with the heart, bring your attention to your heart centre in the middle of your chest and allow it to be relaxed and open. Walk slowly. See what attracts your attention. Allow yourself to linger, looking at what you love. It might be the way the light touches the underside of a fern frond or a drop of water on a leaf. One of my favourite times to experience this state of love with nature is during soft rain. In spring it's exquisite to taste the rain on the rose petals.

Guardianship

The heart opens when we connect to nature through guardianship. The Māori word for this is *kaitiaki*. Kaitiaki encompasses the care of both the physical and spiritual aspects of nature and people. We are part of the whole and so taking up the guardianship of a place includes people. My grandfather showed me how to gather oysters so that more oyster would grow. Toroa (a large bivalve) were very abundant in my grandfather's day. He was very upset when people began greedily raking the toroa beds, ultimately destroying them. If we love to eat something, we need to see its place in the ecosystem and we can begin our kaitiaki there. Sometimes love of a place brings us into guardianship. We find ourselves picking up rubbish and attending in small ways to a place. People have tended to forget, or deny, how important the role of the human is in relationship to the ecosystem. We have a place as a conscious guardian. We are totally dependent on the natural world to live and our survival requires us to attend to our environment.

Sensory Meditation

Find a spot to sit. It can be in your garden. The closer it is to your home the better as it is beneficial to your practice to visit it often. Sit quietly and comfortably, and slowly bring attention to each sense. Begin with looking. Look around you, then look ahead, becoming aware of how the eyes are. Are they relaxed, or focused? Close your eyes, move them left and right and roll them. This helps to bring awareness to your eye muscles. Next, open them and practise focusing, softening your gaze and playing with your peripheral vision. You can do this by looking ahead and then slowly bring your arms forward until you can see them from the corners of your eyes. You can start to play, bringing the peripheral further by moving the arms back a fraction. I recommend furthering your visual experience by practising Feldenkrais or the Alexander technique. Both practices work with eyes.

Keeping the eyes open and relaxed you can then bring your attention to your hearing. Imagine your ears are like that of a deer. What do you hear on your left side, and right side? You can close your eyes and then focus on a particular sound and locate its positioning.

Bring your attention to your sense of smell. Can you differentiate the scents in the air? An animal will sometimes lift its nose in the air to smell. Practise that. See if you can sense where a scent is coming from. When I was a child tramping with my father through different forests, one of his ways of connecting was to smell the air and then his favourite was to smell the moss. You can start to identify what kind of forest you are in by smell.

Bring your attention to your taste. How is your sense of taste and smell connected? Choose different herbs and smell each one before chewing it slowly. I always enjoy exploring the aftertaste of what I have eaten. I particularly love the sweet aftertaste that occurs when I chew something very bitter. Recently I stopped at the Mercer cheese shop and was tasting different cheeses. I bought the ones that had a lingering aftertaste.

Finally, bring attention to what you feel. What is your skin experiencing? Are you hot or cold? What fabric are you wearing? Often our first impulse, when we wish to connect with something, is to touch it. I am sure this is why in so many art displays and shops have a sign saying 'please do not touch.' Velvet, silk and hessian, they all convey an immediate feeling that is experienced first by the body and then the mind. There is the smoothness of fine china, the prickliness of gorse, things may feel wet, sloppy, soft, coarse, crisp, slimy, spongy, metallic and cold. Taking off your shoes and walking barefoot can offer a heightened form of sensory awareness. If you normally wear shoes when outside, you may find that your whole body responds differently to the environment and your posture may change.

Discomfort, Fear and Hazards

Many people experience discomfort in nature. They may be uncomfortable lying on the ground, or sitting in the grass. They often need to put many layers of clothing between themselves and the wild. Some people are afraid to walk barefoot. If this is the case it's important to go slowly as the movement toward connection needs to respected.

If you have fears it is a good idea to take time to examine them. Research to find out if they are based on reality or whether you have inherited them from family or community. Some fears arise through having difficult experiences, being lost as a child or being knocked by a wave. It's also interesting to note where a safe place was when you were a child. For some it was a room in the house. For others it was a tree or a hiding place outside. This makes a difference whether you are naturally more inclined to go outside or inside to seek solace.

People may also feel fear because they do not know what the real hazards in their environment are and how to be with them. Naturally we are fearful of the unknown. Rather than assume that a new environment is safe, take time to observe. A good practice is, when you come to a new body of water and you would like to swim in it, sit and watch it. If it is the ocean, observe the waves, and where the currents and rips are. Are the waves rolling or do they dump? Is there a bar further out? Where it is shallow? Allow yourself to become familiar and then step in for a swim. Someone who often swims long distances in the ocean told me that she will swallow a little of the sea water like a greeting, a blessing for her swim.

Being aware of the hazards in your environment is to know your limitations. Experienced bushmen know their limitations and may choose to make camp for a week to wait for a river to go down rather than cross it in flood. Hazards may be unstable clay cliffs or ferocious stinging nettles. When, as a family, we shifted to Piripai, my father took time to show me where katipo (New Zealand's most poisonous native spider) hid, what they looked like, and how shy they really were. He showed me why it was important not to get boxthorn in your feet and what to do if you did. He pointed out the dangers of blue bottle jellyfish, how the rips worked in the ocean, and the impact of stagnant water. These were the hazards of that environment. My knowing them enabled me to have a greater freedom in my wanderings. This is why it is important to be wised up and teach your children the plants that are poisonous and the plants that are beneficial to eat. Knowledge leads to freedom.

Pay particular attention to what you are afraid of. Investigate the truth of your fear. I have a fear of being charged by wild pigs when I'm in pig country. This arises from the vivid stories my brother told me about pigs up the Mokoroa Gorge. When I was in Germany I went for a walk in the early morning and in front of me on the path I saw a wild boar. He was big and sniffing the air, checking the environment, after which he walked on. I knew that where there was one there were bound to be more and so I stayed very still. Sure enough, more came and crossed the trail. Finally came the piglets. They all followed the path of the leader into an abandoned orchard. I had the privilege to observe them close up. I guessed they were aware of me and had decided that I wasn't a threat. In the past, my fear would have limited this encounter.

One hazard in the New Zealand bush is the tree nettle, a stinging nettle that can ultimately disorient you from repeated stings. A death has even been attributed to the nettle's stings. Flash flooding, exposure from sudden drops in temperature, unpredictable weather changes, and above all getting lost are more common hazards in New Zealand. Knowing your limitations and being wised up to the conditions are the key to venturing further afield.

People often access unconscious knowledge that acts in response to something in nature. It may be that you remember a hazard from one environment that isn't applicable to the environment you're in. For instance, I was teaching a nature awareness workshop and a participant who was from Europe became terribly uneasy about the long grass. She didn't, however, express this and it was only later that I found out that where she came from there were disease bearing ticks that lived in long grass. Carrying our understandings from one environment to another can also go the other way. It's not uncommon for New Zealanders visiting Australia to 'just want to go for a swim' in some innocent looking coastline that does, in fact, contain saltwater crocodiles that could kill.

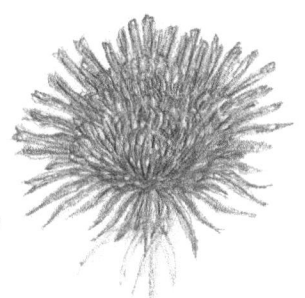

Gratitude

> **never just walk right into the bush**
> **stand at the edge**
> **and watch**
> **when you feel it is proper**
> **you may enter**
> **but always with respect**
> **because you are walking**
> **among your elders**

Gratitude is bound to connection. It deepens our connection to thank and respect every part of the whole. By greeting we are speaking to the intelligence of the life around us, and our place in relationship to it. By thanking we acknowledge its relationship to us. In thanking, it is not the words we use, but our awareness of the creature, element, or person's service that is important. In being grateful, we may glimpse their gesture, their service, and in so doing begin to understand our own place in the implicate order. A prayer of gratitude will centre you and bring you into alignment with your world. From there you might allow yourself to wander, slow down, and open yourself to wonderment.

Prayer of Gratitude

The following is a prayer of gratitude. It is a prayer I perform outside. I often stand in a relaxed pose as this prayer helps anchor me to the physical. Performing this prayer can open our heart to see, in doing so we may feel vulnerable as we receive information and connect to our environment. We may also connect to pain or discomfort. However, if we are able to fully accept and receive what is there in front of us, love arises.

I give gratitude to the plant kingdom
I thank the small plants that cover our Earth and act as a skin to protect the Earth, that give us medicine and nourish us
I give thanks to the seaweeds in the ocean, the algae and the lichen
I give gratitude to the trees, their power, the way they give a home to so many creatures
and I give gratitude to the kinship I feel from the plant kingdom

I give gratitude to the animals
all the insects, the mammals, the small creatures in the earth
all the animals I thank you for the rich diversity to bring and for my kinship with you

I give gratitude to the mineral kingdom
the rocks, stones, crystals
the material force and creativity
thank you for holding us, protecting us and the stories you contain
thank you for gifting us the reminder of history

I give gratitude to the land I am standing on
to the essence and spirit guardian of this land, I greet you and give my thanks to you
I acknowledge all those who have walked here before me on this land
I give gratitude to all those who have loved this place and this earth

I give gratitude to all that is above
the stars that shine their light in the darkness
the moon, for her reflection, rhythms and cycles
the sun the source of our energy

I bring my thoughts to the creation of this universe
and in the quiet and stand in the awe of the creation and immensity of the world

I come to this earth
I give gratitude to each direction
for the medicine you bring
to the seasons, to space and balance
that all things have their time
thank you

I give my gratitude to water
to the rain, the streams, the underground waterways
to the ocean
to the water in my body
thank you for your mystery, for your merging flow qualities
for cleansing and for quenching our thirst

I give my gratitude to air
to breath, and space and light
to wind for cleansing capacity to release the old energies

I give gratitude to fire
for warmth and for its nature of alchemical transformation

I come to earth
I thank this earth and this body for nourishing me and the immense generosity and abundance that is there.
I thank the wildness and the intelligence and the enormous cycle of life and death that I am part of.

Walking

> I wake up my sleeping feet
> with wet sand on a windy night and the slap
> of the ocean foaming
> I wake them on the grit of broken cockle
> shells
> and wild celery adrift in the banked-up
> shells

In the early morning, the world is in the beauty of traversing between night and day. The track that winds its way up the hill from the beach has narrative, homecoming with a towel draped over the shoulder, or the white cement footpath where someone has managed to write 'shit happens'. I step down the hill. I follow zigzag clay patterns ridging the bank. The pohutukawa makes the sandy clay soft underfoot. There are ridges of pathways, ridges on the stone, ridges on the seahorse's skeleton that I find here.

I remember to look up, aware of the first crescent moon rising across from the east during the day and falling away into the west in the evening. I try to name the cloudscapes, or the vista of a headland, the change of forest type. I listen to the soundscapes. In late summer, cicadas build up a dense chorus and as you emerge out of kanuka forest the sounds disperse slowly as if you are part of the symphony.

Poets Dorothy and William Wordsworth walked the wondering walk of the senses. They were revolutionary in that they walked for the pleasure of nature at a time when that was unusual. The Danish philosopher Søren Kierkegaard walked to think. 'Above all,' he wrote, 'do not lose your desire to walk: every day, I walk myself into a state of well-being and walk away from every illness: I have walked myself into my best thoughts, and I know of no burden that one cannot walk away from.'

As I walk, I observe and see what arises within me and around me, my thoughts, patterns, direction and surrounds. Through walking, observing and being in landscape we can begin to understand the language of landscape. We see the patterns of weather and changes of climate. Landscape presents us with a continuity to the past, all the way back into geological time. Being present and beginning to observe the language of landscape is important in understanding who we are.

Walking barefoot increases your sensory awareness as you have to watch where you are putting your feet. I have had a few memorable barefoot walks. One was a two-hour walk in the Tongariro National Park. I felt utterly energised and had a mystical experience. Another time I walked barefoot in the city. People who are used to walking barefoot tend to land with the forefoot or mid-foot, eliminating the hard heel strike and generating less collision force in the foot and lower leg.

Portrait of William and Mary Wordsworth, 1839, by Margaret Gillies

The Wanderer Above the Sea of Fog, c. 1817, oil on canvas, by Caspar David Friedrich

Walking Meditation and Gatha

This walking meditation practice was passed on to me by a colleague and unfortunately, I do not know its original source. Wherever we walk, we can practise meditation. This means that we know that we are walking. We walk just for walking. We walk with freedom and solidity, no longer in a hurry. We are present with each step. We may like to use a gatha as we walk. Taking two or three steps for each in-breath and each out-breath.

> **Breathing in, 'I have arrived.' Breathing out, 'I am home.'**
> **Breathing in, 'In the here.' Breathing out, 'In the now.'**
> **Breathing in, 'I am solid.' Breathing out, 'I am free.'**
> **Breathing in, 'In the ultimate.' Breathing out, 'I dwell.'**

in Your Journal

Take the time to examine what you are afraid of in nature, ranging from small anxieties to real dangers. Write these down in your journal and any stories that are associated with them. Find out as much as you can about these hazards. Are they hazards in your local area? What should you do when you encounter them? How do you avoid getting into trouble in relationship with this hazard? Take note of the moon cycle. What point in the cycle is your favourite? Note down your dreams and see how they correlate to the moon cycle.

Chickweed
stellaria media

Description

I step outside my studio, knowing that somewhere in my garden chickweed will be sprawling out, soft, tender and delicious. It prefers to grow in the 'tended' areas of the garden. Once you discover the sweetness of chickweed it's hard not to keep an eye out for it in the garden. Great in salads, it's also a wonderful grazing herb. It has a slight salty taste that indicates its high mineral content. The leaves of chickweed are oval and grow in opposite pairs. The flowers are small, white and have five petals with deep clefts. The flowers resemble stars with narrow sepals. The fruit are found on elongated drooping stalks and produce tiny yellow-orange seeds. Chickweed readily self-sows and will grow throughout the year though it tends to be more prolific in the spring and autumn than in the middle of summer, preferring the damp and cool. Chickweed soothes. It soothes the whole digestive tract and itching on the skin. Nicholas Culpepper described it as 'a fine, soft pleasing herb under the dominion of the moon.'

Mrs M. Grieves in *a Western Herbal* describes how chickweed does something that she terms 'sleep of plants.'

> Every night the leaves approach each other, so that their upper surfaces fold over the tender buds of the new shoots, and the uppermost pair but one of the leaves at the end of the stalk are furnished with longer leaf stalks than the others, so that they can close upon the terminating pair and protect the tip of the shoot.
>
> Maud Grieves, herbalist, (1858-1941)

This protective gesture can also indicate the nourishing quality of this plant for it is a highly nutritious mineral rich food source. It contains saponins – naturally occurring soap-like compounds – these increase the permeability of mucous membranes, and the absorption of nutrients.

Essence

Chickweed is a remedy to use in times of transition. It supports a person in the first stages of grief, helping to assimilate a situation that is unexpected or where the circumstances are unforeseen. It is gentle and unassuming, yet surprisingly strong and insistent. It has a quality of deep nourishment and assimilation, enabling us to nourish ourselves on all planes.

Chickweed helps us to let go of what is no longer in alignment. This remedy is good for those who cling to what feels safe even though it is outmoded. This remedy is good for those who are unable to let go or step out into the world, particularly when they are anxious and overwhelmed. In our culture, we work in a highly competitive environment. This impacts our nervous system. Rather than be overwhelmed by feelings of inability and not being able to keep up with others, Chickweed helps us to realise the contributions we already make, thus emboldening our confidence and self-esteem. It also assists us to accept differences in others. When experiencing envy, it enables us to look at our own desires and expectations, allowing us to see clearly what is appropriate and supportive in our lives.

Chickweed is a good remedy for children or even infants, helping them through weaning or when they need support through transitional stages of growth. It is connected to the lungs and touches the heart chakra. For those of us who drift on the oceans of life, it will help connect to home. The plant's gesture is nourishing, protective, gentle and encompassing, aided by a delectable sense of humour.

The Shamanic Journey and Visioning

Imaginative Consciousness

Visioning occurs through imaginative consciousness. We experience it with our mind's eye (not seeing something extraordinary taking on material form). Our imagination can be understood as the organ we use for visioning. English poet and philosopher Samuel Coleridge (1772–1834) wrote that 'The imagination opens the doors to perception.' That is the way I understand shamanic visioning, it is through the imagination that we enter into the interior world of the universe and perceive worlds that would otherwise have no form. These worlds can be understood as subtle bodies, dimensional states that concertina, layer up into each other. They are also mirror-like. The imagination in its active state opens up these spaces, allowing energy exchanges within the worlds. The shamanic journey is a process that creates a structure, a narrative, for authentic experience through the imaginal consciousness.

The visionary process may be a sensory experience. The imagination is active through the integration of both the sensory body and the intellect. The sensory body acts as a tuned instrument, an intelligent system of receptors. Sound waves shake our eardrums. Particles of light collide with our eyes. Chemical changes in our mouths stimulate our taste buds. Particles of scent waft into our nostrils. The intellect interprets what the sensory body passes to it. The idea of journeying is not to disconnect from our senses but indeed to enhance them.

> The boy of the fairies beats his drum while men and women passed through invisible doorways into another realm containing magnificent chambers filled with festive revellers eating, drinking, dancing and making merry. After enjoying this otherworldly gala, the men and women flew in spirit to faraway places, such as France and Holland, before returning to ordinary reality.
>
> a 1684 account of 'the fairy-boy of Leith' in Scotland, retold in *Fire in the Head: Shamanism and the Celtic Spirit* by Tom Cowan

Preparing for Journeying

We begin shamanic journeying by bringing the body into a resting pose, lying on our backs, closing our eyes, and letting our body move into an alpha state of relaxation. In this state we are aware, yet relaxed. Within us we access a sustained focus, yet the form of this focus is in a state of inner listening. It is a process of *being with* what we see rather than directing what we see. I often prepare people to journey through a breathing practice that lets go any tension, particularly the tension of expectation, or the fear of not being able to vision.

To experience the shamanic journey, we must first acknowledge that there is energy behind the physical world, that there exists, dimensional worlds beyond the world we live in and that what happens in these worlds may have impact in our world. The imagination can give form to these worlds and make it possible for us to communicate with beings that reside in them. This takes training, and most importantly, a spiritual practice that keeps us grounded in the physical world.

In preparing for a shamanic journey your intention is important. You embark on a journey with a purpose. To enable the answer and the process of intention to be fulfilled, perhaps in an unexpected way, you should offer your purpose or intention up to a benevolent spirit. The preparation required to be able to access and work with the divine imagination comes from the meditative power of being with both the heart and the mind. By divorcing ourselves from either we lose the ability to consciously vision.

You may journey with or without a drum. The drum's rhythm may aid in keeping the connection between the heart and the visionary capacity of the mind steady. It can also give a structure to a journey so that you feel sustained, knowing that you can return to your beginning place like the ball of string that Theseus took into the labyrinth. You may also listen to a shamanic drumming recorded track.

Through mapping and journaling your journeys you will begin to make connections, see the layered nature of the teachings available to you and to discern the qualities of the energies you encounter. Journaling will help give you a continuity and this connection will enable you to explore more and develop a relationship with the dream world. You may find that you experience the energies both physically and emotionally. These moments can be very memorable and healing. Through shamanic journeying you may clarify an enquiry so that you will be able to arrive at insights and answers that shift patterning at deep levels.

Notes on Terminology

The origin of the word *shaman* hence *shamanic* probably originates from the Evenki languages of Siberia and Mongolia, where the term *saman* is still in use. The Dutch traveller Nicolaes Witsen may have introduced the term to Western Europe around 1692. Witsen used the term to describe someone who contacted the spirit world through altered states of consciousness and who crosses over into the underworld to bring back information for the sick and for the tribe.

In modern spiritual circles, *shamanism* has come to mean a spiritual theology connected with nature, a system of knowledge that connects the practical aspects of life with an awareness of the dream world. This sounds promising and yet by putting an 'ism' on the end of the word shaman, there is a danger of it becoming an ideology and a spiritual fad.

I use the term 'shamanic journeying' to recognise the historical basis and cultural borrowing involved in the practice, but wish to avoid being placed in an ideological position called 'shamanism'. I do not consider it appropriate for practitioners of shamanic journeying to refer to themselves as 'shamans'. Shaman, like the word 'druid' or 'tohunga', refers to specific cultural and historical persons. Respectfully borrowing from other culture's spiritual practices is good, appropriation is not.

Difficulties and Dangers in Journeying

Shamanic journeying requires that we trust in our visionary capacity. Growing up in family and community we share a reality. We also communicate with each other to reinforce how we perceive the world around us. If as children we saw or experienced things that weren't supposed to exist and had no way to integrate those experiences, we may have shut down the visioning capacity for survival. Reopening it may take conscious effort. It also requires a connection to the heart. My first advice for those who are struggling with journeying is to go slowly, have patience and be as present as they can with the energy of the heart. If you are ungrounded, often in your thoughts, and tend to flick out of the body, you may also find it difficult to journey. If so, it is a good practice to stay with the senses in your body and to practise sensory meditation every day.

If you grew up where you were not safe and therefore you had to be overly alert and keyed up simply to get through your day then you may also experience trouble journeying. If this applies to you then you should bring your attention to the earth, your breath and to be in a position where you feel safe. You may also feel impacted by journeying in a group as you may experience a merging with others. Imagine the earth cradling you. If you already know your power animal then focus on your power animal.

People who regularly smoke marijuana will often just lie there, think it's all dark and nothing happens. Try and stop smoking for a week or two and then journey. Some people will also find it hard to journey if they have expectations of how it should be and therefore get caught up in their thinking mind, doubting themselves. Recognise what triggers the distraction and carefully come back to where you were in the journey before you flicked out.

People who mix hallucinogenic drugs with spiritual work tend to cling to the experience of power they felt while journeying, and thus enter into illusion. They may be unable to smoothly transition back into ordinariness. Mixing hallucinogenic drugs with spiritual work is dangerous and reckless.

In exploring with the imaginal mind, we may gain transformative teaching, but risk losing ourselves in illusion. Illusion is a powerful teacher if we have the ability to recognise it for what it is. Illusion will fit well with our wounds and our shadows, making it difficult for us to confront. In my view it important to practise shamanic journeying with a group, so that by reflection, journaling and careful sharing we may check how the vision is integrated. This will help to show up illusion. Another powerful way to show up illusion is to listen to the resonance of the body. When something is true, we experience a particular feeling that runs through the body. Before exploring shamanic journeying, we must bring our attention to how we are in our bodies.

Theseus and the Minotaur in the Labyrinth, 1861, pencil, brown wash, pen and ink on paper, by Edward Burne-Jones

The Power Animal

INTO THE WORLD

> Through this type of intense and frequent contact with the powers and qualities of the animals and, eventually, all forms of life, humankind is awakened to, and thus may realize, all that an individual potentially is as a human person. Human completion, wholeness, or religious awakening depends on this receptive opening to the potentialities and sacred mysteries in the immediate environment.
>
> Joseph Epes Brown, scholar of indigenous American traditions (1920–2000)

Through shamanic journeying we can experience a connection with an animal that touches our senses and awakens our awareness – our power animal. It is a profound moment and should not be lost in overinterpretation. We may experience a mystical sensory participation from meeting this animal. It will be our companion whenever we venture into the dream world. The power animal's place is earth and it reflects the power of the individual it is assigned. Kinship and action are qualities of the animal. It acts as a guide in the dream world. It can act as your healer. It can cut through the convolutions of your mind and wake you up when you have become stagnated. Power animals may imbue a physical token, such as an amulet, a picture or a feather. Sometimes people keep these tokens in their home or carry them about.

Finding Your Power Animal

For most visioners, finding their power animal is their first experience of a shamanic journey, their first foray into the dream world. When you are relaxed and have entered the visioning state, offer up your intention to find your power animal.

Imagine yourself in a landscape, whichever landscape you see in your mind's eye. Walk through this landscape until you find a way into the earth, through a cave, crack or door. Once inside the earth you will be greeted by an animal. This may or may not be your power animal. From this point allow yourself to journey freely through different landscapes, spending time with whichever animals come to you.

Feel how you relate to each animal. Your power animal should have a particular connection to you or a prominence in your journey. People may also sense the power animal through the physical body, particularly if feeling is a stronger sense for them then sight. If you have trouble knowing which animal is your power animal spend more time with each. You may even ask the animals directly if they are your power animal. One visioner was unsure what her power animal was, in her vision she went to sleep, telling herself whichever animal was beside her when she awoke would be her power animal.

People often ask if it is possible to have more than one animal. In my view, the answer is a qualified yes. Other animals will appear and work with you. They are important teachers and come through to support when they are needed. However, my experience with people over the years is that there is usually one animal that is particularly connected to them when journeying in the dream world. In some circumstances there may be a shift and another animal may come forward.

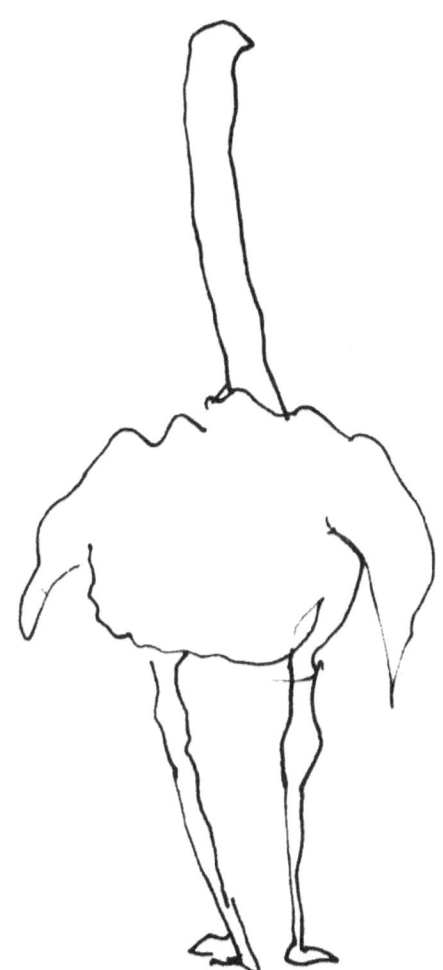

the Power Animal and Individuality

Our power animal reflects our attributes and our individuality. When we transverse the dream world, it is important to retain the knowledge of our individuality. It is our individuality that allows us to be grounded and to be agile in the dream world. In the dream world, the sense of self as the protagonist allows us to experience powerful teachings through narrative. The presence of our power animal as a symbol of our individuality is, therefore, a valuable tool in shamanic journeying.

To understand your power animal is to understand your individual power source. In my training in open form improvisation, we worked with the concept that each individual had different attributes that showed as a power source. Some people were naturally good at abstract movement, others good at words or character. We worked with what was a natural power source for us and developed it. Likewise, the qualities and strengths of power animals allow us to reflect upon and strengthen our own attributes. One way of finding more about your power animal is to research as much as you can about its life history, the environment it lives in and if possible, go and observe this animal.

Separation from and Connection with the Animal Kingdom

Writer and psychologist James Hillman (1926–2011) in his book on dream animals, hypothesized that at a point in our history we separated ourselves from animals and that it was at this point that consciousness became defined. 'We leave the Garden behind,' wrote Hillman, 'Hercules kills one beast after another separating human consciousness from its primordial affinity with animals.' He concluded 'that our consciousness is raised by returning to their teaching.' The theory that a rift occurred in human consciousness separating us from animals is worth contemplating for it may still be lurking within us, interrupting the deepening of our kinship with the animal kingdom. A kinship which through cultivating, we may better know ourselves.

There are, on the other hand, stories that illustrate not a separation but a strong connection to the animal world. Anthropologist Richard Nelson, in an article *Heart and Blood*, describes the intensity and intimate connection between people and deer.

Traditional Koyukon people follow a code of moral and ethical behaviour that, 'keeps a hunter in a right relationship to the animals. They teach that all of nature is spiritual and aware, that it must be treated with respect, and that humans should approach the living world with restraint and humility.'

THE POWER ANIMAL

The capacity of the human mind to experience consciousness through connection to animals and to have a sensory experience of their essential qualities is a pathway to a consciousness of kinship and participation in the whole ecosystem. If we were to play with hierarchy, I would put the human at the bottom of a hierarchical model, for we are dependent on everything to live. Therefore, our role is a role of guardianship. We need the balance of our ecosystem in order to be nourished and live well. Our kinship with the animal kingdom helps us to see the often fragile interdependency of the whole ecosystem. Can we borrow from an ancient wisdom to structure a new relationship between ourselves and the environment? Or is Western society irreversibly committed to the illusion that humanity is separate from and dominant over the natural world?

The Ghost of a Flea, c. 1819 . 20, Tempera mix panel with gold on mahogany, William Blake

Power Animal as Medicine

> 'I'll tell you about it, sir.' I called on him one evening and found Blake more than usually excited. He told me he had seen a wonderful thing – the ghost of a flea! 'And did you make a drawing of him?' I enquired. 'No indeed,' said he, 'I wish I had, but I shall, if he appears again!' He looked earnestly into a corner of the room, and said 'there he is – reach me my things – I shall keep an eye on him. There he comes! His eager tongue whisking out of his mouth, a cup in his hand to hold blood and covered with a scaly skin of gold and green;' – as he described him so he drew him.
>
> John Varley on William Blake

In his book *Animals of the Soul*, Joseph Brown described three ideas encompassed by the phrase power animal.

1. The master guardian or spirit animal that guards all the animals of a given species
2. That it is the essence of an animal or species
3. The guardian spirit, a personal protector

The master guardian is the quintessential manifestation of the animal and would be extraordinarily powerful in that intrinsic central essence. Legends and stories associated with these guardians contain important teachings. But it is the second meaning outlined by Brown that concerns us here. The essence of an animal can be understood as the condensed qualities of that animal. The essence exists in its wholeness and cannot be pulled apart or lessened through interpretation. By observing the power and qualities of animals we may see counterparts to qualities within ourselves.

Once I observed a kingfisher. It alighted on an old flying fox and caught my attention. Its head was slightly bent forward looking intently at the ground. The whole of its body was in a state of focus. There was only one part of it moving and that was its tail flicking. As I observed, I imagined myself becoming the kingfisher and what struck me was the shape of the head. I experienced the sensation of my head energetically shift. The energy in my crown intensified as if I was filled with taut potential. I experienced a baseline state of no tension and an intense focus. These attributes are the essence of the kingfisher.

The essence of an animal is in its intrinsic nature. To perceive it might be like English poet and painter, William Blake (1757–1828) conveyed as a ghost to the visionary eye. It may be perceived as a feeling. It can be distinguished through its appearance as the physical form reflects the essential nature. The essence of an animal can be understood as the condensed qualities of that animal. These attributes or characteristics could be expressed in a simple gesture and the essential quality of the animal could be conveyed in a movement. To do this the essence needs to be observed, understood and absorbed.

the Weka: a Cool Thief

The other day I was sitting around a table with friends and we started to share stories of the different birds in our environment. The fat kereru, the feisty territorial tui, and the weka. The stories of the weka usually bring out a few laughs. One such story was about a weka hiding under a bird feeding table whilst his family had a good feed. It seemed a most difficult place to be crunched under, guarding it fiercely watching everyone with a gimlet eye. The following extract comes from a story by Crosbie Morrison and is about weka on Kapiti Island. To me, the story captures the essence of weka:

Ocydromus earli. Ocydromus australis. Illustration of the Weka, 1873, Walter Lawry Buller: *a History of the Birds of New Zealand*

Presently the light caught a beady eye, there was a vague movement among the shadows of the bush fringe, and then slowly, cautiously, what appeared to be just a section of the grassy and twiggy bush floor detached itself from the rest and became the plump body of the weka skirting ever so cautiously towards the spot that would give him the shortest run across the open grass to that plate of scones. You could almost imagine him measuring the distance with the eye of a mathematician – there was no hesitating or wavering, but just the slow caution that you would expect in the circumstances…

At length he went onto the point he had obviously calculated, then crouched and stretched his neck out and made for the plate of scones. Surprisingly, he didn't run really fast; he seemed more to glide along, powerful legs bent to keep his body close to the ground, neck outstretched ready to grab, and that eye on the alert all the time, as though intent on the goal of his run and yet ready to sheer off innocently the moment he found he was detected. So he got to the plate and picked off not the nearest scone but the biggest one with the most butter on.

Field Trip: a Visit to the Zoo

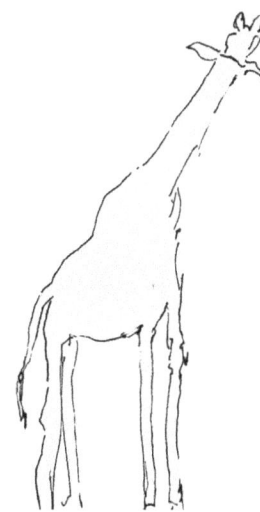

In the process of reconnecting with the animal kingdom, and understanding the essence of an animal, I recommend you visit a zoo, or better an animal park where the animals have a greater natural environment to roam in, as it is a place where you can see and directly come into contact with a range of animals. Zoos have a dark history as places where animals were routinely abused for human entertainment. In some instances, tribal peoples were even displayed in zoos alongside animals. Zoos have gradually changed in how they attend to animals and now have an important role in conservation and this is some relief. Nevertheless, zoos are places where animals are lifted from their natural habitat and held in captivity, it may be the case that animals are physically stressed or suffering from insanity. We should be aware of and sensitive to the condition of the animals we are observing.

Gerald Durrell in his book *The Stationary Ark* argued for the role that zoos should play. Zoos should act as a reserve of critically endangered species which need captive breeding in order to survive. They can serve the secondary purposes of educating people about wildlife and natural history, and of educating biologists about the animal's habits. They should not be run for the purposes of entertainment only, and non-threatened species should be reintroduced into their natural habitats. Animals should be present in a zoo only as a last resort. Enclosures should be built with the comfort of the animal in mind, not for the viewing convenience of visitors. The size of an enclosure should reflect the size of the animal's natural territories. Every animal deserves the food of its choice, a mate of its choice, and a stimulating environment. When we visit the zoo, we should ask ourselves how well it meets Durrell's vision.

Before visiting the zoo, I recommend that you give a thanksgiving prayer. This is the prayer that I did when leading a group on a trip to the Auckland Zoo. The first part of this prayer is to acknowledge the land. When we bring animals that are not part of the natural landscape, not only do we impact the physical landscape but we also may impact the energy of the land.

INTO THE WORLD

We greet the guardian spirit of this land
thank you
we acknowledge all who have walked before us
and to the many animals that have walked freely and no longer roam here
we take a moment to remember you

We send our greetings and thanks to all the animal life in the world
we cherish the ones that still walk with us on our continuing journey
although their natural world has changed
and life has become difficult for them

We now bring our attention to this zoo
we greet these animals
that have made a home here

We give our thanks to the people who care for these animals
We give our thanks to those people who dedicate their lives to preserving the
natural environment so that wild animals may flourish in

We arrive here with respect
we arrive here to learn from the animal kingdom
to remember our kinship
and to come with lightness and an open heart.

[handwritten margin notes: "posture / stillness" and "the small one chases away the zebra"]

THE POWER ANIMAL

When you enter the zoo, wander off on your own until an animal captures your attention. Then stand or sit and really look at the animal. How does it move? How does it position itself? How is the animal in its actions or its stance – alert, relaxed, tense, nervous, energetic, watchful, slow, or considered? Describe the posture in your journal. Consider where its weight is distributed, in the front, rear, or equally distributed? What is happening around the animal? What sense does the animal rely on the most? How happy is the animal in the zoo? Take a close look at the face and the animal's sensory structures. Imagine if you had those ears, that nose, those whiskers, eyes. How would it affect your world? Put yourself in the animal's skin and look out through its eyes. See the world as that animal sees it. Consider how its senses affect its life strategy. How is the animal's body specially adapted to help it survive? What enemies does the animal have?

Write a list of adjectives that describe the animal. Sketch the animal. Now bring it to the medicine. What is the essence of this animal? Bring all the texts and sketches together in one final short piece. These are the words I arrived at for the giraffe – *respectful beauty, deep grace, stretching, sensual, love.*

Ritual

> Lin Fang asked: 'what is the root of ritual?' The master said: 'Big question! In ceremonies prefer simplicity to lavishness; In funerals, prefer grief to formality.'
>
> *the Analects of Confucius* 3.4, translation by Simon Leys

A ritual is a structure. It creates the arrangement of, and relations between the parts or elements of something complex. Rituals enable us to focus, create and transform. A ritual creates a space for invocation and enables receptivity. It aids in creating a bond within a group. Some rituals that I have worked with include creating medicine wheels, creating altars, lighting candles, meeting in co-creative circles, pipe ceremonies, morning walks, tea ceremonies, giving thanks, sprinkling water, and burning sage. There are many rituals we can practise. Some we may practise only occasionally, others we may practise daily. I encourage you to find what rituals work well for you.

Conducting Rituals

I imagine ritual as a pattern or geometry that creates right relationships with energies and elemental forces. Through ritual we create focus and articulate our intentions. The ritual is also about meeting something, for example a particular force or spirit, by creating a space like a room to respect and deepen the giving and receiving of that meeting. Therefore, each part of the ritual and how you are in your heart becomes influenced by your intention and what you are meeting. Ritual brings a consciousness to our actions and this immediately shifts our relationship to unconscious motivations. When conducting a ritual, it is better to allow an interaction to occur, rather than control it. We should avoid rigidity to ritual forms. If changing something about a ritual makes you uncomfortable then reflect on what it is you are afraid of. If you feel that the spirit of the ritual is being compromised, begin again looking at the purpose of the ritual.

If you are conducting a ritual by rote, that is following written instruction and speaking from a set text, make sure you understand the words you are speaking and what you are invoking. If you do not, then you need to take the time to learn and understand each component of the ritual. Think of the ritual as a complex weave of parts and how important it is to understand the nature of the materials you are weaving in, and your participation in this weave. If you are calling in a particular deity, entity or energy (in some of the druidic rituals people embody the gods or goddesses of an ancient tradition) ensure you understand the light and the shadow of that archetype. Ensure you have set in place the balancing force of that essence. If you are calling in angels, find out what they bring, their particular gifts and service to you.

There are many daily rituals that we unconsciously conduct. They mostly revolve around food and drink. In childhood we may have said a prayer before eating or before going to bed. There are rituals connected to learning and work, to space and place. Taking off our shoes, bathing our feet attends to the physical. This sets the stage for the spiritual. In Islamic practice, the washing of hands and feet is mandatory before prayer and all mosques have a special area dedicated to these ablutions. Ritual becomes a bridge between the physical and spiritual.

A Shipwreck in a Stormy Sea,
c. 1823, Joseph Mallord William Turner

the Magic Salt Cellar - Scandinavian Folk Tale

Once there was a poor man. He wept for he had nothing to provide for his wife and children at Christmas time. So, he set out to see his brother who was a rich merchant so that he may beg for food. But his brother threw him out into the cold, providing him with nothing but a few bent nails. On his way home, filled with misery, he met an old man who offered to trade his bent nails for a salt cellar. This the poor man did.

As it turned out, the salt cellar was magic. When the good man turned its handle, an endless supply of not just salt but rich food flooded out. There were words that invoked the ability for it to create salt and words that caused it to cease. When the merchant discovered what his poor brother had, he endeavoured to steal it. This he did. He then boarded his ship, but he did not know the words that made the salt cellar stop creating salt. Eventually, the weight of the salt caused the ship to sink and the sea to become salty. The moral of the story is that incomplete and hasty knowledge for your own ends bodes ill when invoking forces you do not fully understand.

Sacred and Ordinary

By understanding ritual, we can understand the necessity of correctly transitioning between sacred work and ordinary life. The ordinary balances spiritual work. It also brings things into the ordinary. If we were to only work in an enhanced way with all things then we would eventually fall into illusion. All the ordinary everyday things would take on the energy of the sacred and we would lose the ability to be ordinary. Transitioning from intense spiritual work to ordinariness requires a closing ritual and then a consciousness of the transition. The movement into ordinariness will then restore balance. One of the ways this is done for a group is, after the spiritual work is complete, to share food, do dishes, share tasks, even make a joke. This allows a balance to return.

Sometimes when ordinary objects are used in a ritual, they become imbued with energy. They will need to be cleared if they are to be put back to where they came from. Transitioning from sacred to ordinary was understood by Māori and reflected in the concepts of tapu (sacred) and noa (ordinary). Because noa was particularly associated with cooked food, sacred objects could be waved over baked potatoes to remove their sacred energy. Clearing this energy takes time and patience. Be aware that these objects will need their own transition. The role they played is complete but they are still energized by it.

The same applies to people when we partake in sacred work and are energised by it. People often want to cling onto the feeling of power they experienced when they were in a sacred state. If they try to hold on to the feeling of the power they will ultimately enter into an unseemly illusion of power. The movement into the ordinary redresses this.

Lighting a Candle

Start to conduct simple rituals around your work. For example, before you write, light a candle, and as you light that candle put forward what it is that you are writing. When you have finished, state that you have finished and then blow out the candle. Be aware of how you transition to the next action. Bring awareness to the myriad things you do in your day and how you transition from one activity to another.

What Use are Candles and Spectacles if the Owl Refuses to See? 1622 - 24, engraving, Cornelis Bloemaert

Creating a Sacred Place

Shrines and altars are sacred places that can aid a spiritual experience aligned to its particular purpose. They can provide the place for simple ritual and intention for our day. The purpose of creating a sacred place in your home is to bring forward spiritual energies, peace and beauty into your home. Sometimes a small shrine in your home may have a particular purpose such as celebrating the solstices and equinoxes. This might mean considering the qualities of the particular solstice and what you might want to bring attention to. In winter it might be something that represents what you need to nourish and grow so that in the summer it will flourish. In the summer there is a celebration of expansiveness and manifestation.

To create your sacred space, find a small place in your house or outside. It should be a place that will recharge you. Look for pictures of places that have power for you and objects that have a similar feeling. The sacred place is primarily for reminding you that you have power and that you can access it when you need to. Bring to the sacred place objects that symbolize what you desire to invoke. They may also be objects you find beautiful or unique to you and wish to cherish. They can be things that you have found in nature such as bones, feathers, pieces of wood, horns or shells. If you suffer from nervousness you might look for symbols or images of inner peace and relaxation that you can put in your sacred space.

If you feel overwhelmed and carry other people's energy you might like to have images of water, a bowl of water or objects that represent an inner strength. Lighting candles allows you to bring your intention in. Sacred places may also be adorned with things that represent that which we may need to bring forward to support us or remind us of something from our past that we must acknowledge.

The Shrine, 1895, painting on canvas, John William Waterhouse

Awakening Our Inner Selves

Authenticity

As we explore our attributes and what our power source is (and through this become aware of our gift), we begin to bring ourselves into alignment with that gift. The movement to aligning our lives with our gift is to strengthen our sense of authenticity. Authenticity is allowing our natural gifts, medicine and dispositions to flower.

As we move toward authenticity, we may feel a lack of alignment with some aspects of our lives. These aspects may be linked to our imagined or projected self and the movement toward authenticity is showing them up. Imagine two willow trees, one growing wild, the other trained and trimmed by humans to be in the shape of a bird. The tree that is in the shape of the bird is like our imagined self. It may appear superficially beautiful but it is unnatural and takes a lot of energy to maintain it in its state. The wild tree is like our authentic self, growing in a way that best allows growth.

As we align ourselves with our gift, we may experience resistance from others. Resistance arises because we are beginning to change our lives. This may bring us into conflict with the lack of aligned purpose in our communities. We may experience the resistance as a state of limbo between the authentic self and the imagined self in community. In our societies, people can become lost in the imagined self. They communicate with each other from an imagined self. This causes feelings of inadequacy to arise. By connecting and staying aligned with our authentic selves we can ultimately overcome these feelings.

Compulsion to Serve

Author Virginia Woolf (1882–1941) in a talk she gave to women about the professions of women expresses this curious underlying compulsion to serve.

> She was intensely sympathetic. She was immensely charming. She was utterly unselfish. She excelled in the difficult acts of family life. She sacrificed herself daily. If there was a chicken, she took the leg: if there was a draft she sat in it – in short, she was so constituted that she never had a mind or wish of her own, but preferred to sympathize always with the minds and wishes of others… I did my best to kill her. My excuse, if I were to be had up in a court of law, would be that I acted in self-defence. Had I not killed her, she would have killed m**e.**

This compulsion to serve arises out of social conditioning, and guilt. If the reflection we are surrounded by is one that has an underlying message that we are not good enough, we will absorb that into our inner makeup. Woolf's talk highlights the effect of social conditioning and how we internalise, relate to and participate in our culture. I once came across an ancient understanding of trinity that describes three types of self: the individual self, the social environment self and the universal self. We are social creatures and if we are in an imbalanced society it is difficult to see beyond this to bring forward different values and individual evolution. I love the way Woolf self reflects and brings in the court of law, a touch of the relationship between social law and individual freedom and rights.

Virginia Woolf, (1902, 1927, 1939)

Nourishment

> He dreamed a land soft, between two great oceans. With his own hands, Olocupinele planted tall shade trees; he caused rivers to flow, and he made smooth round pools where his Cuna Children would bathe and learn their beauty from their reflections in the fresh cool water.
>
> Story collected by Tomás Herrara Porras, translated to English by Anita McAndrews, quoted in *Cuna Cosmology* (1978)

In the mythology, the Central American Guna people, Guna man and the Guna woman were gifted everything they could possibly want and gifted individually unique gifts by their god Olocupinele. 'Olocupinele settled his Cuna people in the loveliest gardens. Everything so new, so polished, shining! The Cunas clung together, confused, blinded by the great light of Creation.' But they weren't able to be happy in it. There was nothing new to feel or do. They started squabbling and creating weapons to hurt each other. They forgot their god and sought to please themselves.

In the Guna story there was nothing to enable them to desire to use their gifts and their abilities. Sometimes we need the opposite to find ourselves. When everything is gifted to us, we lose the responsibility to create and it is through that creation that we nourish ourselves.

Nourishment typically refers to the substances, food, water, minerals, that are necessary for growth, health and good condition. I use the term in a broader sense to encompass our relationships and our actions that feed, foster and cherish ourselves. When we nourish ourselves, others benefit around us through our role-modelling and our care that moves beyond ourselves. Nourishment resides in balance. Neither greed and avarice nor extreme discipline nourishes. Yet a balance of discipline and self-reward does.

To find out what nourishes you, take time to reflect. Take a mental snapshot of your life and look at your relationships and how you connect with people and things. Our connection to Earth nourishes us. We should explore our relationship with Earth with attendance and trust. To feel nourished is to know that we can take space, and that in the relationship with Earth we are welcomed. Nourishment is not a destination; it is a way of life that enables us to do what we have come here to do.

When we are nourished it enables us to gift to the future as the memory of nourishment also enables us to share and perform our spiritual work. Getting right the balance of giving and receiving also motivates our work. To receive is to be part of change. We receive through our senses. If we imagine the human brain not as a thought factory but as a highly developed receiver then we can become more aware. Remarkably many people block the ability to properly receive, allowing themselves to be programmed into mechanistic thinking. Most people, moreover, choose not to do the things that nourish them. The reason why often lies in ancestral conditioning and cultural patterning that then result in people feeling that they have not enough time and space, give to others too much instead of themselves and subconsciously fear the consequences of nourishing themselves. To grow we need to act with discernment, responsibility and connection to the physical world around us.

The Bear Dance, c. 1870, William Holbrook Beard

in Your Journal

What actions in your life make you feel alive? What are the things you have done in the past that have made you feel alive? Write down what nourishes and what doesn't nourish you. Choose a couple of the things that do nourish you. What do you need to do to bring those things into your life? Write down the blocks that come up when you consider bringing this form of nourishment into your life. Is there support you can get from your community to enable you to do these things?

Structure and Space

Social pressure limits our ability to take the space required to sense and integrate. We also live in a society where we feel pressured around work. A lot of people are doing unnecessary work. To choose to work from an inner prompting that is spiritually directed is a powerful social action. This requires space to practise an inner connection, even if it's only half an hour a day to sit and be alone, or go for a walk and ponder your desires. Taking space can trigger emotions like anxiety and guilt. By taking space we are changing patterns.

Connection brings attention to space and the space within and the space around us. Structure gives us an understanding of relationship and space. Everything physical has structure. Without structure, everything loses form and so within structure there is space. Part of integrating and understanding empathetic experience is to acknowledge space and structure. For a relationship to deepen and for us to explore spiritual concepts there needs to be a structure that gives space to both ordinary and sacred experiences.

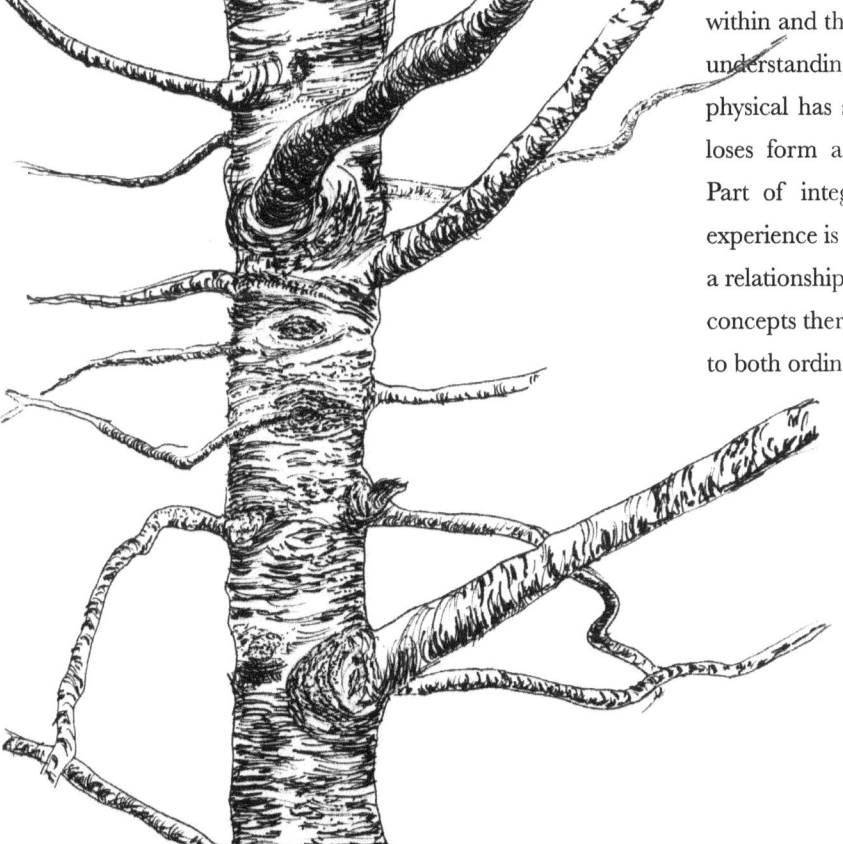

Roles

When we socialise, we are in various groups, parties, dinner parties, family and extended family. We often take on particular roles within these groups. In early societies, everyone had a role and children were destined to fill a particular role. People, for the most part, kept to the role they were born into, if your father was a blacksmith then you would become a blacksmith. The shadow side of this is that these roles can be entrapping or limiting particularly if people born into them had a disposition for something else. The positive side, however, is that people knew where they fitted within the social fabric.

It is worth examining the roles we take up in society, why we take them on and how. Examine the roles you take up in the community you live in and the wider community. Try to discern whether these roles come from social conditioning, arise from your gift and ability, or from something else. Examine how this role protects, inhibits or supports you. If you feel trapped but it is an important role, look at what you might need to change within the role. Observing this over a month can reveal startling things about ourselves so it's worth keeping a note of your thoughts and observations.

Flicking-Out

Flicking-out refers to momentarily leaving our body. People who flick-out often may have suffered from emotional or spiritual trauma. Flicking-out may be a defence mechanism. It can happen in seconds. One minute you may be in your body and seconds later you are out. There are varying degrees of flicking-out. Some people are totally disconnected from their body for much of the time.

To work with flicking-out first you must sense when you might be doing it and examine the triggers that are causing it. This is difficult as people are usually unaware of it happening. Others may help bring your attention to it. If somebody flicks-out around you, pause in what you are doing and think about what triggered it. We often talk about all kinds of things with little regard to the triggers going on in other people. Some flicking-out is very extreme and can cause great discomfort in the person. They need to find ways to come back. Flicking-out often occurs due to related memories in relationship to safety, fear, shame and simply the discomfort of being in the world.

Fear

Fear resides on the edge of our extension into unknown territory. Fear is connected to agitation. Hurt often feels like something that is hard to set to rest. Hurt agitates. By naming the core wound, seeing how to be with it and experiencing what it might be to live without it we begin the process of healing wounds, clearing, cleaning and allowing ourselves back into alignment. Hurt pushes us away from our alignment yet the very journey of realising this and coming back to it brings us insight and understanding.

> The problem with fear is not that we feel it but that we don't feel it. Fear-avoidance and psychic numbing are common ways of handling fear in a culture that continually triggers this dark emotion and yet shames us for it. When we are numb with fear we are oddly unhappy.
>
> from *Healing through the Dark Emotions*
> By Miriam Greenspan

Crisis

In her book *Behaving As If God in All Things Mattered*, author and flower essence developer Machaelle Small Wright writes about the concept of the ring-pass-not. Where we are comfortable, we have a structure in the way we perceive things and how we relate to things. The ring-pass-not represents the boundary of our comfort zone. When we reach it, we have to break down our belief patterning and life patterns to evolve. This is the crisis point. In the tarot, it is represented by the Tower (XVI), where structures and belief systems that do not serve us fall apart.

In crisis, small gestures of balance become crucial patterns that support us. Simple things like that walk at that same time each day, remembering to look up, simple tasks of organization, making a bed are small ordinary actions that can anchor us in the ordinary world through the crisis, so that we do not become restless or dwell on the wound. In crisis we are often vulnerable and being able to stay with this is an important part of the process of transformation

INTO THE WORLD

Lightness of Heart

To keep the heart light is to know that we have the ability to renew, that the heart should not be held down by promises and moral dilemmas. What makes the heart light is alignment to our truth and taking action that arises from our talent. The heart is heavy when others dominate us and when we allow their projection on to us to mould our actions. Forward movement, balance, focus, attention and insight all help to lighten the heart.

Power and the Energy beyond Thouht

As we look into the relationship we have with our own essential power and the energy beyond thought we examine the structured patterns of our cultural beliefs. Our power, our mantel, is not heavy, though perhaps we may be awkward as we pick it up. I think of it as coronet of leaves that cup the tip of cleavers. It is a symbol of the relationship between our own essential power and the energy beyond thought, an energy that flows through us, that is mysterious because it is beyond our full conception, beyond the mind, beyond our existence.

Demon Overthrown, 1902, Mikhail Vrubel

in Your Journal

Take time out each day to be alone and practise sensory awareness through sitting or walking. In your journal do an interview with your body. Look at your hands. Describe them. Imagine a conversation with your kidneys or your heart and lungs. Choose a part of the body and write about what it says.

The Mulberry Tree in Autum, 1889, Vincent Van Gogh

Cleavers

galium aparine

It is familiarly taken in broth, to keep them lean and l..ank that are apt to grow fat.

Nicholas Culpepper, English herbalist, botanist and astrologer (1616–1654)

As I'm writing this, I'm drinking water that has had cleavers soaked in it. It has a lovely cucumber taste and cleanses my palette. When I first discovered cleavers, I was utterly surprised by its tiny flowers, like minute stars, and how the energy in the stem seems to stretch out. It wholly attracted my attention. It was as if it wouldn't let go until I made a remedy from it.

Description

The stems and leaves of cleavers have very fine hooked bristles, which attach to passing objects, like Velcro. It also fastens itself to adjacent plants or shrubs and grows upwards. Its leaves are narrow, lance-shaped and are rough along the margins and surface. They grow around and along the square, and occasionally red-tinged, branching stem. The flowers are white, tiny, and star-like about 3 mm in diameter. It is self-fertile and pollinated by beetles and flies. The seeds are round and covered with hooked bristles. As children we used to call them biddibids and our clothes would often be covered in them. They readily cling to whatever they touch, ensuring dispersal of the seeds.

Cleavers could be invisible. It weaves through the other plants. It moves imperceptibly upwards, divaricating as it goes. Sometimes it is one endless stem showing up amongst the heads of blossom and lemon balm as a small, slightly hairy whorl. I saw one like this yesterday and I could not bring myself to break it. It had moved for so long, on this one small light-footed root, elongating itself, each leaf whorl a corolla for further extension. Usually cleavers tend to divaricate a little more creating new slender structures that reach up and out from these leaf whorls. The positioning of these leaf whorls along the stem can be as precise as the phalanges on your forefinger. In reflection I find a simple, beautiful symmetry in cleavers.

Cleavers has a range of folk names: Everlasting Friendship, Love-man, Catchweed, Grip Grasse, Sticky Willy, Kisses, and Hedgeheriff, each arising from its clinging nature. Hedgeheriff comes from Anglo Saxon *hedge rife*, a tax collector or robber, referring to cleavers' habit of clinging to sheep. Edible and medicinal, it is a valuable diuretic. Can be taken as an infusion or works as a poultice on ulcers and sores or skin problems. It is a great spring tonic as it doesn't grow all the year around and tends to show up in the spring.

Essence

The medicine of cleavers works by cleaving to that which needs to be brought to light. It brings it to the light where it can then be worked upon. It enables us to find intention and be at ease in seeking the energies of curiosity and discovery. Cleavers, by simply existing to seek the light, to seek renewal, seems to cut through all weighty matters. Its lightly anchored root system enables it to let go and move to a new place to grow again. The point between the stem and the leaf is the point of integration. This integration is an acceptance of everything in that moment, exactly how it is.

The cleavers remedy clears the auric field and cleanses. It enables us to receive the appropriate support at any given moment. It has the ability to bring to it the things it needs. This remedy is helpful in putting in place interdependent partnerships, a reminder that we don't have to be self-reliant in everything. It can clear a project of negative or heavy energies and is one of the remedies that can be used in house clearing or land healing.

Clearing and cleansing, it helps us reach out to the divine. It enables us to move out from staying in our own rubbish or old patterns of behaviour. It aids us in identifying and letting go of the old patterns and behaviours, as well as aiding us in reaching out to others when needed. Sometimes there's a leap in our thinking. Cleavers can galvanise that. It calls out to us to wake up to where we are in our lives.

Prayer

> Prayer is an invocation or act that seeks to activate a rapport with a deity, an object of worship, or a spiritual entity through deliberate communication.
>
> Rabbi Steven Weil

> Every word of every prayer, and indeed; even every letter of every word, has a precise meaning and a precise effect. Prayers thus affect the mystical forces of the universe and repair the fabric of creation.
>
> Kabbalistic view of prayer

Cleavers remind me of prayer, it could be that I am reminded of prayer from the quadrangular structure of the stem. The equal length between the whorls and the length of stem, reminiscent of the way prayer divides the day, the morning, noon and evening prayer, or the five-times-a-day prayer.

I imagine the stems as hands. Hands may be positioned for prayer in different ways. They could have the palms brought together like Albrecht Durer's famous drawing. They could be slightly crossed over the chest, cradling the heart. They could be lifted high, palms upward, wrists slightly bent back so that the light might land more gently that way, caught in the threads of the fingers, streaming down the wrists to open loudly through the crown of the head. The hands could also lie open at the sides allowing the chest to be open and the head raised. The hands could even press downward onto the ground, leading the body in prostration to the earth.

The word prayer comes from Latin *precari*, to beg, but cleavers does not beg, not for light, not for mercy, nor justice. Cleavers' prayer starts with deliberate communication, it moves toward and through the air. Its prayer is about alignment, an innate knowing to stand in the bright rain. Cleavers' prayer is like the dance, song, or the yoga position that allows you to enter into forgotten pockets of the body. It is the movement that wells up along the stem, the vital plumbing springing forward. Sometimes when praying we hold ourselves back because prayer can offer a spiritual experience. Someone might experience being touched by something, feel it, smell it or hear it. But it is not physically there.

When I pray, I ask for something to come forward to guide and support me in accessing what is true and right for what I am doing. Prayer aligns us to something higher than ourselves. Prayer could become a dance or a song or yoga position or a movement that is guided by your qi. Prayer can even take the form of spontaneous singing and sounding, these spontaneous sounds are like a shedding and releasing to be in alignment with that force or light. Align yourself to that. Bring yourself into that. Pull yourself into that and in doing so shed what does not belong with that. Prayer opens us to our intention, and to our gratitude. It helps us in shock and it facilitates healing.

Praying Hands, 1508, gray and white ink, gray wash on blue prepared paper, Albrecht Dürer

Prayer to the Great Spirit

Great Spirit
whose voice we hear in the winds
whose breath gives life to the world
we would restore what greed
has taken from the earth

Great Spirit
we are blind and deaf
open your eyes in us
that we may see
open your ears in us
that we may hear
open your compassion in us
that we may have compassion
upon the earth
upon our mother earth

Great Spirit
may our feet walk gently
may our hands respect her
may we learn the lessons
in every leaf and rock
may our strength restore her

Great Spirit
when we face the last sunset
when we come singing the last song
may it be without shame, singing
it is finished in beauty, it is finished in beauty.

the Brain

To draw cleavers is always to wonder whether you need to draw half a dozen other plants to put it in its correct context. Cleavers are never alone. Dandelion with its wind-borne seeds finds its anchor, folding down its leaves, a strong 'this is my space' message. By contrast, cleavers flow in-between like the physical manifestation of a breeze. Cleavers is salty with minerals and juicy with water. Yet it unfolds with natural symmetry, held upright by the invisible, as if partaking of air.

Air can be boundless. It is associated with the mercurial mind, dancing and looping and moving from one idea to another, exploring concepts and finding others to bounce ideas off and then move on. Air is the element of respiration, connecting everything through a constant movement and exchange. Air is associated with communication, sound, expression and connectivity.

the Element of Air

Curiously my work with cleavers led me to reflect on the role of the brain in spiritual work. When connecting with cleavers, I saw in my mind's eye the connective tissues between the two hemispheres of the brain. The hemispheres were communicating with each other, tentatively at first, then stronger. It was a listening aspect of speech. It gave me the inkling that human communication was often a translation of something heard but not quite heard, as if it was trying to convey something deeper in the recesses of my mind. I experienced it, quite vividly, coming from the right ear travelling into the left side of my head.

Later, standing in front of our eclectic collection of physics books, I picked out *The Origin of Consciousness in The Breakdown of The Bicameral Mind* by Julian Jaynes I flicked through it till I came to the chapter on the double brain. In this chapter, Jaynes argues that the speech areas are generally in the left hemisphere of the brain, yet there is a mystery as to a matching area on the right side of the brain, from which people could experience auditory hallucinations. This part of the brain was also connected to the anterior commissure, a bridge of nerve fibres. This transmits the auditory information, that did not come directly from the senses (the hallucination) to the speech areas of the brain. Jaynes' hypothesis resonated with my experience.

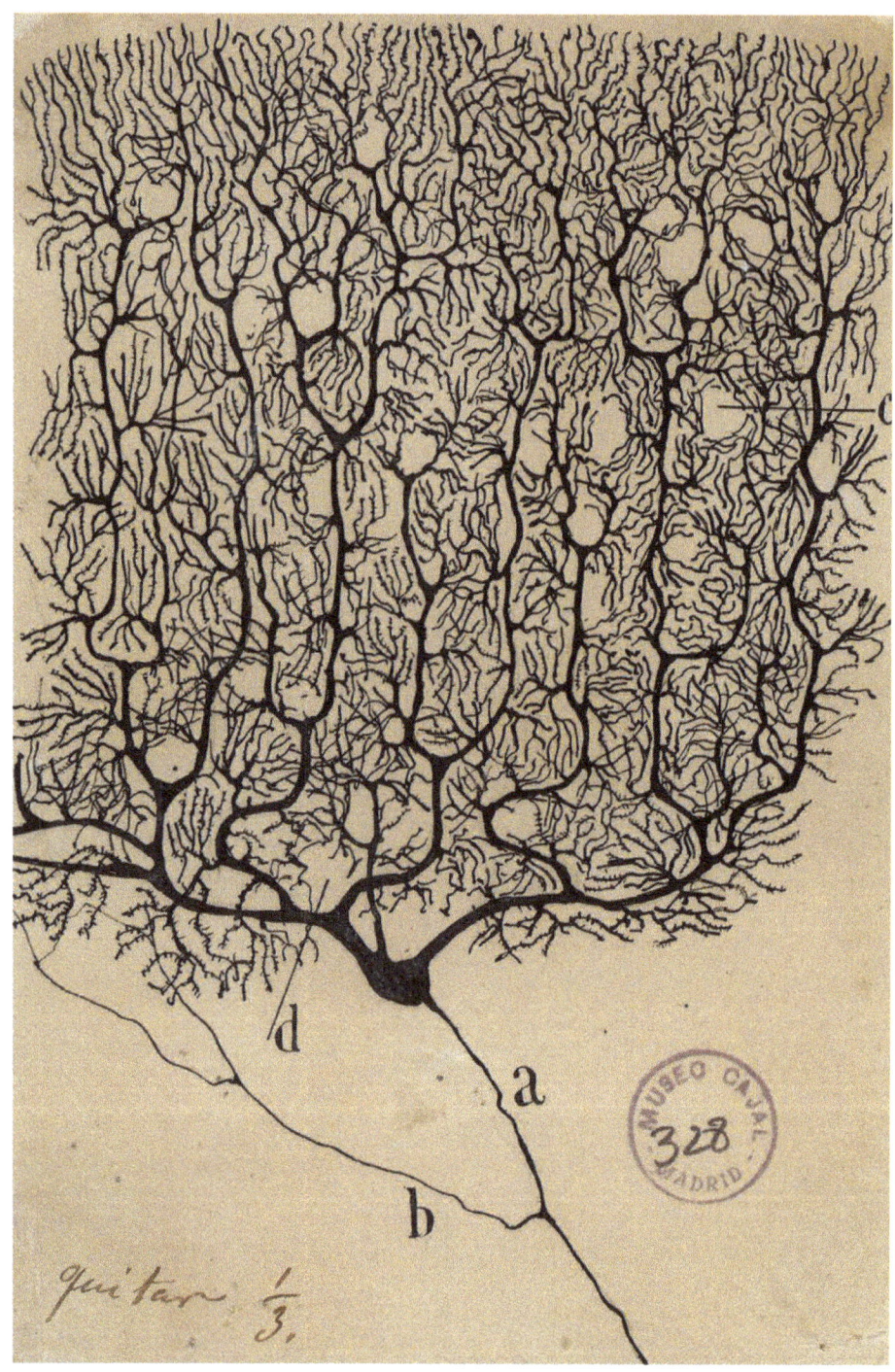

Purkinje Neurons From The Human Cerebellum, 1899, drawing, Santiago Ramón y Cajal (neuroanatomist)

Letting Go

Shortly after this experience, I received a letter that triggered some old pain that I had unknowingly secreted into my heart. A maelstrom of thoughts arose from that pain. I saw patterns of a desire to fix, a desire to please and complete, a desire to be understood, and that is when I saw the owl. It was still light and the morepork swooped above me, landing in a coprosma tree. I felt observed. I went still and returned its gaze. I stepped a little closer and it turned its deep black eyes upon me.

Seeing an owl when there is still light is symbolic for me of surrender. To let go is also to experience a small death. To really let go is also to let go the intent of letting go. At that moment when I saw the owl, something occurred; it was being with what is. I started to look away and imagined being the owl looking at me. I sensed a connectivity from my consciousness to owl consciousness.

the Shadow of Cleavers and Intention

In connecting to the essence of a plant, I look at the medicine it conveys, and through this I experience the shadow. When I connected to the shadow of cleavers, I first experienced a darkness that held me very close. As I brought my awareness to that darkness, I felt fear of being lost and unable to move. It was the exact opposite of the movement that cleavers expresses through its gesture. I felt afraid. I felt lost. I forgot the movement. I forgot what was behind me. I forgot everything. I was stagnant. I was that pool of water that starts to eddy, that starts to go stagnant that then becomes toxic. This is the shadow of cleavers.

When enveloped in the shadow of cleavers, a clear intention functions like a flare that is released upwards. As you allow yourself not to be stuck or clung to by the darkness, the intention carries you forward, through and over obstacles. It generates action. To intend is to activate something that in itself shifts stagnant energy. Intention creates a movement where things have eddied through fear. When you offer up an intention, you cannot know the outcome. Offering up an intention allows receptivity to the unknown that connects to the darkness, that connects to the night.

Indian teacher and spiritualist R. P. Kaushik described how when meditating on the negative state completely and intensely 'there is a complete and irreversible transformation of sorrow or negative silence into a positive state of love and great beauty. This love is at the same time personal and impersonal, individual and universal; a new principle of integrated intelligence comes into being.'

Clearing

Clearing

When I first performed an energetic clearing, I was staying at a friend's house and every time I went into the bedroom I started coughing. I realised that the room was making me cough. At that time, I had never heard of sage sticks, or even energy clearing, but, growing up in Whakatane, I knew about sprinkling water and prayer. I went into the room with a bowl of water and started singing. It seemed very natural. As I closed my eyes, I sensed dense energies and I sang and sprinkled water. I saw these dense clouds cling to the corners of the room before finally dissolving.

Since then I have spent a lot of time observing different energy, what it feels like, whether it is cold or sticky. How it sits in a room or around a person. I also think about where it goes when I shift it. Does it dissolve like a cloud into the air, move into the ground or go to another dimension? I consider whether the energy is caused by the impact of emotions, ancestral patterning, or perhaps unquiet ghosts and displaced elementals.

Entities

A discussion about energetic clearing ultimately leads to the concept of energetic entities. Illness can be understood as an entity. A thought can form an entity. A group has an entity. An addiction creates an entity. Entities are as diverse as the creatures of this planet. An entity is a being that is formed usually through the mind and sits in the etheric plane. It can be understood as an essential quality of something, whether negative or positive, that takes on an energetic form. This energetic form requires a connection of some kind to a physical form, usually either an object or a person.

Sacred objects can be imbued with powerful entities. That is why the looking-after of a sacred object is important and why processes of tapu are put in place to protect them and those who work with them. Over time some entities grow as dark forms. They can pass from generation to generation, or move from person to person. I have experienced entities that manifest like a beautiful scent on a summer breeze or appear in the form of an armoured creature that has outgrown the protective role for which it may have originally been created. One entity that I once cleared took the form of a tiger. The person to whom it was attached had had a traumatic experience as a child and had called the tiger in to aid her. The tiger had done its protective work well, but decades later the tiger remained attached to the person and needed to be cleared. In another instance, I worked with a person whose ancestor had been a grave robber. This had caused a particularly powerful entity to becomes attached to him and this entity had remained attached to his descendants.

I have heard dubious stories of healers shifting extraordinary numbers of entities off people. A woman I knew, who was fairly balanced and grounded, went to a healer who claimed to have shifted around twenty-five entities off her. She went back a couple of weeks later and he shifted twenty more. It all seemed very odd to me. I suspected he was clearing his own delusion or fear. There are occasional circumstances where a person may have layers of more than one entity, but if this was the case, I would look for a past situation, trauma or shock that caused the person to move out of the body. From here you can slowly empower a person to experience being able to sense when they are ungrounded, misaligned and ways to clear themselves.

Attending to the Physical

Sometimes in order to clear something it is not enough simply to do an energy clearing. There may be something that needs to be physically attended to and when that is attended to whatever is causing the disturbance will cease. I was once asked to clear the energy from a room that people were having trouble going into and had been unable to sleep in. On entering I was soon able to sense that the problem arose from the whenua (placenta) of a child. Sure enough, the whenua of a young boy was still kept in an ice cream container under the stairs of the room. Once this was attended to the bad energy disappeared.

Clearing, Merging and Absorbing Energy

Not all energy that needs clearing manifests as powerful entities. Energy disturbances, emotional burdens, shadow projections from others that we take on board, all of these have an effect on our energy systems and will also impact us physically. Sometimes healing is simply about shifting and clearing the energy that is creating the disturbance.

When we engage in a healing exchange, we may absorb some of the energy that we are lifting off a person. By doing a simple clearing between clients, of the room and yourself, you are able to work in a way that has greater clarity and purpose. At one point in my healing work, I hired rooms in Auckland which were also used for psychotherapy. These rooms were never energetically cleared of the accumulated therapy processes, to the degree that in entering the room I could feel the released emotions like an energetic fog layered over each other. I often wondered how therapists could work effectively in the fug of this leftover energy. On the opposite end of the spectrum, there are people who feel a need to constantly and unnecessarily clear themselves. It becomes a stress, similar to people who constantly and compulsively wash imagined germs off their hands. Often, they are simply not able to align or ground.

As a culture we do not tend to transition well between one activity to another. We often don't give space to acknowledge the varying qualities of energy that we use in different tasks. Being more aware of what we carry from one action to another helps us to discern the points of transition and the energy transferral between tasks. This transferral can cause an imbalance of how we direct our energy to the task at hand. The same applies to transition in our roles with people. If we don't attend to how we transition from meeting with one person to the next then we may carry or absorb energy that imbalances our work together. Simple rituals of completion can allow us to transition well.

Another way of clearing energy is to go for a swim in the ocean, river or lake that may help to shift energy. Running, exercise or a sauna will also help clear energy.

Surf Swimming, Hawaii, artist unknown, from the book **The World's Inhabitants,** 1888, Author: G.T. Bettany,

People can experience other people's emotions or even group emotions acutely. They may be unable to discern that emotion as separate from themselves. This may trigger an unconscious protection mechanism and they shut down, energetically stepping back or slipping out of their body. Others will merge with the emotion causing a feeling of overwhelm. Overwhelm leads to anxiety. Practising sensory awareness brings us back into the body and enables us to begin to observe what triggered the emotional picking-up, such as past events. Discerning and recognising when we are picking up on other people's emotions or thoughts is important training, requiring careful alignment with our body.

All relationships have a form of energetic unity and separation. There are some people that are so impacted socially that they move into the subtle worlds around them and protect themselves through merging with another. This merging creates a great loss of energy for both parties. If this is a pattern that is familiar to you, it is important to understand that it may have come from the social conditioning in your family and through shaming. Although this may be a difficult concept to work with, it is in fact quite common. Another key response is being overwhelmed. Overwhelm pushes us away from the heart. It also can be perceived as a consequence of fear in accessing our personal gift. Through recognition of our own social patterning and through working to build sensory awareness and connection we may be able to bring change to these patterns of relationship.

People also absorb energy through judgement. When we judge another, we take energy from the person we judge upon ourselves. I noticed this once when I was mentoring a person who was absorbing energetic burdens from people. I noticed through the energy pathways that this occurred when he judged another person. The judgement precipitated a negative energetic relationship. Rather than thinking you have to clear, look at how you absorbed the energy in the first place.

Be aware that rather than clearing you may need to recharge. There are places that you have a unique relationship with and where you can recharge and claim your own power. Often these places have a strong elemental presence.

The Red Horseman, 1902
illustration for *Vasilisa the Beautiful,*
Ivan Bilibin

Technique

To energetically clear, first take a moment to centre yourself. Stand in a relaxed pose, feet hip-width apart. Bring attention to your breath. In your imagination scan your body, sensing tension. Stretch and shift your weight on your feet to bring forward a pose that feels more relaxed. You might like to do a gesture of putting one hand on the solar plexus and one hand on the heart chakra. You may wish to perform some gestures or mudras (spiritual gestures using hand or body with a Hindu or Buddhist origin, often associated with yogic practices) that allow you to feel more at home and centred in the body. It is important to discern what the original discomfort is, and what it is you wish to clear. Make your intention clear.

From here you may use movement, sound, smoke from a sage stick, a candle, sprinkling water and a prayer. You may put your hands to the ground and let the excess energy in your hands move into the earth. Clearing is about the intention you use. It is useful to work with the elements, water, earth, air or fire and to find your own ritual with these elements. Your voice is a powerful tool in clearing. Singing, or simply making vocal tones can cause energy or even entities to shift.

Smudging is a popular clearing technique and involves moving a smoking bundle of herbs (traditionally white sage) over the person, place or object you wish to clear. Smudging with white sage is an indigenous North American tradition, but using smoke for energetic clearing is common to many cultures and other plants may be used in place of sage. Alternatively, or in conjunction with smudging, you may wish to sprinkle water around the room.

The Lasavia Cleavers flower essence can also be used to clear. You may take a few drops on your tongue and pause, observing any shifts that may occur. Cleavers can also be used to clear a room. You may place a few drops on a stone with the intention of clearing the space, or drop it in a bowl of water which you then use to sprinkle around the room.

Here is a statement of clearing that I have found useful after performing spiritual work. You can speak it while you wash your hands, while smudging, or simply putting your hands on the ground.

I release all judgement,
all expectation and all attachment.
I am free to walk in beauty.

Finding Your Own Clearing Processes

People respond differently to different techniques and elements and it is important to experiment and discover what clearing processes work best for you. To have a number of different ways to clear energy is helpful and it also is a good idea to explore which element you are most at ease with.

You may gradually start to work more deeply with a chosen element and understand it. It is worth observing the different elements, their qualities and relationship with place. The difference between salt and freshwater, and the particular energy of each in clearing, for instance. Or you may look at the role of wind in clearing. Or the differences between clearing at night or during the day, clearing in the top story of a building or standing on the ground. When exploring these different aspects of clearing, remember to balance the elements within you and keep a strong connection to Earth.

It is worth exploring what clearing rituals feel good for you. Rituals help to focus your intention and face the aspect within yourself that may have invited the disturbance you wish to clear. Creating a medicine sphere calling in the directions and putting forward your intention to shift and clear is a good starting ritual.

Physical Cleansing in Our Body

When reflecting on energetic clearing it is worth considering how the physical body cleanses itself. The lymphatic system transports cellular fluids back to the bloodstream, is responsible for the harmony and maintenance of the internal organs. The physical body is constantly maintaining equilibrium through cleansing and eliminating, sweating and excreting, as well as growing and regenerating. When doing spiritual clearing it is helpful to bring attention to your body, think also about your fitness and what you eat and drink. Sauna and massage also give back to the physical body that ultimately sustains us.

Woman Looking for a Flea,
1766 - 1780, print, Johann Feigel

Shadow Projections and Soul Loss

The roles we play out, or have played, in families, and the projections that we carry can cause burdens and energy shadows that we carry and play out in our day-to-day lives. These become so ingrained that it takes real observation and experiences outside of these shadow projections to shift them. Such projections can be understood as archetypes.

The scapegoat archetype is a case in point. I have observed in my healing work that when families are in distress that they will scapegoat somebody. This scapegoat will often be a child who has a close connection to spirit and shows up as the outsider. The shadow projections onto this child can be ongoing. If the child has a healer instinct, they will take this burden on and carry it through life. When someone projects his or her shadow onto someone else, the person who has the shadow projected onto them experiences fear. The fear alone may significantly affect their wellbeing.

Another cause of energetic disharmony is soul loss. Soul loss is usually caused by trauma and those that suffer from it struggle to discern themselves energetically. It's like they have no skin, no protective energetic layer, and constantly merge and absorb other people's energy and feelings. If the person has a strong inner knowing and connection to the physical world this quality of merging can be a tool for identifying illness in others but without that strength, they may not be able to identify what emotions belong to themselves and to others.

in Your Journal

Find two elements that you are most drawn to. In your journal write about them. Create a symbol that represents them. When you meditate on the symbol what do you experience? Think about how you can use these elements in clearing. Write about different places you have been where you experienced heaviness or qualities that made you feel uncomfortable. Are you able to describe these qualities? What happens in your body when you walk into these places?

CLEARING

Travellers Caught in a Sudden Breeze at Ejri, 1832, woodcut, Katsushika Hokusai

Body Dreaming

Body Dreaming

Body dreaming is the practice of using the imaginal mind to see inside a person's body with a healing intention. Perceiving the body as an intricate physical and energetic landscape is integral to body dreaming. Through the mind's eye we can enter into the energy fields of the physical body and see what is happening inside. Working as a healer I have actually seen illnesses, the state of different organs, and the skeletal system. Through body dreaming we can shift and balance aspects in the physical body. When body dreaming, open yourself to what you see; rather than direct the seeing. This is an important concept. I call it *sustained focus without will.*

Training Exercise

Start with your own body. Lie on the floor and get as comfortable as possible. A pillow under the head or under your knees, whatever is comfortable. Take your time. Getting the body comfortable is a form of healing in itself. People are often surprised when they bring awareness to their body how different each side feels. It is when we pause and rest that we become aware of how much tension we hold in our jaw or pelvic area. Note that this isn't a visualisation to relax certain parts of the body; it is an exercise of sustained observation.

Close your eyes. Decide on a part of the body from which you wish to enter. It could be the tip of your little finger, the top of your head, or your left shoulder. Taking the example of your little finger, consider how you mentally move up the finger. Are you being with the flesh, the bone or the veins? How fast are you travelling? Are you uncomfortable with this? If you begin to flick out and start thinking about something else, bring yourself back to the same part of the body, stay with what happens. Don't attempt to scan your whole body. Just be with what happens. Do this for short periods and rest in-between.

When you are ready, call on your power animal to enter your body. Observe how the animal enters your body. This can bring great hilarity at first, particularly those with animals like an eagle or whale. The power animal is a powerful tool in body dreaming. It can also help to experiment with perceiving through the senses of the power animal.

Body Dreaming on Others in a Professional Context

It is important to be conscious as to how we enter into another person's energetic field. Body dreaming helps to bring consciousness to what we are capable of doing unconsciously in relationship to others. In teaching I get people to pair up and take turns in entering each other's dream bodies with their power animals. This process brings forward the ethical protocol of the healer, the importance of consent, trust and observation. Through sharing people learn a lot about their abilities, about healing and receiving healing.

As a body dreaming practitioner I need to be constantly aware of how I observe a person who comes to see me. When I first learnt to see and identify the auric field, I was seeing from a place of being separate. I had to bring awareness to what I was doing. When I realised how often I saw inside people, I had to reflect on the ethics of boundaries. What, for instance, is the point where I energetically enter into the etheric layers of the physical body and how important it is that I ask permission?

When the client, or buddy, is comfortable you may enter into their dream body with your power animal. Observe where your power animal enters. Narrate to the client what is happening. Go slowly. Observe the power animal and share what you see. You may see landscape and symbols. Don't try and interpret them, just stay present and focused. When the power animal leaves the dream body you are finished. Give thanks. Come into yourself and check with the client that they are ok. Take a moment to wash your hands. Clear and ground yourself, before sharing.

Stories

Through body dreaming we may uncover symbols, and landscape which give rise to stories. These stories impact our bodies and sit in various parts of our body, such as the heart or kidneys. They may be stories from crucial points in our lives or from our various relationships we've had over the years. Often the relationships will form a resonance in the body and we can work with the dream body to find the story that underpins them. Sometimes the stories may come from our ancestors. Once someone came to see me about an acute lung condition. Through body dreaming I saw the story in their lungs. I saw a young man in the first world war choking on mustard gas. This turned out to be her grandfather and through then doing healing work for her grandfather, the lung condition cleared up.

Sometimes the story does not sit in a specific organ but resides in a person's overall well-being. It could be a relationship with a parent, where the parent felt despair or inability to act and be engaged in the world. This then manifests as a burden that sits in the energetic field. Anything all-pervading is challenging. I look at how to support a person to clear the burden and then use body dreaming to work with the skin, strengthening the person's boundaries. Skin is an extraordinary organ as it simultaneously eliminates, absorbs and protects.

Symbolic Language

Symbolic Language

> Perhaps we are here to say: house, bridge, fountain, gate, pitcher, fruit-tree, window... to say them more intensely than the things themselves ever dreamed.
>
> Rainer Maria Rilke (Bohemian poet, 1875–1926)

A symbol is an object that represents an idea, a message or an action. A symbol can convey more than words, particularly as we develop our symbolic language through stories, myths and sharing with each other. Take for example a ring. A ring may symbolise a wedding or agreement, commitment and familial duties. In folklore rings can be precious magical items, such as the ring of Andvari in Norse tradition, or they can symbolise spiritual inheritance in stories like *The Wise Jew and The Three Rings*. A ring may also have personal symbolic significance. Wisdom can be encoded in symbols. Sometimes a symbol may be so personal and playful that understanding it brings a feeling of delight.

The romantic poets, Coleridge in particular, viewed the symbol as opening a doorway to a resonance, a vibration of insight that quickens the soul and brings the imagination in. Coleridge described the symbol as, having three characteristics, it must exist of itself, derive from something greater than itself and represent within itself that greatness which it derives from. The symbol was seen as the point of contact between the contingent and the absolute, the finite and the infinite, the sensuous and the super-sensuous, the temporal and the eternal, the individual and the universal. The idea that the object is a doorway through to something greater than it is, is true of symbols that we might receive in a shamanic journey.

In *Maximen und Reflexionen* Goethe wrote that 'In the symbol, the particular represents the universal, not as a dream or shadow, but as a living and momentary revelation of the inscrutable. Consequently, the idea remains eternally and infinitely active and accessible in the image, and even if expressed in all languages still remains inexpressible.' Goethe's words resonate with me, and in my view sometimes the only way an idea can be expressed is through a symbol and this cannot be pulled apart, only experienced.

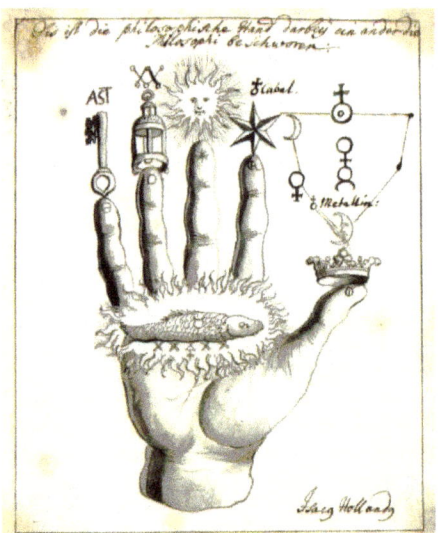

Hand Symbol from the book: **Alchemical and Rosicrucian Compendium**, c. 1760

Revelatory Receiving

Symbols may enter our spiritual practice in a number of ways, through symbols that we see in the world around us and through symbols that we encounter in dreams and visions, and most potently they can occur through revelatory receiving. Revelatory receiving refers to seeing a symbol in a vision in such a striking and vivid way that it triggers a feeling of revelation.

I experienced revelatory receiving once at Stony Batter on Waiheke Island. We were doing a poetry performance at the abandoned World War Two gun emplacements. To prepare, a fellow poet and I did a sound exercise where we made different sounds into the ground. When I sat up and I looked towards the west I saw a remarkable sight: A large benevolent face filled the sky. Every detail of the face was delineated in a white light. And this white light was pulsing. Seeing this vast being was awe inspiring. I felt as if I was having electrical signals going through my body. I didn't know how to integrate this into my life. I asked my friend if she could see it and she couldn't. I turned away and then looked at it again. It was still there. Slowly as the light began to fade from the sky it also faded. At the time I didn't know what to do with this vision. I did the poetry reading. People were drinking but I couldn't drink. Something changed but I wasn't able to identify exactly what that was. Only that things were different after that.

As a young child I had another experience of all-encompassing vision. I was very young, I was in bed and my mother had turned out the light, I was supposed to go to sleep but I felt very awake. In the dark I reached down for a familiar picture book. I just randomly opened it at a page and tried to look at the pictures in the dark. As I opened the book, I saw an extraordinary image of a green face, very old and very wrinkled. Out of the pages emerged two hands with quite long fingernails and they reached out towards my face and touched the corners of my eyes before I managed to slam the book shut and throw it down beside the bed. It was extremely vivid, I even felt the touch of the fingers. When I think about it today, I can't quite put this in perspective. Curiously I never called out to my parents or my sister, knowing that this was something they would not believe.

Later I had revelatory experiences practising latihan with a local Subud group. Latihan is a moving meditation practice developed by the Indonesian spiritual leader Muhammad Subuh Sumohadiwidjojo (1901–1987). The idea of latihan was to surrender to the divine. Part of the understanding in Subud was that God expressed through feelings in the inner body and through symbols. This was an important point in my own continuing journey into symbolic language. There sometimes are challenges in receiving revelatory experiences, where some people fixate upon these experiences and cannot progress beyond them.

Deepening Your Understanding of Symbols

To deepen your understanding, write down your dreams and journeys. Underline the symbols and scenes that have symbolic import. Take one image or word and free write about it. Look at the memories and insights that the symbol invokes. Connect to the power of the image. A strong symbol will have a resonance that you feel and too much interpretation may be a distraction to what it is truly conveying to you.

If the symbols don't convey an immediate personal meaning, slow down. You may find there is a connection between different symbols that crop up. They may all be telling you the same thing but in different ways. Be attentive to emotions that arise at particular parts of the journey and look at how you can expand your symbolic vocabulary through research. You may find a whole area of symbolism that comes through your ancestral lineage. Researching the symbols, you see in dreams and journeys will not only enrich your knowledge but will also be great fun.

I like receiving a symbol that I can work with over time. Some have even become tools that I use in healing work or for energetic support and protection. Colours can also be symbols. I recently dreamed about a lot of turquoise. It was connected to detailed needle work on a doily. I did not immediately understand the symbolic import. It had layers of connotations – memories of my grandmother and her fine needlework, the turquoise stone, the turquoise sky, upper world, teaching, ancestry. I wrote down all the thoughts and feelings that arose from this dream. Sometimes a symbol should not be interpreted at all but simply be held and appreciated.

It can occasionally happen that you get a symbol for someone else. Often when this occurs it is also a reflection for ourselves. Think carefully about conveying this to the other person and let them find the meaning of what you receive before you leap in claiming that you know what it is about. Through their sharing with you it will also add to your understanding of this symbol.

Some symbols are strongly connected with superstitions and it is worth considering where the superstition comes from and what its meaning is for you. Black cats, for example, carry a host of various superstitions. In Germany, a black cat crossing your path from left to right is good luck, while crossing right to left is a bad omen. It is a British superstition, however, that a black cat that chooses to reside with a young lady will bring her many suitors.

When you receive symbolic information take time to consider it. Once in a group I was teaching, someone saw that another person's power animal needed to go outside. They immediately got up to leave the group and literally take that person's power animal in energetic form outside. What they could have done was share the information. It might be that the person needed go outside to become grounded or empower themselves. A symbol doesn't necessitate a literal action.

Sometimes we will see symbols not in dreams and visions but on the street or in the natural world. What lends significance to an object in the natural world is its timing and our relationship to the object. It might be that we see an animal in unusual circumstances, perhaps we see a nocturnal animal during the day. A way of opening to symbolic language is to walk with a particular problem in our minds and decide to open up to the natural world to give us some way of understanding this problem. This is where things in the natural world can become symbols. However, be cautious in reading too much symbolism into what we see on a daily basis and making unnecessary connections between things as this impacts our ability to be grounded. Most of the time that black cat is just a black cat.

By Day She Made Herself Into a Cat,
Arthur Rackham (1867 - 1939)

a walk in the Forest

I did the following walk through a forest in Tongariro National Park. I simply observed what caught my attention.

I am walking in the shadow, through the undergrowth, surrounded by umbrella ferns and astelia. Above me is a kaikawaka tree and in its branches a tomtit. The tomtit comes lower in the branches and begins to follow me but keeping its distance. I lie down on a seat and it comes in close. Its markings are black and white. When it flits it looks like shadow and light.

The umbrella fern divides into four strands on each side, making eight, then these divide each into two, making sixteen strands. It rises straight up out of the ground on a slender stem. The eight strands unfurl simultaneously, forming tight bundles that look rather comical. It's like each frond has equal potential and all are connected to this fine green stem. In that tight bundle of potential, I feel that it already knows its own becoming, a stretched-out fern leaf, the whole journey.

As I walk, I see a small puha growing out of a large stone. The stone is soft, grey, and covered in beech leaves, moss, lichen and this one small sturdy puha. The puha somehow feels like a visitor on the edge of the path. I ponder stone and puha until I come to it again and realise the significance. I experience someone beside me, or is it behind me? It is so strong I look to see if they are there. I hear voices, groups of people and children. I wait to see if they will come around the corner of the track but they don't. The stone reflects self-importance, getting everyone else on the same page, yet nature is so diverse the puha takes the space, small and sturdy on the rock.

The leaves of a five-finger have fallen on the pathway. They make me pause. They are so particular as if there is a language in the way they have dropped and I need to understand the message before I move on. Leaves shaped like hands, the creative aspect, and I still have been lingering with stone, thinking of memory. Memory, story, stone, and collective. These aspects keep flowing through my mind, how we create the memory, that the story is there to serve. I think of the tree, Tainui, growing from the Tainui waka being from somewhere else but also connected to this place. On the path there are twelve larger five-finger leaves and eight small ones.

My attention is drawn by a strong branching tree. I realise that it is a kapuka, *Griselinia littoralis*. In my mind's eye I can see my father pointing out the leaves and showing me the tendency for the leaf to grow asymmetrically. The trunk divides simultaneously into many branches, giving the impression of an upside-down octopus, the branches like tentacles reaching into the air like it is an ocean. The grey warbler sings and sings.

As I continue, I see how when the forest darkens so too does my imagination. I play with fear and distortion, a sense of being lost in the story. As

SYMBOLIC LANGUAGE

in Your Journal

the forest lightens, I am able to find clarity and boundaries. It is here that I see the mountain cabbage. It appears so outlandish, so completely different to everything around it. The ground around is covered with its fronds. The mountain cabbage tree is *Cordyline indivisa* in Latin, at least I think it is. I have a really old Laing and Blackwell book on plants, and the names do change, but I love the book as it is filled with stories. Cabbage trees are tenacious for life, surviving sun, fire, salt water and still able to find soil and root down into it. In reflection I see that my curiosity is my tenacity.

Write down the legends and stories that you were told as a child. Think about the parts of those stories that had symbolic import. Look at different symbols and how the same symbol may have different or similar meanings in each story. A good example of this is the shoe. In Cinderella, it may signify her true self. It might also represent being bound to destiny. In *The Little Red Shoes* by Hans Christian Andersen, it may represent the wild self, the authentic self or vanity. You can go from shoes to feet. In Andersen's *The Little Mermaid*, when Ariel sacrifices being a mermaid to being a human, she has shooting pains in her feet. Feet may represent a pathway, or choice.

Think about your landscape where you grew up as a child. What are the feelings and stories that arise? Turn your attention to the landscape you live in now. How do you see this landscape and your relationship to it? Write down important trees, crystals, rocks and animals, what do these represent to you. Think of a theme and create a collage of images that speak to you. If you are interested in tarot consider making your own tarot cards through collage.

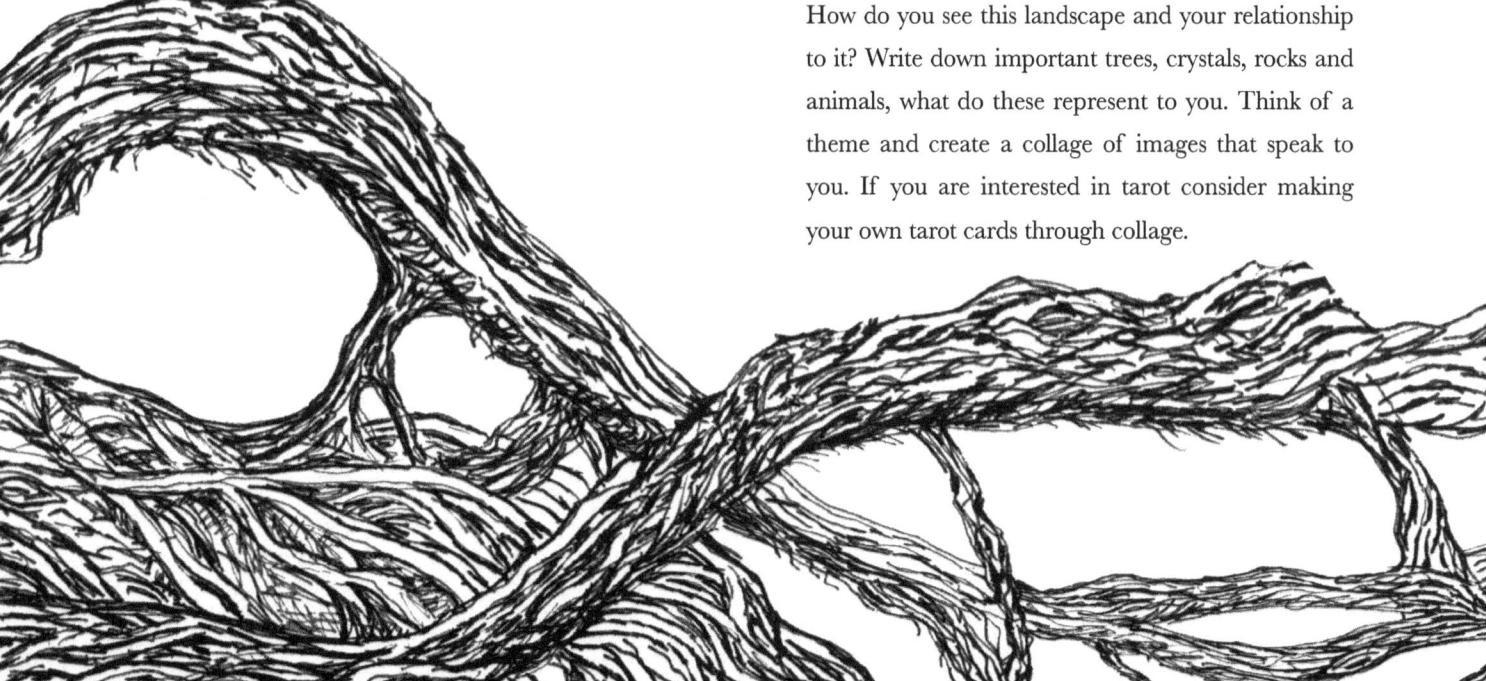

The first thing I notice about comfrey are the leaves. Comfrey is a mass of leaves they are strong. The veins on them are so clear they are embossed. I love how the embossed patterning of the leaves are like archways or maybe more like finger prints or they remind me of how the earth or mud cracks and oval interlocking shapes - the leaf does this. The only time it shows the underneath of its leaf is when its newly coming from the earth in spring. It tends to die back in the winter. The new leaves are fine light yellow green. The hairs underneath are white and so soft they look like fur. As the leaves grow they grow abundantly and straight out of the ground. the stem is. The leaves are long stemed. The stem is hairy so that when you hold it between your fingers its sticky. It forms an oval indent, when I try to draw the simplicity and intricacies of the under leaf I feel as if I will be there for days meticulously attending the leafs blueprint in the meantime its giving an earthy metallic scent. If only I could describe the scent I just can't. The embossing is like a mosaic the veins are such a light green they look like green milk.

Comfrey

symphytum x uplandicum

Background

Comfrey is associated with structure and patterns. This connects it to the spiritual teacher who brings attention to the patterns that help us evolve and also the patterns that may be holding us back. The comfrey that grows in New Zealand is known as Canadian comfrey or wandering comfrey. It is a hybrid, introduced from Russia to England in the second half of the eighteenth century by an English gardener who was in the service of Catherine the Great. From England it was brought to Canada and gradually colonised the whole west coast of North America, and eventually making its way to Australia and New Zealand. It differs from the *Symphytum officinale* (the comfrey of the old medical apothecaries) in that it is softer, and its flowers have a pinkish tinge to them.

Description

Comfrey is a plant of contrast. Its pink flowers are delicate, charming and floating like a pink bell-dresses. The flower unfolds, like a concertina. The racemes – the shoots on which they grow – are botanically described as scorpioid because they curve like a scorpion's tail. The flowers are pink when they first bloom then turn purple, then blue. In contrast to its flowers, its leaves are prolific, large, and grow as part of the hairy stem. This appearance of its cohesive gesture was seen by the old herbalists as a reflection of its ability to join together that which has come apart.

And indeed, Comfrey supports and aids the knitting of fractures and broken bones, from its effect on the soft connective tissues, it also can support the growth of hair, skin and nails. English herbalist Juliette de Baïracli Levy, writes of comfrey that 'It is, indeed, another of the small company of 'wonder' herbs, being good for almost every ill of mankind.' Comfrey contains allantoin. This gives it some important healing qualities that other herbs that are high in silica do not have. Allantoin cleanses wounds by removing the destroyed tissue and stimulating tissue repair. Comfrey can be used to pull poison from a wound.

The veins on the leaves are clearly defined like embossed prints. They remind me of cracked mud, dried by the sun into interlocking shapes.

Each leaf has similar patterns emanating from a curve arching away from the stem. The young leaves are like fingers coming out of the earth and are light yellow-green. The leaf hairs are white and soft like fine fur. Comfrey is textured and strong. It grows straight from the earth and smells of earth and like a wet rock. Nicholas Culpeper places comfrey under the influence of Saturn. Describing comfrey as 'cold, dry and earthy in quality.' Plants with the imprint of Saturn bend their blossom towards the ground. As the leaf grows it curves back over the ground. As the old leaves die, they form a rich damp litter.

Comfrey is full of minerals and silica. The high silica acid content gives it the ability to absorb large quantities of water. It also results in the fine bristles up the stem and under the leaf. It gives the leaves the structured juicy form. Comfrey's long root system can join back together if cut. When I pull it up the roots break off and lie in the ground. Some gardeners fear it getting into their beds for it will grow from a small piece of root. Culpepper describes the roots as 'great and long, spreading great thick branches underground, black on the outside and whitish within, short and easy to break, and full of glutinous or clammy juice, of little or no taste at all.'

Essence

This remedy brings forward patterns – particularly patterns that are subconscious. Comfrey helps us shift and accelerate to meet with new awareness, learning and consciousness. The earth element of comfrey brings to the surface what is hidden and through that healing can occur. This earth element also aids us in integrating changes.

When I first connected to comfrey, I was reminded of an adult that is responsible without being burdened. The gesture was wise and playful. I experienced clear, defined boundaries of roles within relationships and a way of being that was strong and compassionate. When working with comfrey in a daily practice I was able to bring a great deal of awareness to judgement. By putting a light in how we judge and are impacted by judgement it helps us break free from judgement. This includes judgement of self, judgement from others and judgement of others.

I found the remedy supports the ability to contain and work with the emotions, particularly anger. It helps us to shift emotions by allowing us to be present with them without falling into them, balancing grace with groundedness. The remedy enables us to access memory, ancient and contemporary.

The Teacher and the Realms of the Upper World

the Upper World

The spiritual teacher resides in the upper world. Within the concept of the medicine sphere, this is what is above you. You may imagine the upper worlds like the heavens. You may also see them as different landscapes. In these realms there are different beings that have particular roles. What stands out for me in any upper world work is the light. There are often translucent qualities to these worlds and the colours seem more pastel to me. The active principles of the upper world are receptivity and consciousness.

Finding Your Spiritual Teacher

When you are relaxed and have entered the visioning state ask to connect with your power animal. Take a moment to greet and be with your power animal. Then offer up your intention to meet with your spiritual teacher. Imagine yourself going upward into the sky, some people imagine a ladder or climb a tree. You are entering the upper world. This is where your spiritual teacher resides. You may find yourself in different landscapes. Be open to these landscapes that you find yourself in. In these landscapes there may be people and beings that you come across, one will have a special connection to you. This is your spiritual teacher.

When we access our spiritual teacher, we are also accessing a medium of learning and this should be taken into account in our observation of the journey itself. If it is vivid, note the details of the environment of the spiritual teacher. This is important symbolic information.

Jacob's Dream, 1805, pen, ink and water colour, William Blake

THE TEACHER AND REALMS OF THE UPPER WORLD

the Spiritual Teacher

The teacher spirit guide aids us in our work in the world. When I first journeyed to meet my spiritual teacher, I couldn't see him. Everything was very bright. I knew he was a man and the feeling I got was he was very like my father. We were in a garden and whenever I had a question, he would always just show me a plant and that was the answer. From there I had to work with this plant. By studying, observing, and spiritually connecting to the plant, the most curious shifts and teachings would occur and through that I could uncover the theme of the question. I would often end up forgetting the question usually because it was ill-formed, but I always remembered the plant. Through the years of working and connecting with this spiritual teacher, I learnt much about the plant world, how to be with plants and how to grow a garden. The garden that I created became a teacher as well, helping me integrate the often-intense otherworldly experiences.

In connecting to the spiritual teacher, we look at practices, habits, belief patterns and study. We look at how we learn and how we integrate what we learn. The teacher is a guide in our evolution, pushing us back out into our lives with new tools and often a riddle to work with. The spiritual teacher doesn't always give you the answer you would like or expect. The spiritual teacher can help us to discover our innate talents and also guides us on a journey of enquiry. Finding a question is like finding an answer. Sometimes we have questions that actually push away the answer. The spiritual teacher helps us look at how we engage in enquiry and may question our willingness to find the answers.

the Trickster as Teacher

Within the relationship with the spiritual teacher, trust is what enables wisdom to emerge. The opposite of trust is control. This is where the sacred clown, the fool, the trickster teacher arrives. They present you with the unexpected, they wake you out of your routine and shock you into seeing that which you would rather ignore. The trickster arrives when we are indecisive, when we are too afraid to look, when we give our power away, and when we repeat our errors. Author and folklorist Alan Garner in his book *Guizer* describes the fool in a way that resonates with my understanding.

> The fool is where our humanity lies. For the fool is the advocate of uncertainty: he is at once creator and destroyer, bringer of help and harm. He draws a boundary for chaos, so that we can make sense of the rest. He is the shadow that shapes the light… he enters the world like a force without direction, without the knowledge of good or bad.

Through his cunning he changes the world. The fool, the trickster highlights our humanity in the journey from animal instinct to divinity. The trickster teaches us that being innocent will not serve us.

The trickster moves us out of our old patterning by literally waking us up. Patterns can be built up in a community, where everyone has their particular role and a way of acting and responding. The trickster can break up a community and a community has to change. Change in such a way as there is no going back. The trickster will use the shadow parts of us and any shadow that the community is built upon. It can be a fearful process, as an individual has to face their shadow and access an inner strength. Part of such an evolution is to act in the face of a fearsome truth. I see that ultimately the trickster acts as the catalyst for evolution.

The Norse Trickster God Loki, from an Icelandic 18th century manuscript

Places of Learning

I once had a vivid dream. In this dream I entered into a very beautiful yet formal garden. In this garden stood a building with archways atop tall marble pillars. This place, a university as I perceived it, had myriad rooms. I entered into these vast rooms where I encountered a few people discussing philosophy, other rooms were libraries of books. I eventually entered a room where there was a teacher I deeply respected. I felt as if I had entered the wrong place and was about to go when he stopped me and told me that this was a place of learning and that I belonged here and could come back at any time. It was an experience where I felt that I could access anything I wanted, yet a part of me couldn't receive the teaching because I didn't respect myself. To learn I had to respect who I was.

In another incident, I had a visionary journey in which I travelled on a boat through the upper world to an island. The whole island was a medicine wheel. Immediately upon disembarking I felt its extraordinary power. The teachers on the island actively ignored me. The message was clear: 'go and do the work and perhaps we might be interested.' Both the university and the island are what I call places of learning. They are places that exist in the dream world where we can access important teachings. You may visit places of learning through shamanic journeying or through dreams.

When you arrive at a place of learning you may need to sit in the atrium, or an equivalent place because often teachers need you to prepare to meet them and it's important to give time for this. There may be something that needs to be attended to, before going further. If you are eager to begin with and then experience a freezing, a blocking, a shutdown, or a running-away, then there is something that you must first attend to before exploring the place of learning. This is the first teaching. Sometimes we may be shown some of the inner rooms of learning and experience a sense of 'look, this is where you are going. Now go back and begin the work that is required.'

THE TEACHER AND REALMS OF THE UPPER WORLD

Wisdom and Knowledge

Learning

In teaching the medicine sphere I may ask the group to stand and face east. I would ask each person how they felt and what sensations they experienced. Some might not feel much difference, but when they turn to the north or another direction and I ask the same question most people describe a different feeling. It is this conscious comparison of experience that leads to enquiry. People begin to relate to the directions in a personal way. This leads to a desire to learn more.

We learn best when we are led by our curiosity. Curiosity can be an odd mix of excitement, focus and vulnerability. Being led by curiosity requires that we give space to follow and explore where it leads us. When I draw the silvery felted lamb's ear, *Stachys byzantina*, I become curious in a number of ways. I observe that its seed head is similar to another plant; this makes me wonder if they are in the same family. I desire to touch its soft furry leaves. I wonder where this plant grows in the wild and why its leaves are so furry. When I try to draw it, I want to convey that furriness. I find my skills lacking. When we are on the edge of our ability, we tend to feel frustrated and make personal judgements about our talent. This is the time to discern between talent and skills. Discipline and time are required for learning a new skill.

In learning, we need to be at ease with states of not knowing. Imagine a house with a strong foundation, you can trust that the structure will uphold you. If you have a house in alignment with your values, perhaps with rooms that have particular intention, then your talents can flourish. Many people tell me that they read a lot but can never recall the information. A good way to absorb the knowledge that you read is to shut the book and pause a moment. Is there a shape, a symbol or image in your mind about what you have read?

Knowledge can be elusive. Other times it can enter painfully with an edge of truth. What we have pursued we then resist. Some knowledge is used for domination or comes from a place of manipulation. Watch out for knowledge that is drip fed. Knowledge, truth and therefore wisdom, changes us. From there we can only move forward into unknown territory. Knowledge leads to the unknown.

Integrating Extraordinary Experiences in Your Journal

In teaching plant spirit medicine, I encourage people to become the plant. This form of learning through journeying and other spiritual practices can affect people in extraordinary ways. When learning occurs outside of people's rational understanding, they may emerge from the experience with a feeling that something happened but they don't quite know what it was. The rational mind says 'what was that all about? Now we need to get on with life so let's forget about it. It doesn't have any use for you anyway.' Most people are familiar with this kind of dialogue. The key here is to acknowledge that something did happen. Try not to immediately adjust to what feels familiar, rather stay with the unfamiliar. To help to integrate an experience that occurred through meditation and journeying we need to pause and share and write.

I have noticed that those people who are particularly rational and analytical find such experiences challenging. They may feel uplifted and excited, yet be uncertain how to integrate or use the experience. If this is the case for you, you may simply need to give it time. It may take a few days before you notice that something is different or that you have an understanding of the experience. I think of it like a book you don't get at first, then later you understand it easily and wonder how come you thought it was so difficult before.

In the evening take a moment to contemplate. Then, in your journal, write about your day as if you were writing down a dream. How were you with the events throughout the day? Try this for a few evenings and see how this brings awareness to the day. Do your best not to be too analytical. How best do you learn? Write down your favourite and your most difficult times of learning. What was happening that made it difficult? What was happening that made it easy?

> I have a fairly large collection of books and my two main rooms are lined with bookshelves. Kurmos showed great interest. What were they and why did I have so many? I explained to him that they contained facts, ideas, speculations and theories, accounts of past events, stories invented by writers and so on, all of which were written down, put into print and made into books which could be read by others.
> His comment was 'Why? You can get all the knowledge you want by simply wanting it.'
>
> quoted in the *Gentleman and the Faun* by Robert Crombie, Scottish scientist, (1899–1975)

Nga Kete O Te Wananga - the Three Baskets of Knowledge

by Leanne Tamaki

The three baskets of knowledge are central to my understanding of learning. Hearing the story of how Tane retrieved the baskets from the heavens and learning what each basket represented was a crucial turning point in my ability to learn and integrate spiritual concepts. Because I feel very close to this story, I asked Leanne Tamaki of Tuhoe descent to write up her understanding of the three baskets of knowledge. This is her understanding.

Story aids our understanding of reality: as a guide, as a blueprint for our actions, behaviours, cultural and social mores. Story is an expression of our world-view. Story reveals the connection and relationship between all things – the celestial, the cosmos, the human. In connecting to story, our perception and understanding widens and deepens. This is being in relationship-to and being in relationship with story.

These words, recounted here as a *karakia* (incantation, chant, prayer) invoke the spirit of determination, agility and fortitude that the kaitiaki (guardian) Tane embodies and employs on his journey to acquire the three baskets of knowledge. These baskets contain knowledge that is beneficial to humankind. In other tribal traditions it is Tawhaki that acquired the baskets, but in this telling it is Tane, progenitor of humankind and kaitiaki of forests. In the karakia the story has been shortened. There are more intricacies and layers to be discovered, just as there are varying iterations of the story. Whatever its iteration, however, Tane's story has the same function – to illuminate and disseminate knowledge.

Familial relationships are accentuated in the story. The teachings vary but family is always important. Tane is chosen by his siblings over his brother, Whiro, to undertake the task. While Tane is acquiring the baskets and the kohatu (stone) Hukatai and Rehutai, his family build the wharekura – the first house of learning and the place where the kete and kohatu will be placed. His brother Tawhirimatea who governs the realm of the weather accompanies him for part of the journey. Tane having observed the elements understands that the winds in the heavens could foil his quest and calls upon Tawhirimatea's power to help him.

In this story, we are Tane – he is the progenitor of humankind and thus we are of him. Because of this relationship we have access to the bounty provided by the forest, his realm. When entering the forest, we ask permission before entering. We do this with respect for Tane and those beings within the space and for the privilege of access

Tenei au, tenei au
Te hokai nei i taku tapuwae
Te hokai nuku
Te hokai rangi
Te hokai o to tipuna a Tane-nui-a-rangi
I pikitia ai ki te Rangituhaha
Ki Tihi i manono
I rokohina atu ra ko Io Matua Kore anake
I riro iho ai nga kete o te wananga
Ko te kete Tuauri
ko te kete Tuatea
ko te kete Aronui
Ka tiritiria, ka poupoua kia Papatuanuku
Kia puta te ira tangata
ki te whai ao
ki te ao marama
Tihei Mauri Ora

Here am I, here am I
here am I swiftly moving by the power of my incantation for swift movement
Swiftly moving over the earth
Swiftly moving through the heavens
The swift movement of your ancestor Tane-nui-a-rangi
who climbed up to the summit of all the Heavens
To the summit of Manono
And there found Io-the-Parentless alone
He brought back down the Baskets of Knowledge
Tuauri
Tuatea
Aronui
Portioned out, planted in
Mother Earth
The life principle of humankind
comes forth into the dawn
into the world of light
There is life

afforded to us. The act respectfully recognises our relationship to and with Tane, and with ourselves. Our relationship to story and how this connects us to the celestial and the cosmos underpins this.

Rehua, a messenger of Io conducts vital cleansing rituals that acknowledge Tane moving from tapu to noa. This ritual holds teachings about role, responsibility and acknowledgement of states of being. In the physical world, the essence of the cleansing ritual is articulated in different ways. When leaving a cemetery or burial site you wash your hands and sprinkle yourself with water because these spaces have a different state. It is a space where the physical body is continuing its transition and returning to Papa. Tapu honours what is occurring and gives space for the transitioning. Water is used to clear and cleanse: the act of the ritual acknowledges and moves you from the state of tapu to noa.

When Tane agrees to undertake this task, he is approached by Rehua and asked which path he will take. To which he responds 'by Te Toi Huarewa and te aratiatia.' Whiro, who was not chosen and wants to attain the knowledge for himself, tries to ascend by the incorrect path. He fails and is forced to descend. Knowledge should be acquired by the correct path and for the greater good is one interpretation of this story.

The baskets – the gifts which Tane attained and gifted to humankind are called Tuauri, Tuatea and Aronui. There are different interpretations as to the type of knowledge each basket contains but I follow Maori Marsden's interpretation:

> Tuauri – beyond in the world of darkness. It is the real world behind the world we sense. It is a place of creation, gestation, evolution and refinement before manifestation into the natural world.
>
> Tuatea – the world beyond space and time, beyond framework. It is infinite and eternal. It is the place of divinity. It is the eternal world of the spirit – the ultimate reality.
>
> Aronui – is 'that before us', before our senses. It relates to the natural world and what we learn through observation and in relationship with it.
>
> Rev. Maori Marsden, tohunga, scholar, healer and minister

the Three Wisdoms

In a vision I once experienced three wisdoms. It was a profound and vivid experience. In the following passages I invite the reader to share that experience.

the first wisdom

The first wisdom appears to me as a luminous white being, pointing upwards. I see myself in a field, and he desires me to look upward. I have trouble raising my head. It is as though my head is stuck to my chest. I wait in this state and see myself at the beginning of a conscious evolution. As I become aware of this, I am able to move my head.

The first wisdom accesses the connection to source, acknowledging that there is an energy that moves behind all things. The Kabbalah describes *Ein Sof* – God as Infinity. The essence of divinity is found in every single thing. To know this is to experience trust in the eternity of life. Physical form is like a mask. In the unity we can meld with form. The unity touches our personality, our difference. This is the cosmic law of unity within diversity.

The luminous being brings his forehead to mine. This is the remembering that we all share the unity. The luminous being is tapping at my chest. I have to wait again. There is something in my chest like a shadow. The being tells me that when the unity comes into form it creates a shadow. Splitting occurs and that is why we need to remember and practise the unity. He presses his hands together. This is his mudra. This is an expression of bringing the two parts together in wholeness. He touches his lips to my forehead. This is the release of this knowing into my being.

the second wisdom

The second wisdom is a blue being. As he first appears, he is indigo. As he takes form, he becomes cobalt blue, then Prussian blue as he lifts up into the air. He uses his finger to form blue energy lines across my body from left to right. The first line crosses my forehead. The second line crosses my throat. The third line crosses my chest. The fourth line crosses my solar plexus. The fifth line crosses my navel. The sixth line, my hips, and the seventh my knees. He draws a circle on the ground around my feet. He then draws a line down the centre of my body. As he does so, the lines he had drawn across my body become rings around me. He tells me this is the 'blueprint' and I need to look at it. He then crosses the line above my head and this also forms a ring.

He shows me the meridian lines in the body, the internal energy lines. The other lines are the external energy lines of the body. I begin to perceive that there are distortions in these lines and that there is knowledge in them. He shows me other important lines. One is the ancestral line. Its colour is indigo. As he shows me I see that I need to work with this line. He shows me a green line. This is connected to nature. The second wisdom shows me the universal web, a vast array of connection points and energy lines.

He points to the ancestral line and the nature line. 'Always make sure that these are clear and strong,' he tells me. He shows me arcs across the sky, the speed of light, the movement behind matter. His mudra is the interlacing of the fingers and thumbs leaving the forefingers touching lightly and pointing upwards. He opens out his chest, lifting the breastbone, and indicates for me to do the same. This is standing tall and being in alignment. He stands on my head and leaps off. He is gone. It's a reminder that the second wisdom is connected to the mind, the mind aligned to the heart, integrating what we know into the world. This is the message of the second wisdom.

the third wisdom

The third wisdom is green and appears behind me on my right side. He plays with my right arm and hand. He shows me that action needs to have a connection to the other wisdoms. He tells me that we must know our talents and sacred gifts. He shows me how the work of the gift is to grow by doing. He shows me that it is not enough just to do, but we have to do with an understanding of ourselves. He shows me the story of how Maui slowed down the sun. By slowing down the sun he was able to access the power that is inherently in us. It is also knowing that great force and power must be directed and disciplined. The wisdom points at my throat. I experience an insight into adornment, celebration of the physical and the act of balance within the physical world. I experience his gesture through the brightness and joy of his eyes. His look makes me look at myself. To stand in his gaze is to see truth. The third wisdom tells us to see the truth of our form and look at how we act in the world. The mudra is about connection. His palms are open and facing up to receive. Then he crosses them over his chest as if to cradle the heart. We must celebrate how we have lived and what we are doing.

Belief Systems and Patterns

> The greatest enemy of the truth is not lies but firmly held beliefs.
>
> Arthur Schopenhauer, German philosopher (1788–1860)

> Belief, in fact, is every human's greatest foe. More people have believed what life is than people who have learned what life is.
>
> Estcheemah, indigenous American elder

Because of the nature of my work I feel deeply uneasy about belief, and belief systems in particular. My view is that spiritual work should be experientially driven, not belief based. Belief systems have the potential to generate rigid expectations around spiritual experiences and ultimately lead to dogma, blindness, and exclusion. Beliefs, moreover, can distort genuine spiritual experiences, as people will mentally warp the experience to fit their beliefs. We must walk the line between having structure in our practice and creating a belief system with care. The more we desire change, the more disturbing our thoughts, fears, anxieties and prejudices appear. Beliefs and belief systems then appeal to us because they seem to ease our difficulties and offer certainty, however, they are often only sublimating our urges and fears.

I also see the importance of looking at how our beliefs will structure an experience. I recently met someone who wanted to share with me about a group who she was part of where they were connecting to an alien ship within the earth. She called it an 'earth ship.' She went on to share how they were the first people to be accessing this special wisdom that these alien beings were disseminating for earthlings. I was curious and asked her what these teachings were. As she shared, I recognised ancient earth wisdoms that are often told in old stories. I wondered whether this ancient female wisdom could simply be that, and nothing to do with aliens in the earth. I thought from her story that where the belief was distorted was where the ego considers itself special, that she was among the first people to be accessing this wisdom, the only people who can have this healing or knowledge. This creates a culture of exclusivity and does not empower the participants.

Temperance

Rachel Pollack in *Seventy Eight Degrees of Wisdom* describes the tarot card, Temperance (XIV), as showing a person whose behaviour is connected to the real world but in a way that is more meaningful than before. 'Temperance,' she writes, 'indicates the ability to combine spontaneity with knowledge.' It's the bringing together of the disparate elements of our life that is key. We often try to separate and parcel off parts of our life so that they don't freely interconnect, particularly with their spiritual life and ordinary life. I consider however that it is important to integrate our spiritual and ordinary lives and this is what temperance means to me. In the Smith-Waite deck (1910) Temperance depicts an angel, one foot in the water and one foot on the land, the water represents the unconscious world or the dream world and the land represents the 'real world' of events and people. It's worth comparing Temperance with the Star (XVI). Here the figure is no longer stiff and calm but naked and fluid more immersed in the watery element of spirit. The Temperate personality acting from an inner sense of life and purpose links the two realms. This walking the two worlds is often how the shaman is described in literature.

Smith-Waite Tarot Deck, 1910,
illustrator: Pamela Colman Smith
academic & mystic: A.E. Waite

Questions to Ponder

You don't have to find answers to these questions. Approach them more as a personal meditation, something to muse on from which other questions may arise. You may wish to write the questions and your thoughts down. Take one thought pattern that you no longer wish to have in your world. How would you create a ritual to release it?

1. As a child what stories impacted you? How did this change your way of being in the world? Was it changed positively or negatively by this story?
2. What was the overriding message you were told growing up?
3. What is your innate attitude to spirituality?
4. How is critical thinking a healthy and important tool in your learning and awareness?
5. How do you give your power away to someone you think is an authority?
6. How can we learn without the desire or need to give away our power or authority to others?
7. What is your understanding of self-responsibility?
8. What do you value? Is this in alignment with the belief system you grew up with?
9. What does it mean to have spiritual strength?
10. Can you identify a pattern, value, or emotional response you have that comes through ancestors or social and cultural conditioning?

Observational Meditation

Meditation refers to the practice of focusing the mind. Taking space to meditate becomes important in a culture of distraction. Observational meditation is best understood as being present to what arises within. It is an intensive practice and it is perhaps best to start with ten-minute blocks – rest and then begin again for another ten minutes and slowly increase this practice. It's important to do this meditation with attention. Don't drift off.

Begin by observing something or closing your eyes. Then bring awareness to your observation. Observe your thoughts or sensations that pass through your body. Be with yourself. Observe your thoughts but don't join them. See how they nudge and flow and hook you. It's time to see what you are actually thinking and how those thoughts impact your everyday life and others. Observe how the energy of disruption may arise. Stay with this inner observer. Don't fall into these thoughts and feelings. Adhere to this. When you practise this enough you start to observe the observer and find a natural way of being with the energy beyond thought. At this point, a change may occur. In his book, *Light of Exploration*, spiritual teacher R. P. Kaushik describes it thus:

> This explosion releases a tremendous energy. It is not a blinding flash; it is not even a psychic experience… It is a light inside oneself within which there is no difference between the experiencer and the experienced. Such is the light of exploration. Only with this light can we enquire into the meaning of meditation… It is an ongoing discovery of the movement of life – life which is not limited to your life or my life, but the life which is a totality – an immensity has no name, but nevertheless is.

Contemplation

Contemplation is reflective thought done in a way that is restful. It is also the action of looking thoughtfully at something for a while. In this state there can be integration of events, pieces fall into place of their own accord. I once read a passage in a book where resting under a tree all day was an important and profound experience, sadly I have forgotten the book, but I often think about that passage. If Isaac Newton hadn't rested under the apple tree, contemplating, then he would not have come up with the theory of gravity. Contemplation is the moment when the artist takes time just to look. I like to contemplate as I potter around or look at things around me, particularly in the landscape.

Bittercress
cardamine hirsuta

Description

The gesture of this plant is small, humble, often invisible and yet its essence is bold and bright and sharp. It goes unnoticed in most people's gardens and there is very little reference to it in most herbals. It's a great little salad weed, its botanical name, *cardamine*, is from the Greek words for heart and subdue, the plant having once been used as a heart sedative. It is a small rosette-based annual, up to twenty-five centimetres tall, and a member of the mustard family. When, in the early spring, it flowers, the stems grow upright with few leaves and put forth small white flowers that quickly turn to seed. It can tolerate the cold, and Hugh Wilson in his book *Stewart Island Plants* noted it grows around huts and houses there. I let this plant grow wild with the chickweed and in the early spring my whole garden was covered in small white flowers.

Essence

Bittercress has an alert, fluid quality. It is responsive and connects us to our hearts. It reminds us that our actions are best when we are aligned with our hearts. The nature of bittercress is bright, sharp, of the trickster, and playful.

Bittercress is a remedy that helps us to take action at the right time while also allowing space to be restful. The remedy helps us to examine how we act and what we are acting from. It gives us clarity and perception, shows up rigidity and holds us to account. The cress creates a pathway towards the notion of embodiment. It has the ability to go through immense change and yet stays true to the essence. Therefore, as an essence it helps us to go through change enabling us to trust that what is true for us will come through. What I love about this essence is that it enables the ability to be disciplined without being overbearing upon oneself and on others.

The negative aspect of bittercress is slothfulness and procrastination, feeling unable to push through to the next stage of something, a state of being prepared to give up. Slothfulness is a reaction to work rather than creating space to relax.

The Warrior

Call me forward
when you are timid of your true nature
when you require courage to stand up in community

When you lose your voice, sing like a river
when you are diminished, find your standing place

Embody me and I will help
you connect with yourself
in order to be
with this situation
or that relationship
or with yourself

I bring perspective
and may balance
with softness
or with strength

the Warrior Spirit Guide

The warrior spirit guide takes the form of a woman or man and has a strong connection to tribe and community. This connection is to the essential identity of the tribe. They serve the ancient lineage and are not bound to individuals. Even though they may travel great distances, place is important to them and they have a strong connection to their specific landscape. The warrior resides in the middle world. This is the dimension that corresponds most directly to the world we live in, its past and its future.

The warrior spirit guide aids you in responding to everyday challenges, relationships and situations. They help with everyday awareness, taking responsibility, and having the courage to be true, even if it goes against our cultural or social conditioning. Practices connected to the warrior include self-discipline, physical fitness and wellbeing, and understanding the use of our will. The warrior aids us to observe what initiates our actions and reminds us that we should act out of grace and not fear.

The warrior teaches us to be present. The presence of the warrior has a natural authority that they will show if they see that something needs to be reflected back to a group or community, particularly if there is a distortion away from truth. They may do this in subtle ways without having to be outspoken. In the warrior, the will is an important force. The warrior process is about strategy, understanding of timing, facing your fears, burning off self-importance and ultimately facing the unknown. The warrior gets us back to being real.

Finding Your Warrior

When you are relaxed and have entered the visioning state ask to connect with your power animal. Take a moment to greet and be with your power animal. Then offer up your intention to meet with your warrior spirit guide. Journey with your power animal to the middle world. There you will find various people. One of them will be your warrior spirit guide.

Greet your warrior in a way that is appropriate for them. You may wrestle, bow, hongi, or simply exchange a glance. Observe the posture of your warrior, consider when you may take on such a posture. The warrior serves a tribe or community. Look at the nature of the relationship between the warrior and their community. Ask to be shown what your warrior brings to their community. Consider how that relates to you in your life and in your work.

A warrior will have tools or weapons. These may be songs, gestures, dances, swords or taiaha. Take time to look at these tools that the warrior uses. Go deeper and see the subtle processes and symbolic meanings and uses of these tools. Ask yourself how you can bring these tools into your life. The warrior may present you with a shield. The shield may have symbols on it that represents what the warrior serves and is aligned to. If you vision a shield, you may like to create a shield and paint these symbols on it. Farewell your warrior in an appropriate way. Consider when and how you can call upon them.

Aztec Warriors, early 1540s, artist unknown

Blame and Projection

> As they pushed steadily inland, took over the vital waters handed on to the bushman by his long line of ancestors, killed off the game which had sustained him unfailingly through centuries, plundered his honey, destroyed the pastures of his bees, dispersing the quick swarms, and systematically eliminating not only the natural amenities of his life but also the necessities of bare survival. As I grew up, I looked in vain for some flicker of conscience in regard to this sombre picture of our beginnings… First one must vilify in one's own spirit what one is about to destroy in others; and the greater the unadmitted doubt of the deed within, the greater the fanaticism of the action without.
>
> Laurens Van der Post, Afrikaner explorer, journalist, author and soldier (1906–1996)

Laurens Van der Post's description of the genocide perpetrated by his ancestors is an extraordinary facing-up-to of loss of these people, 'the bushmen' who had a strong connection and love of their land. 'The bushman,' he writes, 'was there solely because he belonged to it. Accordingly, he endeavoured in many ways to express this feeling of belonging, which is love, but the greatest of them was in the manner of his painting.' To annihilate a whole people, one has to project onto them all manner of savagery so that there cannot be any connection to the heart, or sacred care for their lives.

Part of practising warrior medicine is to confront patterns of blame and projection in our societies. Blame is a common response to misfortune and dissatisfaction. Throughout history whole groups of people, villages, and entire countries have blamed others for their misfortunes. As people project blame, they create inner dialogues of anger and resentment. Their thinking consists of retaliation and justification. Such projection creates strong mental barriers so that the belief system of blaming can be likened to heavy armour. We can see projections of blame by reading between the lines of newspaper articles. The projections in these stories can be revealing, particularly if we fit somewhere within that story.

When critically reflecting on blame and projection, we must also recognise a truth – our society is unbalanced and unfair. Cruelty, greed and misuse of power exist. Extraordinary imbalances of wealth and opportunity are a malaise in our society. Patterns of blame may therefore arise from genuine grievances and in such cases, this needs to be acknowledged. The warrior is aware of circumstance and how we think and act.

Petty Tyrants

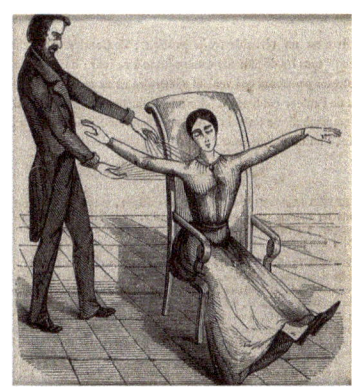

Blaming, I have often witnessed, requires an audience, and the best audience is one that shares the dissatisfaction of the blamer. Belief systems are enforced through the echo chambers we create. If we are caught in a cycle of blame, we should identify where we are disempowered and what actions, albeit small, that we can take to shift that ground. The prayer of gratitude unfolded with dedication aids us to shift out of cycles of blame. I think of this prayer like a bridge that allows us to walk over a mire of bad feeling without getting caught in it.

People can shift from blaming others to blaming themselves. This is a process of inner ferment. There is the danger that people may fall into mental torment, fear and anxiety, believing themselves to be a burden to others. Blame then leads to self-judgement and shame. The best warrior process, in this case, is to become bored with the judgement and shame but interested in the ferment itself. The ferment is like a boiling up of suffering and pain. The ferment can act as a catalyst to positive or creative action. The prayer in this place expresses whatever is in the inner – whether it is tears, shouting, sound or song. This expression allows the burning off of self-importance. Thus, it is possible to transmute blame into inspiration. We can then work with morality, look at service, community and work that expresses our gift. Once the action and practice have begun, the focus shifts to creating discipline.

A Mesmerist Using Animal Magnetism on a Female Patient, wood engraving. Mesmer Franz Anton, (1734 - 1815)

The warrior becomes most important and can be understood with the greatest clarity when he or she is juxtaposed against their foil, the petty tyrant. Petty tyrants arise in our daily lives, they are people who try and exert power over us, or emotionally trigger us. The word petty refers to the flawed and human aspect of the tyrant. They may be acting out blame, judgement and projection patterns. They may be worthy of our compassion. To the student of warriorship, a petty tyrant is welcome for it is through facing them that transformation occurs. A warrior is fortunate if they meet their foe upon the path, otherwise they would have to go and look for one.

American anthropologist Carlos Castaneda (1925–1998) in his book *The Fire Within* categorises petty tyrants into four groups – those that persecute through brutality and violence, those who create unbearable apprehension through deviousness, those who oppress through sadness, and those who torment by making warriors rage. I prefer to distinguish between types of petty tyrants by using the medicine sphere. By visualizing the petty tyrant within each of the four cardinal directions I arrived at four different archetypes.

In the East, I see the petty tyrant who is impatient, wanting things happening at once, needing and demanding that you work to their will and desire. They may inspire you, yet at the same time are burdening you and distracting you. We can confront this petty tyrant through work with the element of inspiration. We may need to examine our fears of instigating our own work and developing the focus and discipline to build a project from our own inner desires. When in relationship to this type we should act in a way that inspires. Inspiration is a spark that ignites a sharing of ideas that then connect and build on each other.

In the north (south in the northern hemisphere) I see the petty tyrant as the fighter and rebel, emotional, goading you into fighting while mistrusting you. The north tyrant will question your authenticity and how your actions align to your thoughts. The north is the height of the sun, radiance and strength. The fighter may press you and trigger you to come out and fight, thereby coming out into the day and revealing yourself. The fighter may distort how you present yourself to others in a direct pushy way. Your emotions may be displayed and chaos ensue. The fighter may approach you suddenly so that you are unprepared. If you were to approach this tyrant as a mirror you might see how it finds the wounds that you keep hidden and pulls them out into the light, making you feel defenceless and vulnerable. The fighter is often emotionally based, reactive and trigger happy. They will speak their mind in a rush but will become aggressive if you respond in like. The way to approach this petty tyrant is to look at your resistance to bringing forward your work towards fruition, to look at your vulnerability at revealing yourself and see the patterns of protection that you put in place, particularly around the heart. By forcing us into the light the north tyrant can actually push us into doing our work. When someone mistrusts us, it is worth examining why.

In the west, I see the enchantress, the illusionist and the shadow magician. These petty tyrants are the hardest to confront. They build up our self-importance. They love to make us feel special, even put us on a pedestal. They are masters of illusion and create distractions that enchant us and cause us to lose ourselves, even to the point self-delusion. It is a powerful and hollow journey. If you try to break free from the illusion you may trigger drama and further illusionary enticements. These west tyrants try to entrap your power and mana and they work on the etheric levels. Some are masterful in their ability to create diversion through hallucination. They can also be hypnotic and charismatic. They entice you with a desire to transcend the mundane, to be free from pain, to be loved and be important. The reflection that we use to confront this tyrant is finding beauty through humility and listening to your own inner feelings and responses to what feels true. It is also becoming humble, looking at our work in correct context. We can also acknowledge the power of the energetic connections we form in our relationships and the reality of the etheric world. In dealing with the west tyrant, the warrior process is in learning to express structure and form boundaries that help to anchor us and build our understanding of the world beyond the physical. Ritual can be helpful here.

In the south (north in the northern hemisphere) I see the petty tyrant who takes power through knowledge. They hold knowledge in a way that reflects a superiority, they are your judge, your critic or even the specialist who might hold your life in their hands but feels that they do not need to consult you. They are often threshold guardians, who block your way when you are about to deepen your understanding or take things into your own hands. Knowledge is about transformation and this petty tyrant reflects your own fears around your power to change through knowledge.

If there is a dominating person in your life, they are likely to be a petty tyrant. It's hard to imagine that the neighbour who annoys you could come under any of these categories, yet persistent negative behaviour can become a torment. Where there is dominance, anger will arise. Anger is a desire to access your own potential, or power. When someone creates dominance, they create an illusion and demand that people participate in the illusion.

The petty tyrant in your life may not be a tyrant to everyone. Rather it is their particular relationship with you that requires work. You are acting to transform the relationship, not the person. The self-importance that resides within us is the mirror of the petty tyrant. It is wasteful to expend energy on being offended.

Having identified a relationship of domination, consider how you respond to domineering behaviour. Do you serve dominance? Do you rebel? Do you fight? Do you cut off or do you appease it? Part of looking at what you do in relationship to those who dominate is to look at what you are most afraid of because it is your fear that creates your own suppression and control. Examine the situation from a larger perspective to see that you really are dealing with a petty tyrant. Sometimes the petty tyrant is a person who is demanding you to wake up and partake in life.

In freeing yourself from the petty tyrant you look for what is binding you to that person. Open your thinking, find strategies that shift old patterning. Examine the core mirror of the petty tyrant and uncover what the tyrant is pushing at. Look at what time of your life you are being reminded of. Take note of the weakness of the petty tyrant and the underlying motive behind their behaviour. This is often where you must dig out your own pain and shadow. Meditate, observe until you get it. Identify the old patterns of response: fighting back, cutting off, losing out, giving over power. Once you have identified the pattern break it. The petty tyrant may be right on your path, standing between you and what is truly important to you. Change your responses and move past them. Clarity of observation enables you to cut through and move through the energy that desires to control your power. Control can become an invisible power, control that seems invisible is usually because it's an unquestioned way of behaving and all that is required is to see it.

Metanoia

When we become conscious of the patterns of our belief systems and accumulated assumptions, we may experience a kind of healing crisis brought on by a disruption to these patterns. This can be disconcerting. Sometimes these disruptions disturb us with impulses that are not in alignment with our values or our inner being. Engaging in spiritual warriorship enables us to recognise these patterns and change our thinking. This is metanoia.

When I am under stress it is difficult to hear others or receive communication. This is where we can miss an opportunity for a real shift in a situation. This inability to listen under stress is an instinctual reaction to defend or act aggressively towards what we perceive as an intrusion. Will, used wrongly, may override others under these stressful situations, and thus cause harm. Spiritual warriorship is the correct use of the will. It is exciting to employ the will in a creative and holistic manner. This is the process of metanoia.

Death and the Unknown

The warrior spirit guide can lead you in a shamanic journey into a place of death and the unknown. This is a powerful journey and one that should be approached with caution. It has the power to transform us. The direction of the medicine sphere into which we enter for this journey is the southeast (northeast in the northern hemisphere). This is the place of entering into the place before and through creation. It is the place of endings and beginnings, of death and birth. To prepare, you must do work on shadow, emotions and the ability to put down burdens. The warrior becomes the warrior through the process of facing the unknown. The warrior goes through death as part of their initiation.

As we begin our journey, we enter the unknown. Entering the unknown is like entering into the void. When you come into this energy, emotions are triggered or touched. Aloneness resides here, a feeling of not quite fitting. You're not what you were and you haven't quite become. There is grief of what you have to shed, and there has to be a place of grief in this transition. Carrying a burden is connected to being afraid of the unknown. It is like we cannot walk into the unknown without carrying a lot of things. And yet, the more that you walk into the unknown the more you need to lay them down. This is the process of surrender. When you journey into this place you will experience the great falling-off. Things like the cloak-of-energy-from-other-lifetimes will fall off you.

When you shed these, you may feel naked or broken. These cloaks cover your brokenness.

The great-falling-off becomes the process of death. There is a vulnerability in death similar to the open sensitivity and vulnerability in coming into the world. This pathway reveals your brokenness, the wear and tear of these lifetimes. Courage is required to be with this. It is your essential nature that makes it through. Imagine the warrior way as being alert, conscious and innerly still. When I walk before dawn or at night without a torch, my senses need to be sharp. If I think too much about things I could slip or lose my way. An animal has a quality of presence and we can translate this quality into the concept of the heart-mind – understanding and seeing the mind in the body and to meditate with the mind through the body is a dynamic state of being in the heart. There is intelligence in the heart. Allow yourself to bring attention to the sensing heart, the receptive heart, the observer in the heart.

There is a place before you arrive, a place where you sense that something is changing that you are coming through. This is the place that must not be hurried. This is the place of the accentuation of your spirituality. There can also be an experience like death where you walk through an illusion. You walk through the illusion into this place of truth. This place is where you may feel forsaken, that you've been abandoned, that all your life is wasted. This is a place where despair may be all-encompassing. The moment of utter darkness is a moment of arrival. The utterly beautiful, and deepest despair, sit for a second beside each other and in each other; so that it feels like a trip of a switch and you have come through and yet also this place could be the deepest ravine that you fall into.

The warrior may also be a companion for others as they transition into death. They allow the shedding and the surrender to occur without disruption to this process and understand the intense sensitivity that a person goes through as they shed their worldly actions and protections. If you cannot recover from your death in arriving into life then you may have to go back and release your death so that you are *in* life.

INTO THE WORLD

Standing Meditation

Standing still is perhaps one of the oldest exercises, the ability of the hunter to stand still for long periods of time, watching, waiting, stillness before action. Standing still for periods of time opens us to energy that flows downward through the body. At first you may feel tension or pain. This gradually lessons. The body has postural muscles that react against gravity and act without volition. Postural muscles are strengthened through intent and practise. The balance required for riding a bike is an example of training postural muscles. In yoga, there are postures that also strengthen these muscles and a range of good standing postures such as warrior poses. Standing meditation is a beautiful practice. I find it gifts me spaciousness in the way I approach my day.

My practice is to find a quiet place (I practice standing meditation outside). Stand with your feet hip distance apart and parallel. Soften the backs of the knees so that the pelvis relaxes downward. Bring your attention to your feet. Sense where the weight is. Rock a little on your feet until you feel centred. Gaze straight ahead of you. Move your head a little so that you find an alignment where the muscles in your face and neck may be relaxed. Smile gently. Float the tongue so that the tip is on the roof of your mouth. Float your hands up so that they are in front of your lower abdomen. Stretch out your hands as if you were holding a ball with your fingers pointing toward each other but not touching. Breathe deeply. Soften your gaze.

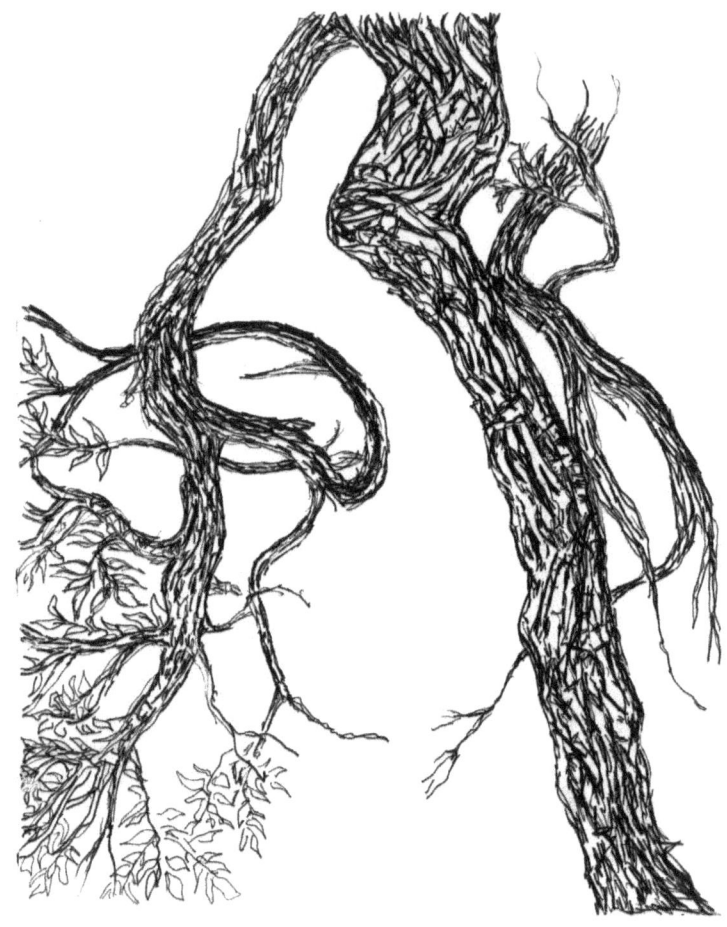

If we observe a tree, then it is possible to embody the essence of that tree in our posture. Through posture we can embody essence. When we embody essence through posture it is possible to merge with the thing and yet retain who we are. We may call into the power of what we are merging with.

192

Presence of Action

Presence of action refers to a state of attention while moving. Practise this move any way you choose. You may walk, crawl or simply move your fingers. Bring your deepest attention to your movement and slow it down. Allow the movement to be fluid, to have connection. Then speed the movement up. Play is essential in this exercise as it about exploring movement as if it were new to you. There is narrative in movement, there is story, reason, and intention. We learn this through training and practise.

Movement can show up our unconscious patterns. They may be emotional and impact how we move. When you bring attention to movement you also observe your unconscious movement. The state of action and attention will eventually be at one with each other. I call this presence. The practice and awareness of movement allows the whole of you to be present in action. Through movement we can experience divine energy. Instead of the will moving the body, the body surrenders to the universal energy. Imagine a mingling of energies internal and external to the body. These are the energies that now move the body.

a Samurai Warrior's Creed

I have no parents – I make the heavens and earth my parents.

I have no home – I make awareness my home.

I have no life or death – I make the tides of breathing my life and death.

I have no divine power – I make honesty my divine power.

I have no means – I make understanding my means.

I have no magic secrets – I make character my magic secret.

I have no body – I make endurance my body.

I have no eyes – I make the flash of lightning my eyes.

I have no ears – I make sensibility my ears.

I have no limbs – I make promptness my limbs.

I have no strategy – I make 'unshadowed by thought' my strategy.

I have no designs – I make 'seizing opportunity by the forelock' my design.

I have no miracles – I make right-action my miracles.

I have no principles – I make adaptability to all circumstances my principles.

I have no tactics – I make emptiness and fullness my tactics.

I have no talents – I make ready wit my talent.

I have no friends – I make my mind my friend.

I have no enemy – I make carelessness my enemy.

I have no armour – I make benevolence and righteousness my armour.

I have no castle – I make immovable-mind my castle.

I have no sword – I make absence of self my sword.

Anonymous Samurai, fourteenth century

Faith in the Third-Day Moon, Portrait of Yamanaka Yukimori, a samurai known for his great strength and loyalty, served the Amako warlord during a time in Japanese history referred to as "Sengoku", 1886, colour woodblock print on paper, Tsukioka Yoshitoshi,

Dandelion

taraxacum officinale

> The root growing downwards exceeding deep, which being broken off within the ground, will yet shoot forth again, and will hardly be destroyed where it hath once taken deep root in the ground
>
> Nicholas Culpepper

Description

Dandelion is a plant of contrasting elements. Dandelion didn't grow in the sand dunes where I grew up, but it did grow everywhere in the town. Perhaps it does not like sand. People tend to confuse dandelion with other similar plants like hawkbit and even nipplewort. And sometimes dandelion can be puzzling to identify because it is so variegated depending on where it is growing.

Even the flowers are variegated some rich-yellow, many-petalled, others paler with fewer petals. It is difficult to examine dandelion in its individual parts for it is connected to all of its aspects. Each part leads us on to another as if it insists we see its diversity as part of a greater whole.

Dandelion possesses a hollow stem that supports a brightly emanating composite flower head that is sensitive to the sun, opening at dawn and closing at dusk. There's one flowering on the edge of the garden, as I write. I can see it from my desk. It's closed because it's stormy and raining. In fine weather the petals are outstretched, but if it's about to rain the whole head closes up. When it's open and the sun is out, I often see bumble bees alighting on its bright yellow platform. Dandelion pertains to the earth. It makes fast to the earth in an upright manner. The stem will grow higher if it is growing amongst tall plants so that when it flowers it may be in the sun. Even the seeds that are designed to be carried by the wind, have a perfect anchored parachute shape allowing them to float down to earth in an upright manner. The seed head is like a convex station for silvery stars with an earth centre of brown seeds.

The leaves are without hairs and the margins of the leaves are jagged like teeth where one of its folk names 'lion's teeth' come from. The leaves grow close to the ground in a floret. The root is long and has a bitter taste, though I must admit I like chewing on it when it is dried. It breaks off easily and you will have to dig it out carefully if you want to keep it intact.

As a child I was told that if you smelt dandelion you would pee your pants. We also would look out for the seed heads and blow them counting how many times, to get the actual time of the day. If any friends had warts, we would break the stem and let the white milky substance drip on to the wart. If it was done every day it would make the wart go black which seemed an exciting and curious phenomenon. Its folk names reflect these customs as it is also called piss-a-beds, blowball, cankerwort, and puffball.

Dandelion has a long history as a healing plant. Its botanical name *taraxacum* is derived from Greek *taraxos* meaning disorder and *akos*, remedy. Many years ago, an herbalist told me that the leaves were for the kidneys and the root for the liver. The leaves contain vitamin C. It's a diuretic and tonic. The main target organs for dandelion are the liver and the gallbladder. It's also a general stimulant. The chaffinches in my garden love the seed. I pick the leaves for salads, and I dry and grind the roots to make dandelion coffee.

Essence

Dandelion's essence is nourishment. It contains the qualities of both the earth and the sun. It's a remedy that enables relaxation throughout the body, knowing all is well. It is a tonic that allows us to access joy within the body. It reminds us to celebrate with others and to stretch out when despondent.

Its essence has a strong elemental presence. Rich, grounding and no-nonsense. It goes deep into the earth, reminding us we are of the earth and responsive to the natural environment. It enables us to sit back without having to prove ourselves or make out that we are more than who we are. Curiously it's an essence about how we experience space within ourselves and how we allow that experience of space within our lives. As we enter a healing process, it can help us where we are vulnerable and enable us to draw back when necessary. It supports nature awareness meditation, giving the observer a sense of complete connection.

On the physical plane, dandelion helps clear toxins from the body while on the energetic plane it helps us to shift the energetic toxins and challenges of the modern world. Its strength is that it stays fully connected to all aspects of itself and therefore helps integration after a spiritual process, healing or states of shock. It's good to use after soul retrieval work.

the Sun

> From among the leaves, which always abide green, arise many slender, weak foot-stalks, every one of them bearing at the top one large yellow flower.
>
> **Nicholas Culpepper**

Life is dependent on the rhythms of the earth. As the earth turns on its axis in the course of twenty-four hours, we have day and then night. As it travels in the course of one year, we have the seasons. Sunlight is earth's predominant source of energy. When we attune to the sun, we encompass in our understanding rhythm and therefore the timing of actions, when to retreat and rest. The dandelion flower symbolizes the solar rhythm, it also symbolizes the spiritual meaning of the sun. The sun is the creative force. It is involved in life and death. When we are connected to solar energy, we feel able to be ourselves through all things, we are aware of our individuality, we shine our light. The idea of working with the solar force is that things will turn out well.

the Seed

> ... and the head of down becomes as round as a ball; with long reddish seed underneath, bearing a part of the down on the head of everyone, which together is blown away with the wind, or maybe at once blown away with one's mouth.
>
> **Nicholas Culpepper**

The seed inside of us, our blueprint is like our innate gift. I think of it as an exquisite microcosm that is unknown until it starts to grow. People often skirt around their potentiality, to see in others their gift and to express desire to live other people's lives. There is a constant looking elsewhere rather than to be with what is truly their own. It is the fear of our own potentiality and the fearsome nature of the journey not only of discovering this essence of self but in the creative expression and giveaway of this seed.

Think of the immense diversity of seeds in the world, their resilience and ability to withstand extreme conditions. Boneseed, for example, floats on the ocean for months coming from South Africa, then washing up on the shorelines here in perfect casement. If you want to hurry a peach to sprout you have to hit it, break the hard, outside kernel, otherwise you will have to wait two years before it sprouts. Some New Zealand seeds take three years to sprout. Some seeds, such as certain species of magnolia can stay fertile after thousands of years underground.

In the autumn when many plants go to seed, they shed their leaves while putting all their energy into their seeds. This can be a metaphor for the times when we need to shed the things that are no longer serving what we need to grow, and express our gift instead.

Dandelion Knight, 1899, Walter Crane

The Beneath

Connecting with Our Spiritual Ancestors

> The stories and epics that I knew were important not because they represented people and events whose existence and occurrences could be verified, but because they were lessons to me, and to anyone who cared to listen, about who we are and how we should live our lives. I teach and I write mo'olelo – not history, perhaps as you all know it. I tell stories.
>
> Jonathan Kay Kamakawiwo'ole Osorio,
> Hawaiian historian

> I arise today
> Through the strength of heaven
> Light of sun
> Radiance of moon
> Splendour of fire
> Speed of lightning
> Swiftness of wind
> Depth of sea
> Stability of earth
> Firmness of rock
> Through the creator of creation
>
> Celtic Prayer

Our spiritual ancestors are the ancestors that support the education of our soul. They take us back through an unbroken line to our source. To meet the spiritual ancestors, we enter a shamanic journey with the intention of connecting to these ancestors. We meet with our power animal and journey to the place of the ancestors. Our spiritual ancestors may be a single person or a group. There may be a circle of spiritual ancestors and they may welcome you to join them. They may be people of any historical era. Their look or dress may surprise you. In any case, they are people that we have a deep spiritual affinity to. Discovering your spiritual ancestors is about creating a powerful connection to where we came from. Therefore, some people who embark on this shamanic journey may find themselves talking to a tree, a rock or a waterfall.

Our spiritual ancestors aid us in finding out about the qualities of our soul path and support us in bringing this aspect into our lives. They help us look at our own potential. They may give us the connection to where we came from. It is there that you may look at the archetypal powers at work in the spiritual lineage. You may realise your exuberance or understand your love of snowflakes or simply realise why you love to live by the sea or close to mountains. You are finding your spiritual family and with relief you realise that you are not alone. When you return you may have work to do, or you may feel more committed to your service.

Discovering your spiritual ancestors may be disconcerting as you may come across raw and wild power that you don't feel comfortable with. When this occurs be observant of your discomfort. What are the patterns of fear and desire that may suppress this energy? Some energies are difficult to integrate or may not have a place in our world. We often have no space to dance ecstatically or experience merging with a force, in such a way that we are held by elders.

Each time we connect to these ancestors we may experience something different as we evolve along our own path. Nevertheless, I have always experienced a deep abiding thread in journeys to the spiritual ancestors that consistently reveal recurring symbols that remind me of my work.

Sharing stories with others helps to integrate journeys to the spiritual ancestors. These stories can be the stories that we love and relate to most. They may be family stories or folk tales, or the myths that we responded to as children. These can become indicators to us of our physical heritage and a connection to our spiritual ancestry.

the Wise One

In shamanic practice, the wise one is one of the four spirit guides assigned to us that assists in accessing our wisdom. The wise one's abode is in the depths of the earth. In the medicine sphere its placement is in the south (north in the northern hemisphere). This is a place of retreat from the world as we seek wisdom within ourselves. There are thresholds where we have to trust in something to enable us to move through the darkness as we enter into the experience of wisdom.

To find our wise one, we begin a shamanic journey. We meet with our power animal and offer up our intention of meeting our wise one. In the visioning state we will find ourselves in a landscape. From here we must find a way into the earth. As we descend into the earth, we will at length meet our wise one.

The wise one can take the form of a mythical creature, animal or human. There can be a neutrality in its response to you, as you would expect of an ancient being who may be more amused by the serious antics of your life, than indulgent. It can bring to light what is happening around you, even that which you may not want to see. It brings perspective, a shift in the way you perceive things. In meeting the wise one we may experience a sense of space and timelessness.

Finn McCool and the Salmon of Knowledge

The twelfth-century *Macgnímartha Finn* describes how the Irish folk hero Finn McCool (Fionn mac Cumhaill) attained his wisdom. Beside the well at the bottom of the sea grew nine hazel trees. At length the tree fruited and their nuts were eaten by a salmon, a salmon that became known as the Salmon of Fec. There was in those times a wise and powerful druid named Finnegas. Finnegas knew of the Salmon of Fec and knew also of a prophecy that whoever should eat it would gain the wisdom of the world. For seven years Finnegas laboured to catch the Salmon of Fec, before he finally snared it. He then gave it to his apprentice, Finn, to cook, but forbade him to so much as taste it. Finn put the salmon on a spit to roast and when it was cooked, he laid it before his master. But as he laid the fish before his master, Finnegas saw the look of wisdom in his eyes and asked if he had tasted the salmon. Finn replied that he had burnt his finger on the spit and put this in his mouth to ease the pain. Finnegas then returned the plate to Finn to eat, saying 'You have eaten of the salmon of knowledge, and in you the prophecy is fulfilled.'

I have shared this story because of the way knowledge is embodied and transferred. Stories are important to me because they contain so many layers and each time I read it or hear it told, I find myself connecting to another piece. I particularly like how although Finnegas knew of the Salmon of Fec and laboured to catch it – it was Finn who accidentally received the wisdom. There is something about how wisdom can bypass knowledge and yet the two are connected. It also shows how destiny can override the best-laid plans. The story also has a personal meaning for me because my wise one comes in the form of a salmon. But the most interesting aspect of the story is the way it explores wisdom through embodiment. I use the word embodiment to refer to the process by which an entity or force moves into our bodies. Such experiences can be overwhelming, even frightening, but the story illustrates how they can also be powerful and gifting.

THE BENEATH

Salmon eggs are laid in freshwater streams at high latitudes. the eggs hatch into alevin or sac fry. The fry quickly develop into parr with camouflaging vertical stripes. The parr stay for six months to three years in their natal stream before becoming smolts, which are distinguished by their bright, silvery colour with scales that are easily ~~washed~~ rubbed off. The majority of species of salmon migrate to the ocean for maturation. In these species, smolts spend a portion of their out migration time in brackish water, where their body chemistry becomes accustomed to Salmon osmoregulation in the ocean SALMON make amazing journeys, the salmon of Llyn Llyw is the oldest sometimes moving hundreds animal in Britain. of miles upstream against strong currents and rapids to reproduce.

INTO THE WORLD

the Underworld

The underworld is a world under and within the earth. It's a place of darkness. This darkness could be the rich and fruitful place of the un-remembered and disowned aspects of oneself. It is also a world of entities, unusual beings and myth. It is an underworld, a place without light, the place of the seer. The underworld is often called the lower world in contemporary shamanic practice and the two terms are interchangeable.

> You gods, whose is the realm of spirits, and you, dumb shadows, and Chaos, Phlegethon, wide silent places of the night, let me tell what I have heard; by your power, let me reveal things buried in the deep earth, and the darkness. On they went, hidden in solitary night, through gloom, through Dis's empty halls, and insubstantial kingdom, like a path through a wood, in the faint light under a wavering moon, when Jupiter has buried the sky in shadow, and black night has stolen the colour from things.
>
> Virgil. *Aeneid* BkVI: 264-294
> the Entrance to Hades

I do, however, have a preference for the term *the underworld* because of its rich associations with a large body of folklore across cultures and languages. When I do a shamanic journey into the underworld, I often see the bizarre, the mythological, things I do not understand and things that do not fit easily into my everyday reality. Sometimes there is an absurdity, like the world of *Alice and Wonderland*. Occasionally this absurdity causes a sensation of awe and fear.

Psyche and Charon, 1892, lithographic print, A. Zick

Earth Beings

The underworld is a place where we may cross a threshold to realize our potential and receive a gift. There is a Japanese folk tale that provides a good analogy for the kind of things the underworld can gift us. In the story there is a little old woman who loves to make rice dumplings. One day one of the dumplings tumbles through a crack in her floor. The earth opens up and she follows this dumpling into the underworld. Her journey into the underworld is a tale of bravery, laughter, absurdity, fear and magic. Ultimately, she returns to the world of light with a magic paddle that enables her to create an endless supply of rice dumplings from a single rice grain.

The underworld is a place where we can meet our shadow, and unearth the shadow patterns and unconscious forces that impact our life. I find it a place of exaggeration and yet the things I vision in this world, change occurs in my personal, ordinary everyday life. On occasion, journeying to the underworld has seemed like a bizarre dream that I've known to be important but can't quite figure out why, yet simply having that dream has caused things to shift. I've recognized a truth, a truth that lies behind the façade. In the underworld you can uncover people's masks.

As part of my personal spiritual practice, I spent a night alone on a sacred hill. During the night I had an extraordinary psychic experience. I was physically pulled up into the air by a powerful force and then thrown to the ground. This happened several times until I had the experience of a doorway opening into the hill behind me. Earth beings came out to meet me and welcomed me into the hill. Peace descended.

Over the years I have slowly got to know these beings. They are nutbrown in colour with deep happiness lines etched into their faces. They have unusual ears that are pointy and wide. They are family and community orientated. They attend to the earth energies. They taught me a lot about land healing, earth energy lines and the protocol in approaching land. They love all the earthy root vegetables, particularly dandelion. They love the sun but do not stay out under its rays as its too bright for them. I find them a warm joyful people. They usually come up to the world of light only in the early morning or late evening.

Once when I was sitting and meditating outside, an earth being came and visited me, he was persistent and respectful. He held his head on one side and looked at me as if asking 'Are you going to come and play or are you going to ignore me?' I had that sense of resistance when you feel like all the demands of your life are tapping away at you. I think of it as the resistance of the threshold – this encounter was going to shift something in me. When I looked through his eyes, I saw the plants weaving together in their energy states. When he lifted his head to look, he beautifully transformed as if the world of light was almost too much for him. He was ready to plunge down into the warm earth and he was inviting me to follow him. I did.

A lot happened in those pathways under the earth. He showed me things that I don't yet fully understand. I found places that can cocoon us, and that part of our spiritual journey is to shed them. To do this we need to trust and be safe and allow the earth to support us. I received a sense of how important space and time is for us to create changes. Through safety there was a regeneration of energy. There were spaces in the underworld where I was in a deep blackness, a pocket of weightlessness, no gravity. The earth being told me that this is the earth's breath. This particular part of the earth was regenerating energy. He told me that we are losing these pockets. He expressed this rather matter of factly. The nature of his being was total joy yet as he told me that these pockets were now rare there was stillness, perhaps a sadness, in his stance.

Journal Extract

The following is an extract from my journal that describes a journey I took into the underworld:

I go down into the earth and meet a small man. We walk along an earth line. It's like a vein. We come to a fire and we sit with others like him. There is a concentration around the fire, fire and smoke. They observe the smoke, watching its patterns. They bring out a pipe, which they fill with sweet herbs. As they pass this pipe around, they always bring it to the centre fire first before passing it. The pipe is white clay. When it is finished, we stand up and file through into a cave of water. The water seeps out of the rock all around me and falls into a deep chasm. They leave me here.

I feel alone here. It's like I don't understand something. I sit here and wait. The rock is very black. I bring attention to the rock. I wonder what kind of rock it is. It's so black in this place I can't see anything. I sense the rock as greywacke. It transmutes to pounamu (New Zealand jade), then to obsidian and then back to pounamu. I feel as it does these transmutations that I become the rock that it transmutes into. As I do this, I experience the almost opposing qualities of obsidian and pounamu.

My feet become restless. I become aware of this immense chasm that the water is dropping into. I jump into this and fall and fall until I land in a place of small stones and it's very dry. I think I am in Wales. There are beings that come forward and dust me off and touch me with their hands. They then pat me with the soil, it's like a welcoming. They guide me. I allow them to lead me. They lead me deeper into the darkness. It is very dark. I would call this place the place of complete darkness. The air is very close and very old. I slowly become aware of a light. This light is unusual as it emanates from a woman. I feel a great affinity for this woman. I feel like I know her very well. As I stand in front of her my mouth fills up with dry fig leaves. I open my mouth and take out these leaves and place them on the ground. As I stand up, I find I am naked and the beings are brushing my skin. As they brush and brush my skin, I shed shame. There are more leaves in my mouth, I take them out and drop them on the ground. I see water and a willow reflected in the water, all the while more leaves are coming out of my mouth. I find a whole stem of willow coming out of my throat and as I let it go, I feel clear and more connected to myself.

I find myself sitting down, I have a book in front of me and I'm writing. There are very old manuscripts here and the paper is crumbling. The words fall into me. There is an old man and he is walking by a stream. The willows bend over the water. I think the man is from China. He lies down on his front and stretches out his hands towards me with a book in his hands. I also lie down and stretch out my hands and receive this book. The book is red, and it absorbs down through my body particularly into my legs. There are bees here and as I come to sitting, they are crawling on my ankles. I am both restful and yet have a restlessness in my heart. I open my mouth and birds fly out. There is a tui and my father is here. I start to write. I start writing about shame and how it impacts all our relationships, how shame can wrap our feet and cause us to walk on pathways that are not ours to walk. I find I am coming back rapidly. I see the pipe and the beings with the pipe and I come through a doorway.

When I open my eyes from this journey, I feel clear and refreshed. I observe the goldfinches feeding on the dandelion seed, the small cobwebs wrapped around the rosemary, the late afternoon sun outlining the grape leaves. I am back with many symbols to ponder on and a feeling of release that makes me feel that it is possible to find a way to bring forward this gift.

the Element of Earth

As an element, earth has rhythm to it. It is always moving, changing, and dynamic. There is a whole vibrant universe existing within the ordinary yet we are able to create an organizational stability and work with it. This is the nature of earth. Earth is about creation and our relationship with the material world.

Earth is connected to understanding our tools. Consider tools for art purposes, brushes, pencils and pallets, or for gardening, forks, spades and snips, or for crafting, chisels, needles and pliers. When we get to know our tools well, know them like friends, we are able to create *with* them rather than make them do our will. We must attend to our tools in relationship to the environment. The tools I need for my garden, the clothing I wear, how I want to adorn myself – these are related to the quality of earth and when we do it well, we can feel light.

When I sit with the quality of earth as an element, it is death that comes to me, and in death there is birth and life. At the time of writing, it is February and there is a drought. Where the earth isn't covered, cracks are forming in the clay. Plants are seeding and dying back. The angelica's dry and brown seeds hang in skeletal umbrellas. There is death and with it a particular smell. This smell has an odd dry sweetness, the smell of dry yellowing grass, of dusty insects, of small lives giving themselves up to the sun. The top layer of our earth is the debris of life and in it live a community of decomposers, a vital ecosystem, intimately connected with the growth of plants. Earth is loam and soil, fecundity, dryness and clay. It acts as an anchor, integral to the whole, inside and outside of us. Through earth, the natural world, and the ordinary existence, we can spirituality balance ourselves. In connecting with earth, we are less likely to become confused or suffer from illusion, as may happen when we engage with the other elements. It is with earth that we cultivate the spirit.

Talking to the Earth in Your Journal

Talking to the earth may be done alone or with others. If you are in a group, form a circle. Kneel down and bring your forefingers and thumbs together to form a cup. Start talking into the earth. Begin with giving thanks, thank everything you can think of. You might want to hum and sing a little bit. Slowly start to sing or sound into the earth. The simplicity and power of this is profound. Sound has a vibration and when it is sung into the earth it seems to reverberate through each person in a way that will connect each person to the heart.

Start to write a poem or a prayer that is talking to earth. How do you put words to a conversation with earth?

Reflect on when in the day your energy is at its lowest and then look at the times of the day when you have the most energy. How do you best utilize these times? This is understanding your own rhythms through observation. Take time to look at the different rhythms of the year particularly the solstice times and the equinox. Think of simple rituals you can do to celebrate and acknowledge these points within the solar rhythm of the year. Fast write about the following: how is the sun's energy stored, how do we partake in this stored energy? Create a discipline for yourself where you observe the rising and setting of the sun for seven days. How do you describe the particular qualities of these times of the day?

Sunrise 1913, oil on canvas, Otto Dix (below)
Red Sun, 1935, oil on canvas, Arthur Dove

Earth

East, fire, animals,
up to the sun down to the earth,
to the fire within

North, water, plants,
up to the moon down to the earth,
to the water within

West, earth, mineral, stone,
up to the mountain down to the earth,
to the minerals in our bones

South air, birds, flight,
up to the stars down to the earth,
to the breath in us.

Earth Prayer

earth
may I walk gently upon
you
may I walk in your
rhythm
may I be your lover

earth
with these hands may I
grow a garden
with this body may I
open my senses
with kindness may I
connect

earth
may I be like a child
in your presence
playful

earth
I am in awe
of your wild
of the raw forces
through you

earth
I thank you
I thank you
I thank you

Scotch Thistle

cirsium vulgare

Description

The first thing that draws my attention when I observe this thistle, are the soft silvery hairs under its leaves and stems. They catch the early morning light and appear to glow silver. A small hunter spider sits on the stem. Its leaves are symmetrical, each with a longer spine and two smaller spines on each side. As I draw its leaf I think about patterns and I wonder what we do when we see these patterns within ourselves. How do we change? Perhaps it is the courage to acknowledge our mistakes. I think of a joyous courage as I try to draw that combination of softness, sharpness and symmetry.

In New Zealand, this is one of our most abundant thistles. It is a biennial, germinating in early spring. In its first summer it forms a rosette. In its second summer, between November and March, it flowers. The composite flower heads are purple and the seeds are attached to feathery down that is carried by the wind. As children we considered these seeds to be fairies. I also have a memory of sneaking out of school with a friend, climbing over the back fence into a large patch of thistles, getting the flower head and eating the little nutty piece underneath it. The leaves of Scotch thistle are spiny on the upper surface. It has deep lobes, tipped with strong spines. It has a strong central taproot. Scotch thistle can grow quite large, forming well-branched shrubs up to a metre and a half high.

Background

The Scotch thistle became an emblem of Scotland during the reign of Alexander III (1249–1286). According to legend, a Norwegian army under King Haakon IV of Norway landed stealthily on the coast of Largs at night. To ensure that they kept the element of surprise the Norwegians advanced barefoot toward the Scottish stronghold. Luckily for the Scots, however, one of the invaders stood on the spiny point of a thistle and screamed in pain. The Scots were alerted to the presence of enemies and were able to repel the Norwegians.

With the desire to plant something symbolic of their country, a group of Scottish settlers ceremonially planted the first scotch thistle in New Zealand at Petone, near Wellington, during their St Andrew's day picnic in 1840. The thistle flourished. A Wanganui settler later established a thistle patch around his raupo hut to deter 'barefoot' intruders. By 1859, only nineteen years after the first thistle had been planted, New Zealand was so infested by this botanical invader that Reverend Richard Taylor reported great patches of thistledown floating in the Cook Strait.

Essence

I made this remedy from a particularly large and magnificent specimen in a friend's garden. It was, without doubt, the biggest thistle I have ever seen, and we partook in much laughter and joy in admiring its form. Its presence certainly couldn't be ignored. The essence of scotch thistle contains feelings of joyousness and invincibility. When I observe the whole plant there is an uprightness and aliveness that makes you want to celebrate, even if life is full of challenges. It seems to say 'yes I am alive and I have cause to celebrate.' It helps raise the energy – particularly when you have that feeling of being sunk down to the pit of your stomach. Scotch thistle is a remedy to aid those who have suffered and survived hardship. It gives hope and life aiding recovery from depression or wounds. It brings courage. It contains a quality of elation yet has a feisty edge. My friend Oraina, on meditating with scotch thistle, visioned swords on the ground and dancing on the roof all night before going to battle. It aids us to let go all the non-essentials and just step forward.

Thistle Fairy, 1932, Ciceley Mary Barker

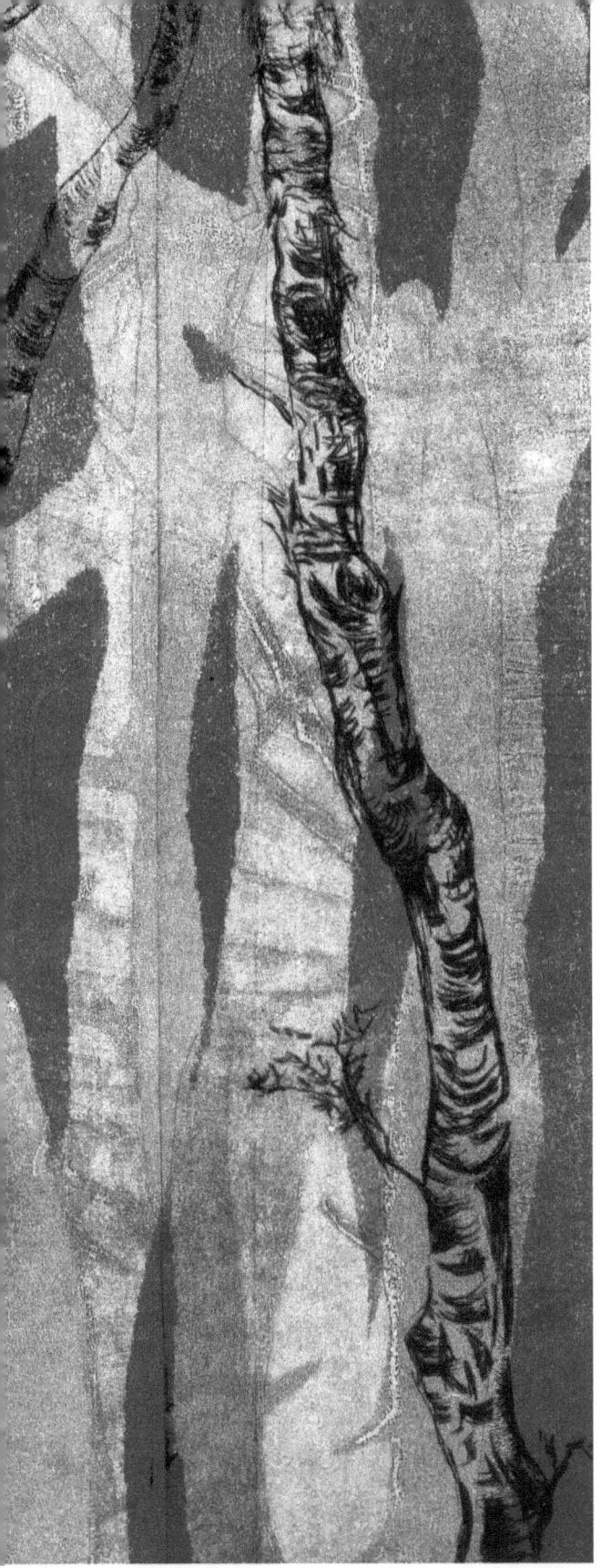

Ancestral Work

Ancestral Work

As I begin to write about ancestors I want to handwrite in my notebook. I start looking for my fountain pen, I think about the colour of the ink and the feel of the paper – this perception of the beauty of script and paper comes from my mother and through her from my grandfather. My grandfather wrote many letters, and instilled in us the way that different letters should be written. We were taught how to begin and end, and how to properly write the address on an envelope. I visualise the aspects that make up who I am, weaving together my lineage, my ethnic group, the land I was born in, and the land I reside in. I am the result of all kinds of accidents, influences, and choices made by my forebears. I come out of stories that I identify with and these, in turn, show me how I react and respond to life's circumstances. When we look into ancestry, we are finding the stories that connect us to who we are, how we came about, our origins and our myths.

The ancestors come through from the land, through our ethnic group and through our lineage. In finding who we are we touch into concepts of identity, myth and mana. How we perceive ourselves through these connections and also to become aware of how others perceive us. People who for the first time find they were secretly adopted, are usually stricken by this information for they are stripped of their identity.

Whakapapa

> Papa is anything broad, flat and hard as a flat rock, a slab or a board. 'Whakapapa' is to place in layers, lay one upon another. Hence the term whakapapa is used to describe both recitation in proper order of genealogies, and also to name the genealogies. The visualization is of building layer by layer upon the past towards the future. The whakapapa includes not just the genealogies but the many spiritual, mythological and human stories that flesh out the genealogical backbone.
>
> Ross Himona

Many of us have no sense of this genealogy. Yet all of us have stories and as we do spiritual work on our ancestral line, we may uncover parts of our genealogy. There may be gaps but slowly we can gain a sense of something, a weave is the way I visualise it, that we are part of. Himona describes it as 'te Here Tangata,' a rope of mankind that stretches back into the past toward the instance of creation, and on into the future. We can draw consciousness out even further, seeing ourselves as part of a vast weave of people, land and nature, a humbling perception.

Acknowledgement of ancestry leads to the understanding that our participation in life is intermingled with ancestry that is within us. When we gain understanding of the wholeness that ancestry presents to us, we begin to acknowledge all those who have walked before us.

Sobonfu Somè begins her talks with a beautiful prayer. In this prayer she acknowledges all those who have walked before her. This is the prayer that she translated from her dagara language.

> **I call on the spirit of this land**
> **the spirit of my ancestors**
> **especially the spirit of**
> **all the wild wise women**
> **who have ever roamed this earth**
>
> all the wise women
> who have brought forward their medicine
> all the wise women
> who have been the warriors,
> the protectors of life, the bringers of life,
> the ones who are responsible
> for us being here
> to come and join us at this time
>
> through,
> it is only through your presence
> **for it is only through your blessings**
> **that we can achieve what we are here**
> **to achieve**
>
> so please bring us your wisdom
> your guidance
> bring us your ways
> the ancient ways that are sometimes
> forgotten
>
> bring it back into our consciousness
> into our mind,
> our spirit and into our soul
> come and shake those bones in us
> so we can remember
> come and allow us to dine and commune
> with you
> once again, as we use to do with you
> come and make the old ways
> as natural to us as possible
>
> may all the wild women
> from all the traditions come and hold this
> place sacred
> and open the gateways of wisdom,
> of knowledge
> so we may enter and drink from the well
> of the long wisdom that women hold.

My Ancestral Journey

Genealogy was not something upheld by my father. My sense is that he wanted us to forge our own lives with values that arose from a love of nature, science and the arts. He was an atheist and an existentialist – life was about how you lived it now. My mother's father, on the other hand, was proud of his lineage. He told us about being fifth generation New Zealanders. He told stories about his mother and grandmother. My grandfather's stories always drew richly on the landscape of the estuaries where his grandfather settled in Howick and later where he settled in Matakohe in the Kaipara. His sense of place was deeply embedded in the estuaries and by the sea. Our life, our lineage began in New Zealand, everything beyond it was not remembered. It was as if our genealogy ended in a vast ocean.

In a shamanic journey, I once journeyed back through my father's lineage and arrived at an oak tree. This oak tree had also symbolic import in that I felt we were a people who tended to stay put. I researched my father's family origins through the paternal line and they came from the area around Oldham near Manchester. It seems they never left this region which originally had large oak forests which were felled for the construction of ships during the Age of Sail. My great great grandfather broke with tradition; he left on a ship for Australia with his wife Elizabeth and their four children in 1848.

I recently travelled for the first time to Oldham, Manchester, finally crossing that vast ocean, that gap in my lineage. This was my father's lineage, and the land where my ancestors had resided for as long as any records showed. The hotel I had booked was, unbeknown to me, situated near the source of the Medlock river. One day as I was walking back from Oldham, I found myself intuitively following the Medlock. When I realised what was happening, I had already crossed a lane and was at the source of the river. It was in a small paddock, unprotected from the cattle and heavily polluted with effluent. Standing there amongst the cows, the rain and the wind, I was suddenly hit by something profound, a sense of ancestral place that took me by surprise. As I trudged up the hill to Bishop's Park, I started crying.

It was only in retrospect that I realised that this river would have originally been a landmark in my lineage and that this river, like so many rivers during the industrial revolution, and after, had been badly treated and polluted. Rivers are powerful metaphors in understanding lineage and ancestral connection. To the dream traveller, the flowing river gives direction, it also continues to flow through different landscapes. Sometimes in working through difficult and traumatic events in a person's lineage I sometimes get them to travel back to a time of greater strength and wisdom. From here I get them to imagine a small trickle of water like a spring that can move through the lineage to the present day.

Ancestry Imprinted on Land

The people who lived in the place that we reside in imprinted their relationship with the land into the land. The actions they performed and the stories they told that are intimately connected to the landscape exist still as a vibrational memory. When I visit a country, I like to take long walks, preferably to hike and sleep on the ground for a few days. It is in this way that I can experience the people who were there before me. It is through that resonance that I may also, with respect, connect with the place. I can also be influenced by the land and have feelings and sometimes experiences of these people.

When I open up discussion with different groups of people around connection to ancestry and place, the discussion moves to people's feelings of intense connection, sometimes a sense of displacement and feelings that where they reside has stronger implications for who they are and identify with than their ethnicity or their lineage. One woman who was born in New Zealand but the rest of the family was born in the UK experiences a distinct difference between herself and the rest of her family. She puts it down to where she was born and the place she resided in.

It's thought-provoking to acknowledge that we may have absorbed ancestral nuances embedded in the land that we grew up in, though in doing so it is important that we do not deny our actual heritage and remain vigilant in our awareness of the impact of colonisation on that land. In my view, absorbing ancestry though land, happens through elements. The elements of a place whether it is the wind, the type of soil, the forests or the hills and mountains, mould the people of that place. It manifests in their food, their stories, and their language. Even though new cultures, ethnic groups and languages may colonise a place, they may find that as they imbibe and be in that place, they become more sensitive to ideas and ways of being that are of that place. A conversation I overheard at a market illustrates a case in point. One stall holder was sharing her childhood with another. She had grown up in chalk country in the south west of England, with softness, lilac bushes and gentle beauty. The other grew up in West Auckland. One story was harsh, the other gentle. Both were speaking English but all the nuances in the language expressed the place they grew up.

I grew up in Piripai. When I was a child I used to vision an old woman who smoked her pipe watching where the tide and the river met. Somehow, I connected to her as an inner teacher and guide and she would remind me of that landscape, watching this exchange of waters where the essential essence of the river mingles with the ocean. The sand dunes had the element of death, a place to merge with, or to go over to, letting go the things of the world. As a child I wandered this landscape and I came across an urupa (Māori cemetery). The actual grave site was on the highest point of the sand dune close to the river side of the spit. At the time I did not realise the full import of this but as I was a sensitive child, I was very careful and respectful. I visited the burial ground regularly. When I visited, I would feel the expansion of the place and I learnt to naturally respect its tapu. I felt personally impacted when people started doing motorbike races nearby.

Much later I learnt that this urupa was named Opihi. It had never been formally closed but was rarely used. Many Ngati Awa chiefs are said to be buried at Opihi. A woman, Mihimere Mokai, was buried there in 1938. A number of babies were buried there in the early 1960s and were the last funerals held there before 2003 when the urupa came into use again and kaumatua, Sam Jaram, the grandson of Mihimere Mokai was buried there. He was interned according to traditional funeral rites. Men were the only ones allowed in the burial party and they removed all their clothes. In the old times, men would undress on the town side of the river and row the body by dinghy to Opihi. I have often pondered how those sand dunes helped form who I am, their openness to the elements, the wildness, the loneliness and the urupa.

When I walked the hills behind Margetshöchhelm in southern Germany I sensed the ancestral energies residing in the fields, in the rocks and in the trees. I particularly sensed it in the early morning. It was as if their time accumulated overnight and let its breath out in the morning. It was so strong I felt as if their bones were speaking through the plants and fields. It reminded me of folk tales, like *the Singing Bone* or *the Silver Plate and the Transparent Apple*, where secrets are buried in the earth, and then trees grow from that earth, and then if a pipe is whittled from them, and then played, its song expresses the truth, usually about a secret or a murder.

In Nomadic societies people travel to the same places over time. These pathways and routes across land come to impact the land with different kinds of stories. Where were the good stopping places, the difficult traverses, the sacred places, the abundant peaceful places? The energies of these pathways are also embedded in land. People who are sensitive may pick up these pathways even though the nomadic peoples of that time no longer visit them. We may even get an inkling of their stories.

in Your Journal

Exploring your sensitivity to land you might want to think about how you pick up and take into yourselves the ancestral energies that are embedded in land. Sometimes we have different sensitivities. Some people will have sensory experiences of a particular time and others will have a different experience of people that may have inhabited the place earlier, or later. What is interesting is to start to become more able to read landscape. In relationship to land, the ancestors had sacred places which were often connected to their stories about arrival and connection to place. These stories also helped to embed their connection to that place. New Zealand has an interesting history of place names with some pakeha place names reverting back to Māori and some place names like Glenomaru in South Otago is a combination of Scottish and Māori words. Many Māori place names describe the features of the landscape, sometimes they are a reference to a story of origin, often they were named after an important ancestor and an event around that ancestor. Otarawairere, a bay in the Whakatane district means the birth canal where the Ngati Awa tribe was established. Many English place names in New Zealand were also named after towns in England and have very little connection to the place itself, these displaced many of the Māori place names. An example of this is Christchurch. We may have forgotten the history or the stories and so I encourage you to find out about the stories relating to the place you reside in, and consider how you relate to these stories. Pick half a dozen place names from your area and research the origin of those names. Write the answers in your journal.

Consider the following questions. What were the qualities of the landscape where you grew up that you think you may have taken upon yourself? What were the stories that you remember about the people who lived in that place before you? What about where you live now? What are the essential qualities of the place where you live now? How do you relate to them? What is the importance for us in knowing this? Write your thoughts and answers in your journal.

the Ancestral Ally and the Place of the Ancestors

The ancestral ally is a being from our lineage that we call forward to support and guide us in healing and shifting ancestral patterning. To connect with this ally, you journey shamanically to the Place of the Ancestors, first connecting to your power animal and offering up your intention to journey there. The Place of the Ancestors is in the upper world and has a time and landscape that is particular to your vision.

When you journey to the Place of the Ancestors you may visit places of power – geographical zones that possess a quality of noumenal energy. Places of power are connected to people. Often these places are meeting points of two or more elements, such as the top of a mountain, or a hill where there is a vista and a feeling of sky touching earth. It could be a place where two rivers come together or a cave where we experience space yet are under the earth, surrounded by rock. These places will also support us and give us information about ourselves.

When you have reached the Place of the Ancestors call forward the ally and wait to see who turns up. For some people, the act of calling someone forward from their lineage is challenging. It takes trust and the ability to call for support and receive it. I like to work with an ally in ancestral work as they help to anchor me and give me support when uncovering difficult and sometimes harrowing experiences. Meeting your ancestral ally can also be an exciting and cathartic experience.

The ally shares with us its world, a world very different from our own. It may help you in negotiating challenges and co-operates with you in a particular activity. The relationship with the ancestral ally is one of mutual aid. They often combine different abilities or have access to different resources that work to mutually benefit both us and them. Just as they enhance our world, we enhance theirs. Our learning of their world is as beneficial to them as it is to us. Having a connection to an ally helps us to understand the protocol of their particular world. They have ways of responding and being that are different to ours, and it's worthwhile taking your time to get to know the diversity of beings. They can be teachers, guides and even unusual friends.

Ancestral Pattering

To become more aware of what I carried from my ancestry, I free-wrote on the subject of ancestors. I started to write about my hair. My hair is very thick and springy and when I was a teenager my mother didn't like my hair and was always wanting to control it. I started to feel shame at going to hairdressers and I always considered my hair as wild. As I grew older, I started to appreciate the wildness of my hair. I wrote about my mother's hair and my grandfather's hair. I loved, how my grandfather's hair, though cut short back and sides, was so thick and bristly. I loved to push my hands through it when he would let me. I moved from hair to their love to excel in what they did. My grandfather was a sportsman and a teacher and when he was young, he excelled in running. I thought of the stories he told about his grandmother's prize-winning cooking competitions. I realised they were a competitive bunch of people but they valued humility and never boasted. Writing down these stories made me look at my own drive for perfection. I wondered how much of that had arisen through inherited patterns of behaviour.

As we develop a sensitivity to the influences of our lineage, we can begin to perceive their presence around us and it is powerful experiencing that connection, albeit subtle. I often sense my mother like a musical tone, a vibration that is around me when I practise art making. It is not always there, but enough for me to be aware of it. When I work with the essences, remedies and plant medicine my father will come in like a curious presence. Sometimes I perceive a trickster like playfulness, and I become more awake, alert to what is happening around me. I was given a symbol from my father once, the gingko leaf. These symbols can be reminders and help us in remembering we are not alone, that we are part of a lineage. I see this lineage as a weave of influence, of knowledge and stories.

If you are adopted then you have two lineages to work with and connect to. If you experienced love and family and support in your adopted family you will find a connection through the lineage of the adopted family, where their presence can be experienced and connected to. Finding out the story of your adoption also helps bridge the connection with the biological family. If you have a parent or grandparent who was adopted or you do not know their lineage you may discover more through shamanic journeying. You may even meet someone from their lineage in the dream world. Both lineages have importance.

When teaching ancestral patterning I usually ask people to share stories they may have heard about their families. As we share, we connect to each other and we have more stories to share on similar veins. We start to make the connections that happened in their lives that may be happening in ours. Uncovering stories helps us to understand ourselves. Healing and shifts can occur simply by finding out about our stories. On the other hand, secrets in lineages can

Heirlooms

create blockages that are like feelings of shame or disquiet yet you don't know why. Sometimes these stories can only be uncovered through shamanic journeying or altered states of awareness where the intention is to perceive what these secrets are.

Think about your mother. What attributes have you inherited from your mother that you need to value and grow? What have you inherited from your mother that you need to let go of? Ask the same questions about your father. The answer may come through writing in your journal, simple contemplation or sensing into the wisdom of your body for a feeling or a vision. This can be profound and you may even be able to look back down the line to see how those attributes have been passed from one person to another.

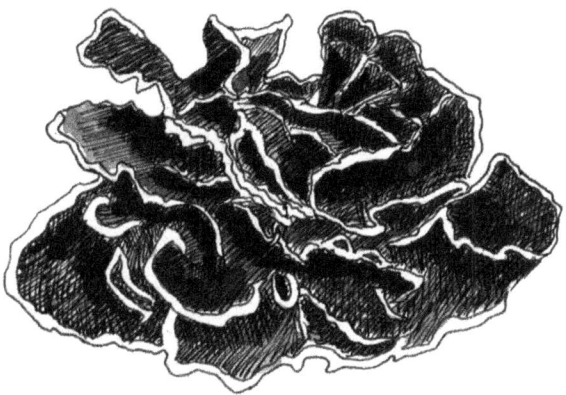

Heirlooms can connect us to our ancestors in varying degrees of potency depending on the object. It may be something our grandparents cherished, their favourite chair, cup, or jug. I have my grandfather's bread knife. The blade is thin and worn with years of sharpening. When I use it it reminds me of him. Objects such as these contain the imprint of the ancestor and we may connect to them through the object. Some heirlooms are passed down through many generations, they may become imprinted with many different lives and stories. Treasured objects like taonga that are passed down or placed on the land in sacred caves or places of power enable particularly clear pathways to the ancestors. They represent a continuum of their presence, mana and wisdom.

Objects may also contain troubled energy. They may be imbued with family conflicts. Other times they seem as if they carry an imprint that feels overbearing and we may baulk at the responsibility of being the caretaker of such an object. In inheriting a stolen object it's important to attend to this, as these objects, particularly if they are sacred to another people, may impact a whole lineage. By possessing this object, you may end up partaking in the original theft.

Andrea Reischek arrived in New Zealand in 1877 to work with Julius von Haast to help arrange the newly built museum in Christchurch. He was a taxidermist, collector and treasure hunter. Shortly after he arrived in New Zealand Reischek looted a sacred urupa, writing:

> Before me lay a fallen hut, the one time palace of the great chief, Ngapui Tirorau… I lit my dark lantern… I crept into the fallen hut. Within lay two rotted and carved coffins, and close by were cases of death-offerings, wooden clubs, stone axes, tuki-tuki, etc. I took the stone and wooden tools with me and went outside. From the hut itself I took the long middle post made of totara, on which was a beautiful tekateka, or carved figure, representing the face of Chief Titorau fully tattooed. I carefully dragged the post to the river and sawed off the head. So I would leave no trace, I let the sawdust fall into the water. I then packed the head and the other things into my rucksack, put out the lantern, and turned off homewards.

Reischek showed no understanding or respect of the sacred nature of objects which he stole. Objects stolen in such a way continue to be imbued with powerful negatively impacting energy. Which is best cleared through a ceremonial return of the object.

Marcus Lloyd of the Mangatu hapu of Gisborne described the feeling of having sacred objects finally returned to his people. In an interview with the *Gisborne Herald*, Marcus said:

> Ancient treasures of my ancestors were returned to the people after having been stolen by European settlers from a sacred cave 100 years ago. Tears flowed as epochs merged and the portals to our past were thrown open. Moments like these are history in making. These sacred treasures lay undisturbed in a burial cave for ages and are direct links to our ancestors and the traditions of our past. Such things being taken from us are due to colonisation. In this instance, it was the descendant of the person who stole the taonga who felt compelled to make right the misdeed of her ancestor. In doing so she has restored some manner of respect to her family. Now, all our old ways and treasures are returning. So is the knowledge of the ancestors and surely the mana. I'm a happy man right now.

In the best way, such treasures from the past restore our connection to ancestral lineage and allow us to evolve because we sense the connection to origin in a way that is more immediate and alive.

The experience of feeling the presence of the ancestor through the treasures of the past connects us to eldership and the role of the elder in our community. Eldership is about passing on traditions that create security, a sense of belonging, a sense of place, and a cultural continuity through generations. Ellders were essential in creating a dynamic, nourishing community. They also challenged and initiated their people. In the best sense, they became the peacemakers and guardians. The breakdown and destruction of our cultural heritage has created a tragic loss of place and mana in our elder

Sharing Stories

In my view one of the best ways to work with ancestors and help restless spirits find a place of rest is to share stories. First create an altar, and bring a group of people together in a co-creative circle. Practise connection to the medicine sphere and bring that to the altar in the centre. You might want to bring photos or objects that represent your connection to your ancestors to the altar. The participants should then light candles that represent the directions and the centre. Using a rakau or talking stick each participant then takes time to share with others the stories that they know they can share. Sharing stories in this way can be very powerful. When you have finished sharing remember to give a closing ritual. Give thanks to the ancestors and finish with a prayer that acknowledges the ancestors and their place in our lives.

Forgiveness

Forgiveness is a heart-based process. In many ways I think of the word forgiveness as to mean give without reserve. We move into processes of forgiveness when we cannot move on through pain and wounding. Sometimes when we are working through the process of forgiveness it can feel physically painful in our hearts. I see forgiveness like a grace, and there is something immensely humble when forgiveness arrives. It is like a sudden vista in a dark image, it may arrive through understanding and often through hard personal work, where we may glimpse a release from the perpetrator of the past.

I was working with a group of women recently around forgiveness. One woman brought up the fact that she had put photos of her ancestors up on the wall but couldn't bring herself to place a photo of her father up and realised that she hadn't forgiven him. That got us exploring forgiveness. We decided to look at what happened in our bodies when we couldn't forgive somebody and what happens in our bodies when we do forgive. We asked this question and meditated on the receiving. In answer to the question to what happened in my body when I couldn't forgive, I felt like a child unable to move, holding tightly to a shameful moment. The feeling when I was able to forgive was very upright and full of mana. When we shared, our experiences were similar and we considered that forgiveness was an important process in healing ourselves and particularly allowing us to move through challenging and often traumatic experiences.

We then began to explore the question of how we forgive. We realised that we needed to think about who we needed to forgive and then ask the question how. We considered who from our past we needed to forgive and then opened ourselves to receive how do we do this. My experience was profound. The person I needed to forgive suffers from schizophrenia and had a big influence in my childhood. My receiving around how I was to forgive him was to see him in all his illness and his wellness. I saw that I had tried to see him in his potentiality for goodness or from being wounded by the terrible actions that occurred through his illness. In seeing him in his entirety I felt oddly released. It was difficult to face, yet I became at peace. In looking at it I saw how I had softened my seeing by seeing through the heart. I also saw how this person had possibly triggered my wounded healer archetype.

As we discussed our experiences, we saw that ultimately the process of forgiveness was to do with self-forgiveness. To receive this was first to perceive how often we are our greatest critics. To have forgiveness for the self is to cradle one's heart, and tears came as I arrived at compassion for myself.

There is a great meditation where you rest back and imagine yourself cradled by the earth, as if the earth is holding you. With your hands you gently cradle your heart. In your mind's eye you move back through your life and cherish the life you have participated in. Reflect on what you have given and then those in your life who have given to you. It is a meditation of gratitude for your life. I see it sitting well with the process of forgiveness.

Forgiveness is part of the healing that is important in ancestral lineage. Sometimes it is not possible to rush this, sometimes we may need help to come into a place of heart or to be able to even begin to start such a process. My experience is that some events in our life need time and process and we cannot will a forgiveness process. We have to arrive at it.

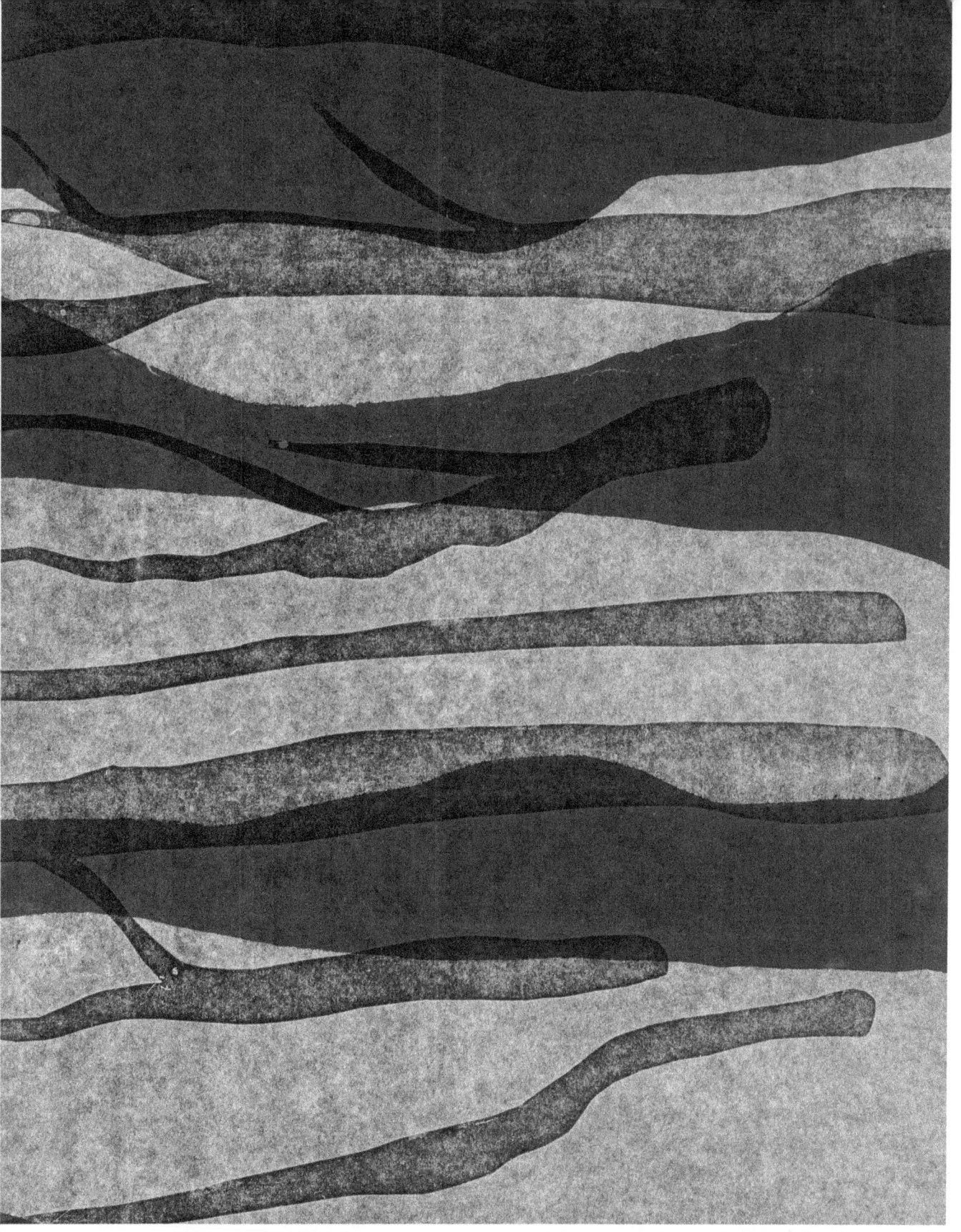

Origin

Before there was any light there was only darkness, all was night. Before there was even darkness there was nothing. Of these things it is spoken in our karakia, those chants given down from ancient time that name all the ancestors of the Māori people. It is said in the karakia, at the beginning of time there stood Te Kore, the Nothingness. Then was Te Po, the Night, which was immensely long and immensely dark:

Te Po nui,
Te Po roa,
Te Po uriuri,
Te Po kerekere,
Te Po tiwha,
Te Po Tangotango,
Te Po te kitea

The Great Night
The Long Night
The Dark Night
The Intensely Dark Night
The Gloom-laden Night
The Night to be Felt
The Night Unseen

The first light that existed was no more than the glowing of a worm, and when sun and moon were made there were no eyes, there was none to see them, not even gods. The beginning was made from the nothing.

Māori origin myth

Myth is the twilight speech of an old man to a boy. All the old men begin at the beginning. Their recitals always speak first of the origin of life. They start by inventing this event which no man witnessed, which still remains a mystery… The speech of an elder in the twilight of his life is not his history but a legacy; he speaks not to describe matter but to demonstrate meaning.

extract from Divine Horsemen: The Voodoo Gods of Haiti by Maya Deren (1917–1961) Ukrainian American filmmaker and voudouist.

Changes of shape, new forms,
are the theme which my spirit impels me now to recite,
Inspire me, O gods (it is you who have transformed my art),
And spin me a thread from the world's beginning
Down to my own lifetime, in one continuous poem

Ovid, *Metamorphoses*

> Before the earth and the sea and the all-encompassing heaven
> came into being, the whole of nature displayed but a single face,
> which men have called Chaos: a crude, unstructured mass,
> nothing but weight without motion, a general conglomeration
> of matter composed of disparate, incompatible elements.
> No Titan the sun god was present to cast his rays on the universe,
> Nor Phoebe the moon to replenish her horns and grow to her fullness;
> No earth suspended in equilibrium, wrapped in its folding mantle of air;
> Nor Amphitrite, the goddess of ocean,
> To stretch her sinuous arms all round the earth's long coastline,
> Although the land and the sea and the sky were involved in the great mass,
> No one could stand on the land or swim in the waves of the sea,
> And the sky had no light, None of the elements kept its shape,
> And all were in conflict inside one body: the cold with the hot,
> The wet with the dry, the soft with the hard, and weight with the weightless.
>
> Ovid, *Metamorphoses*

Early Morning Observation

I live in a valley and sometimes I walk down from the house to the studio to write. If I am very early and the stars are out, I lend myself to stargazing and let my imagination go. These luminous points in the sky give a certainty, when the dawn is still a long time arriving. In the deep silence of the early morning, soft cloud forms, moving up from the horizon. It is the time when the ruru is still about and the songbirds are still resting. I walk a little more down into the valley and sit back, looking up.

All the small details of my life talk away to me. I let those voices grow smaller, detail, tiny lines in the earth. I touch these lines that are like small wings. I am a detail, small in the great movement of the universe. Within the detail of my breath there are tiny microscopic beings. The tilting shifting universe, life is teeming around my knees, my hands. I lose my sense of proportion. I am taken back to when I was a child and as I dropped off to sleep, I could be as big as the universe and as small as an ant. I experience myself so small I don't know what to do with it, but to stretch out my foot to check I am still here.

INTO THE WORLD

Spiritual Work and Science

Islamic artists wrote in gold on fragile leaves to remind us of our transient nature. They gifted their exquisite art to kings, princes and califs to remind them of the true nature of our lives. In my mind I visit the clematis, flowers like white stars drape over the kanuka in spring. I see the small white pratia in the short mountain summers, the light fairy-like koromiko flowers, the dragonfly and the butterfly, transient delicate beauty and the nature of the tiny part of this life is the counterpoint to a star and the vastness of the universe. The light slowly seeps into the sky, outlining form in silhouettes. I love this time when the light is so inconspicuous.

Spiritual work and science in popular thought tend to be juxtaposed, the doctor juxtaposed to the healer, critical thought juxtaposed to faith, and verifiable facts juxtaposed to feelings and intuitions. This is not the way that I see things. To me, scientific enquiry and spiritual work converge in that they are both about deepening and exploring our understanding of the extraordinary nature of existence. Faith and belief are not my view of the foundation of spiritual work. Rather, I see my work as being founded in understanding experience and curiosity, elements that are also foundational to the pursuit of science. Reading scientific work has been an important branch in my own spiritual journey. In this final chapter on origins I touch on some areas where science overlaps with my work.

Genesis occurs repeatedly in a timeless ocean of Nirvana. In this new picture of the universe, our universe may be compared to a bubble floating in a much larger ocean, with new bubbles forming all the time.

Michio Kaku, American physicist

early - before dawn drawing in darkness. stars the early chill beauty silhouette of the pohutukawa and the shadowed hills the more routined difficult of the truth

saturday 9th February

The Creation of the Universe

When I contemplate the creation of the universe, I experience awe. This awe arises as I see myself as part of a bigger picture, a picture that is mind-boggling and extraordinary. As someone engaged in spiritual work it is my view that we should engage with scientific understandings and contemplate their implications. If we follow concepts of lineage and descent to their ultimate origin it leads us into the abstract realms of cosmology.

In the beginning of the universe, Howard Alan Smith writes, there was an infinitesimal point. It began as a hot, dense and intensely energetic speck. Time began at the beginning of this burst of radiation. This burst of radiation expanded outward from this infinitesimal point, in a process called the big bang. The universe evolved in its present form and is still expanding. The infinitesimal point from which the universe expanded is the very space you occupy here. The cosmic light created then, surrounds you now.

The universe is composed of four forces. The first force is the electromagnetic force. It enables magnets to push or pull each other and electrical charges to attract or repel one another. It binds electrons to orbit the nuclei of atoms and governs their collective behaviour. The second force is gravity. Its charge is gravitational mass. Gravity is the force that holds the moon in orbit to the earth. The moon's gravitational pull causes the tides in the ocean. Gravity keeps the earth orbiting the sun and constrains the sun in its path through the Milky Way and binds together the galaxies in the universe in a network of clumps and filaments. The third force is called the strong force. It exists in the microscopic nucleus of an atom. It holds together the protons. In the nuclei, the positively charged protons repel each other it is the strong force that holds them together and keeps the atomic nucleus in a stable configuration. The strong force is the strongest of all the forces. The fourth force is called the weak force. It is the weak force that helps to enable the sun and normal stars to shine. These are the four forces of the universe.

In the beginning there was nothing and from nothing there was a speck and in the speck was incredible energy and immense heat. The four forces were united, each a different aspect of the same force. As the universe expanded, it cooled. And the four forces differentiated from each other. The first period is when gravity assumed an identity separate from the other three forces. The second period occurred when the strong force became distinct from the weak force and the electromagnetic force. These first two periods occurred within microseconds. The third period lasted about three hundred thousand years. The fourth period has not yet ended.

INTO THE WORLD

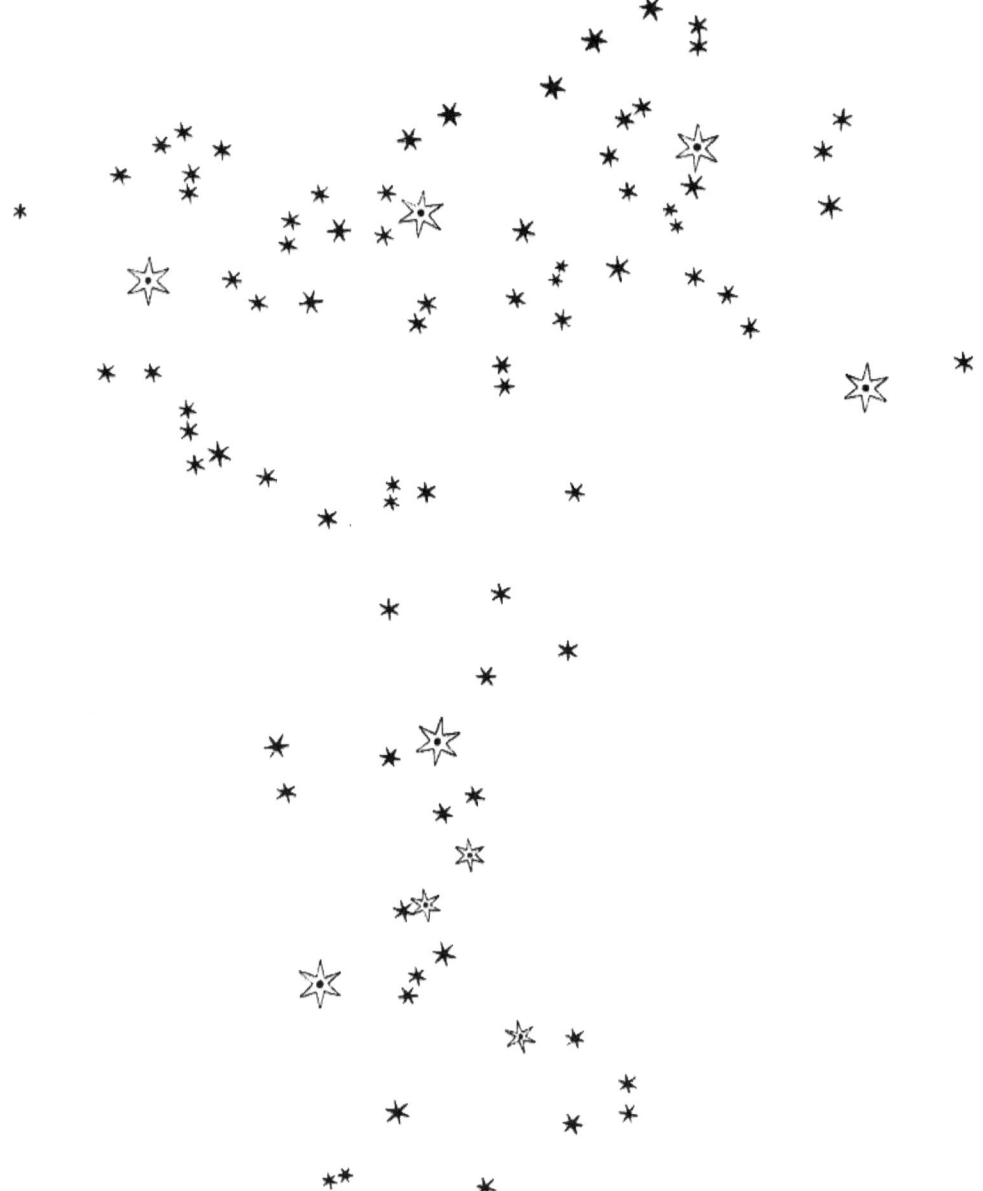

The Rope of Mankind

The lineage arises from the beginning point, that, that is without limit, that, that engenders all things. The beginning of wisdom is the awe of this. When we consider lineage, it is difficult to know where to begin. Our connection that goes through our parents, grandparents and so on doubles with each generation. If we go back ten generations, we are looking at a thousand forebears. If we go back further, in just a thousand years we are looking at four billion forebears. This is clearly absurd, but this absurdity reveals the truth of how closely related we all are and how closely related all our ancestors were to each other. As we follow our lineage further back we have ancestors that are also the ancestor of chimpanzees. Further back still we have an ancestor that is our ancestor and the ancestor of all backboned animals. Ultimately, we can follow out ancestry back to the first microbial life forms where we share an ancestor with all life on earth.

Like most of my generation, my view on human origins was influenced by Jakob Bronowski's *The Ascent of Man*. My imagination was filled with images of savage enterprising men making a living in a hostile environment on the savannah, walking on two feet to see above the tall grass. Before spreading out across the world. Unfortunately for scientific consensus, Bronowski's classic hypothesis was disproved in the nineties when studies of fossilised pollen found alongside a range of the early bipedal ape fossils demonstrated that they evolved in a forest environment. There has since been little consensus around the environmental selective pressures which caused human evolution. Personally, I am most drawn to the hypotheses championed by Sir David Attenborough that abundant waterside environments had a crucial impact on our evolution.

Increasing archaeological finds of ancient hominids, meanwhile, keep pushing back the date of human evolution, in some cases to before the time when the common ancestor of chimps and modern humans lived. While it is generally agreed that modern humans evolved somewhere in Africa, before migrating outward along the coasts, not all hominids evolved in Africa. Neanderthals evolved in Europe and interbred with migrating homo sapiens from Africa. Some modern humans still have some Neanderthal genetics. Other extinct hominids include the Flores Man who was only about one metre high and whose only fossil evidence is found on the Island of Flores in Indonesia.

The origin of humanity is a fraught, cross-disciplinary and controversial area of research. But I see the extraordinary diversity of human lineage like a braided river. Ross Himona uses the term Te Here Tangata, the rope of mankind, and visualises himself with a hand on this rope which stretches into the past back through generations to the instant of creation and on into the future for at least as long. The perception of being part of that is humbling. We are part of a vast weave of people, land and nature.

The Pleiades - Galileo, 1610

Ethnic Groups and Belonging

> An ethnic group is made up of people who have some or all of the following characteristics: a common proper name; one or more elements of common culture, for example religion, customs, or language; unique community of interests, feelings, and actions; a shared sense of common origins or ancestry, and a common geographic origin.
>
> **Statistics New Zealand (New Zealand government ministry)**

In writing this book I became aware of the complexity and pitfalls involved in writing about ethnicity, its politicisation, its shifting definitions and the ever-present shadow of twentieth-century racial theories which make the subject so prickly. It is all made more complex by the understanding that human cultures are best understood as a continuum and ethnic labels are all too often arbitrary. I could not, however leave out a discussion on ethnic belonging because issues related to ethnic identity have come up time and again for people in my spiritual work with them. Ethnic belonging is a thing and the cultural differences between groups have a real effect on people. At the same time superficial judgement and discrimination of people based on their perceived ethnic group remains prevalent in modern cultures.

In understanding ancestral patterning, we must look not only at our parents, grandparents and great-grandparents' patterns of behaviour but at the culture that they were part of and were impacted by. It is also important to consider how we and our ancestors were judged by others on the basis of our or their ethnic group. The way we identify with a group impacts how we work in the world.

When teaching ancestral work in Germany one of the patterns we uncovered was the recurrence of shame. There were many stories around shaming, from small village shaming where a parent acted differently from the norm and so the child carried the shame of being different, to stories of cultural shame of being German after the Second World War. These issues of culture and identity impact our ability to access our true desires and live with integrity. I sometimes wonder about the impact of missionary Christianity on New Zealand. Their certainty around their laws of behaviour would impact a more open culture. Shaming was also embedded in Christian missionary culture.

Survival in racist societies tells another story. Ethnic identity may have to be hidden and connection to the group lineage may be cut for survival reasons. I recently picked up a newspaper at the Nelson airport and read a story of a woman from Australia who was always told she was part Māori. When she finally decided to find her Māori ancestry, she discovered that she was not Māori but part Aboriginal. To protect her grandmother from being taken away for being 'half cast' they told the officials that she was part Māori. This confusion of identity impacted two generations. Her father struggled to hear and integrate this news due to his strong sense of aversion to being identified as aboriginal. History is full of persecution and slaughter along perceived ethnic lines. The trauma of these events has the power to impact people generations later.

Ethnic identity is also connected to landscape as cultures are shaped by their environment. Simon Schama in *Landscape and Memory*, writes that 'National Identity would lose much of its ferocious enchantment without the mystique of a particular landscape tradition: its topography mapped, elaborated, and enriched as a homeland.' It is not just identity that is connected to landscape but our spirituality is also embedded in the landscape. Spirituality is connected to living within a complex ecosystem of relationships. Prayer, meditation and other spiritual practices that arise from cultural practices that directly related to survival of the culture and the individual within a place.

A healthy way of accessing our group heritage may be to connect to a collective mana built upon sharing stories. Jonathan Osorio in *Gazing Back* writes:

Ancestry is what is left, after the loss of people and lands, after the seizure of our government, after the loss of language and the steady demoralization of our people young and old. We are still able to connect to the dizzyingly vibrant days when our chiefs numbered in the tens of thousands and our people were as numerous as the sand and stars. We do not connect with them in symbolic and imaginative ways only; through our mo'olelo and mo'okü'auhau, we may treasure our own lives as continuations of theirs and take pride in grafting our stories and our lineages onto the ones that they established.

There is strength and mana in knowing where we come from, both the good and the bad. Separating or discerning these influences from who we are authentically is impossible because they are part of our authentic selves. We may discern the shadows from the positive, the old patterns from what is now required. Yet how we respond in our relationships and how we project onto others may still carry imprinting from periods in history that impacted our ancestors. It is important in ancestral work to become aware of what we carry through our line that could be hampering our ability to express our essential nature.

Morphic Resonance

Within this discussion of origins, I would like to draw attention to the work of Rupert Sheldrake. Sheldrake, a biologist and researcher, developed a hypothesis which he called morphic resonance.

Each species has its own fields, and within each organism there are fields within fields. Within each of us is the field of the whole body; fields for arms and legs and fields for kidneys and livers; within are fields for the different tissues inside these organs, and then fields for the cells, and fields for the sub-cellular structures, and fields for the molecules, and so on. There is a whole series of fields within fields. The essence of the hypothesis I am proposing is that these fields, which are already accepted quite widely within biology, have a kind of inbuilt memory derived from previous forms of a similar kind. The liver field is shaped by the forms of previous livers and the oak tree field by the forms and organization of previous oak trees. Through the fields, by a process called morphic resonance, the influence of like upon like, there is a connection among similar fields. That means that the field's structure has a cumulative memory, based on what has happened to the species in the past. This idea applies not only to living organisms but also to protein molecules, crystals, even to atoms.

Memory, according to Sheldrake is not housed within our bodies, but in our energetic fields. How a person behaves during their lifetime, what they think, what they do, how they act, what they see, all feed back into the shaping of the field in its changing and in its evolution. According to the morphic resonance hypothesis all fields contain memory, even the field of a hydrogen atom, its only memory being that of its structure. Its structure is established through repetition of action. The electron passes around the atom's nucleus in a certain orbit reinforcing its behaviour until it becomes seemingly unchangeable like a law of nature.

I am not suggesting morphic resonance provides evidence for my experience of inherited ancestral patterning, rather I think Sheldrake's understanding of memory is worth contemplating. The idea that memory is contained in the fields of things and people has been a useful lens for me when looking at ancestry and consciousness. Evolution and change can happen as we shift our patterns, causing us to look at the habitual actions we take that no longer serve us. By changing these it may create a discomfort and unsteadiness in the field. It is thought provoking to become conscious that through our actions and our thoughts we can shape a field that is larger than us and will survive after we die.

Connecting to the Circle of Elders

Before beginning this journey find a place where you are comfortable. You may wish to have photos of your ancestors on the wall or a shelf nearby where objects that connect to the best aspects and values of your ancestors are displayed. Once you are comfortable you may begin your journey. Once you have entered the visioning state imagine your mother standing behind you. Imagine her mother standing behind her, and all the mothers of their mothers behind them in a line that stretches for many miles across the landscape. Alternatively, you could do this through the paternal line. Imagine a continuous line. Journey in spirit form down the line until you come to a circle of elders sitting around a fire. See yourself as part of this circle, imagine spending time in this circle. In a journey like this there is a quality or an essential feeling that you may experience. Ask the elders for a talisman. Find ways of remembering this talisman. When you return from the dream world you may wish to henna it on your skin or recreate it physically to wear. Having a talisman like this helps to remind you of the values and stories this journey brought up for you.

Free Writing

When free writing it is best not to think too much but just to write and allow the stream of consciousness to flow on to the paper. No one is judging you on your writing, it is only for yourself to reflect and discover what comes from it. Begin by writing about money. What is your relationship with money? Write about fears, abundance, and poverty. Then write about food. What are your values around food and what kinds of food do you love? How do you like to eat and what time of the day do you like to eat? Write about intimacy. Are you physically intimate as a family or aloof? Write about ambition. How are you impacted by the ambitions of your parents or grandparents? How were you supported or discouraged in what you chose to do? Write about religion. What belief patterns did you inherit and how are they of value today. Write about marriage. Write about the values and processes around marriage for you. Write about your childhood home and how that reflected the values of your parents. When you have finished, look at what you have written. Can you discern the elements of your life and attitude toward things that you have inherited?

In this world

the order of the universe

and its purpose

and our mind

and matter

behave as a wave

in this world

a wave stretches out

both before and behind its crest

and efforts to contain it only make it diffract

causing it to spread even more

although a wave

is found mostly in one place

it will have presence well away from that one place

in this world

we are inescapably involved

in bringing about

what appears to be happening

great forces are moving

elements, particles

in all the outer

in all the inner

layers

as we come closer

and closer

and closer to earth

these forces stabilize

they transform

they find their place in relationship to each other

this entry into the microcosm

things become dense, smaller

within them the essence

becomes concentrated

if there is no access from that point of

concentration

to its wilder state

to its atmospheric process

through the shutting off from that

the energy can become stagnant

and poisonous

when there is disconnect from source
it may create distortion
and yet the seed has to become disconnected to
know itself

for in the seed contains the source
the elements recognize potentiality
they greet it with force
they hum
they are difficult
they are there
the seed may be full of the potential of its limbs
yet it cannot move them
it may be full of the potential of its mind yet it
cannot create
in the process of 'tzimtsum'
known as the contraction
God withdrew Himself
from a part of Himself
to make room for the created world to come

the seed is left
in the darkness

in the darkness it is hard for the seed
to be with itself
for it feels in that place the aloneness

the noise of the elements
the rushing of the stars
these are absent in the darkness of the earth

in time
it might hear its own
encapsulated light

in time
a small
trusting towards
inner light

the point of arrival.

Appendix
Lasavia Vibrational Remedies

This appendix offers a brief introduction to the Lasavia vibrational remedies, and a summary of the wild weed collection, which is dealt with in more detail throughout this book. Readers who wish to have a fuller understanding of vibrational medicine, and the Lasavia collections in particular, need refer to the Lasavia Essence Book.

Background

Vibrational medicines have been used by many peoples across space and time. Ian White, in his book *Bush Flower Essences*, details how Australian Aboriginal people would eat the flower to obtain the beneficial effects of the plant: 'The essence, in the form of dew made potent by the sun, would thus be consumed with the flower.' White goes on to say that if the flower was inedible, they would sit among them to absorb the healing vibration. In Medieval Germany, Paracelsus (1493–1541), an alchemist, physician, astrologer and philosopher, would collect dew from flowers to treat physical ailments as well as emotional imbalances in his patients. The name most associated with vibrational medicines in the modern era is the English doctor, Edward Bach (1886–1936). Bach began his career as a surgeon before taking a post at the London Homeopathic Hospital where he worked in Bacteriology as a pathologist. He started to prepare vaccines using homeopathic methods and gave a paper proposing that vaccine therapy was closer to homeopathic than allopathic medicine. He saw both homeopathic and allopathic medicine with mutual respect and recognition.

Later when he created the vibration medicines he is famous for today, he named them remedies. Today they are known as *Bach Flower Remedies*.

My view is that when we engage in the healing properties of vibrational medicine, we engage in a relationship with the consciousness of the particular plant, animal or mineral. People often perceive of medicine that they take as something that only serves themselves, they forget that the medicine itself has a consciousness and that by imbibing the medicine they are partaking in that consciousness. Vibrational medicine opens a gateway into the consciousness of the medicine and the healing occurs through that relationship.

Production

The Lasavia remedies that I create are connected to landscape, and to the time that they are made. The kanuka that grows in the sand dune of Piripai and the kanuka that grows in the valleys of Waiheke Island are different kanuka. They have different qualities and yet they have the same essential quality. In making a remedy I connect to the essential note of the landscape the plant is growing in. I also listen intuitively for the appropriate timing to create each remedy.

Each Lasavia remedy has within it the physical components that transmit and preserve the essence of the plant, animal or mineral that it embodies. These physical components are water and the preservative, brandy or occasionally apple cider vinegar. In creating a remedy, I put water into a small glass bowl (sometimes I use a stemmed parfait glass). This vessel has no patterns on it, is clear and able to transmit the light to the water. When working with plants I usually transfer the physical flower or part of the plant I am making the remedy from into the water. For animals I connect with the animal and working in accordance with it and the elements I ask that the vibrational essence of the animal be transmitted into the water. The sun activates the water to 'potentise' the remedy. The remedy is then bottled and allowed to sit. This process can be likened to an energetic fermentation process. The remedy is 'still working.' When this is finished, the process is complete. I preserve the remedy with equal quantities of brandy. This is called a mother tincture.

Stock bottles contain approximately four to six drops of the mother tincture. The transferring of the mother tincture to the stock is a meditative process. It is the time when the remedy shows itself. I often find the experience potent. It requires neutral concentration and I usually rest briefly in-between making stock bottles to ensure a clear transition. The stock is what practitioners should use and the stock bottles are also used to make up all dosage mixes. Mother tinctures should not be taken directly but the stock concentrate may be used as a direct remedy.

Using the Lasavia Remedies

The Lasavia Remedies are safe and easy to use. You may prepare a small dosage bottle by mixing 15% brandy with 85% water or 90% apple cider vinegar with 10% water. Drop six to eight drops from the remedy selection of remedies you wish to use. You may also drop the remedies in your drink bottle or glass of water. You may take drops directly from the stock bottle but take care not to touch your lips or tongue with the glass dropper. The remedies may also be beneficial when rubbed gently on the skin. Places on the body that they can be applied are on the forehead, the soles of the feet, wrists and the palms of the hand. This can be helpful for babies. Another way to take remedies is in a bath. Cleansing and protective remedies can be dropped around a room or other space.

Sometimes a dosage bottle is for a particular time or crisis. You don't always have to take it until the bottle is finished. I find a lot will shift within the first three to four days so it's a good idea to take the drops regularly at least three times a day for the first three days. A practitioner may give specific instructions as to how long you should take the remedies for and how often.

If you are an intuitive person, you may already notice how particular remedies seem to jump out at you. I encourage you to listen to this, pick up the remedy in your hand and sense how it feels before reading about what they do. Another way to choose is to muscle test or use a pendulum. If you are unsure, you can always read what each remedy is recommended for and pick the one most appropriate to your situation.

Healing with Remedies

Healing is often about a shift in how we approach our lives. Illness can even be a key in our own healing process. Bach's therapeutic goal in *Heal Thyself* was that each person takes responsibility for their life. He argued that all human beings hold within whatever they need for their own healing. Thus, there is no longer a reason to fear illness. Illness is spiritual. It is connected to the journey of the soul to correct itself. The key is often the power of our mind and the process of the heart.

Another aspect of healing is uncovering what is hidden, to uncover what is behind an illness and to come to the root of it. When we use a vibrational remedy, we bring forward what might be hidden or we look at the gesture within the plant that would create balance through the likeness to our own personality. The healing that we can experience with the vibrational remedies may be subtle but have big consequences.

The Wild Weed Collection

A weed is usually defined as a plant that, in your perception, is in the wrong place – the gardener forever digging up the plants that take over the garden bed, the plantain, the dandelion, the buttercup, the thistle. The way I perceive the word 'weed' is a plant that is common and overlooked yet very often has great medicinal value. Weeds and humans have often grown together, there is a compatibility between the two and therein dwells the medicine. The weeds that I have made remedies from have all been introduced to New Zealand either accidentally or deliberately.

Developing a more intimate relationship with the weeds in our own back gardens can lead us to discover rich, forgiving and abundant friends. In making these remedies I was surprised by their potency and their strong relationship to humankind. Some of these remedies feel like a joyful shouting in my ear. It was hard for me to weed the vegetable gardens without some kind of general explanation to them about giving space to broccoli, or rows of carrots. I ended up having whole beds dedicated solely to chickweed and bitter cress. I feel enriched by my relationship with these plants. I encourage you to get to know them for yourself. Take a moment to taste the dandelion leaf or place the flower in water to drink or gather the chickweed and the cress for your salads.

Chickweed – *Stellaria media*

Chickweed is used for times of transition. It supports a person in the first stages of grief, helping to assimilate a situation that is unexpected or where circumstances are unforeseen. It is gentle and unassuming, yet surprisingly strong and insistent. It has the quality of deep nourishment and assimilation, enabling us to nourish ourselves on all planes; physically, emotionally and mentally.

Cleavers – *Galium aparine*

Cleavers clears the auric field and cleanses. It therefore enables us to receive the support appropriate for us at any given moment. It has the ability to bring to it the things it needs, a reminder that we don't have to be self-reliant in everything. This remedy is helpful in putting in to place, and assisting, interdependent partnerships. It can clear a project of negative or heavy energies. It is a remedy that can be used in house clearing or land healing.

Comfrey (Russian) – *Symphytum x uplandicum*

Comfrey enables us to access memory, ancient and contemporary. The power of what is hidden becomes present. The remedy creates an ability to contain and work with the emotions, particularly anger. Comfrey helps us to shift emotions by allowing us to be present with them without falling overwhelmingly into them, balancing grace with groundedness. The remedy helps us break free from judgement, judgement of self, judgement from others and judgement of others – bringing light to the state of judgement.

Bittercress – *Cardamine hirsuta*

Cress moves with responsiveness to a situation, while connecting us to our hearts. It reminds us that our actions are best when we are aligned with our higher selves. Slothfulness and procrastination are negative states when we feel unable to push through to the next piece and are prepared to give up. Bitter cress allows us to move out of these states and into action. It is an essence that allows us to take action at the right time, with a balance which allows us space to be restful without guilt.

Dandelion – *Taraxacum officinale*

Dandelion contains the qualities of both the earth and the sun. This remedy enables relaxation throughout the body, knowing all is well. It works like a tonic. It goes deep into the earth, reminding us we are of the earth and responsive to the natural environment. The essence enables us to sit back without having to prove ourselves or make out that we are more than who we are. This essence enables us to protect ourselves when vulnerable and to know when to draw back. Its strength is that it stays fully connected to all aspects of itself and therefore helps integration after a spiritual process, healing or states of shock. It's good to use after soul retrieval work.

Scotch thistle – *Cirsium vulgare*

Scotch thistle encompasses the feeling of joyousness and invincibility. When I observe the whole plant it has an uprightness and aliveness that makes you want to celebrate, even if life is bringing challenges. A remedy to protect the one who has suffered and survived much hardship, this remedy gives hope and life so that they may recover. It brings courage, the quality of elation and a feisty attitude. Scotch thistle helps us to let go all the nonessentials and just step forward.

Annotated Bibliography

Pre-modern Texts

Aurelius, Marcus. *Meditations.* Translated by Martin Hammond, Penguin Classics, 2006.
In addition to being Roman Emperor and conqueror of Parthia, Aurelius, is one of the most important philosophers and advocates of stoicism.

Confucius. *The Analects of Confucius.* Translated by Simon Leys, W.W Norton and Company Publications, 1997.
Ley's translation is designed for lay readership and almost all classical Chinese terms are translated.

Ovid. *Metamorphoses.* Translated by David Raeburn, Penguin Classics, 2004.

Plato. *The Republic.* Translated by Tom Griffith Cambridge: Cambridge University Press, 2000.

Virgil. *Aeneid.* Translated by Frederick Ahl, Oxford University Press, 2007.

Indigenous Lore

Allen, Paula Gunn. *The Sacred Hoop: Recovering the Feminine in American Indian Traditions.* Beacon Press, 1986.
Allen provides great insight into the society of Laguna Pueblo people with whom she grew up.

Brown, Dee. *Bury My Heart at Wounded Knee: An Indian History of the American West.* First published Holt and Rinehart 1971, this edition, Bantam 1973. Brown's classic work on North American indigenous history is an important read for anybody who wishes to understand more about the horrors of American colonisation and why cultural appropriation is such a sensitive subject.

Brown, Joseph Epes. *Animals of the Soul: Sacred Animals of the Oglala Sioux.* Element Books, 1993.
Brown, Joseph Epes. *Teaching Spirits: Understanding Native American Religious Traditions.* Oxford University Press, 2001.
Brown is one of the more reputed sources on North American indigenous spirituality. He was instrumental in bringing indigenous knowledge into American universities. He is not, however, of tribal identity himself.

Castaneda, Carlos. *The Fire Within.* Washington Square Press, 1984.
Castaneda's work is controversial, as some scholars have questioned whether Don Juan Matus, the Yaqui elder from which he received much of his knowledge, actually existed. Castaneda does, however, have academic defenders and the authenticity of Don Juan is unlikely to ever be definitely proved. We should, in any case, not let this detract from the strength of Castaneda's spiritual philosophy.

Cowan, Tom. *Fire in The Head: Shamanism and The Celtic Spirit.* HarperCollins, 1993.

Davis, Wade. *Shadows in the Sun: Travels to Landscapes of Spirit and Desire.* Island Press / Shearwater Books, 1998.

Davis, Wade. *Light at the Edge of the World: A Journey Through the Realm of Vanishing Cultures.* National Geographic, 2001.
Davis spent several years living among many different tribal groups in South and Central America. He is best known for his discussions on the use of psychoactive plants in American spiritual practice.

Eaton, Evelyn. *The Shaman and the Medicine Wheel.* Quest Books, 1982.
The Shaman and the Medicine Wheel was Eaton's last book, published when she was eighty years old and one year before her death. Eaton's background was as a novelist. She was Canadian European.

Marsden, Maori. *The Woven Universe: Selected Writings of Rev. Maori Marsden.* The Estate of Rev. Maori Marsden, 2003.
Rev. Maori Marsden was a tohunga, scholar, healer, minister and philosopher, of Tai Tokerau (mixed northern) tribal identity. Marsden was an Anglican minister and a graduate of the whare wananga.

Meadows, Kenneth. *The Medicine Way: A Shamanic Path to Self Mastery.* Element Press, 1991.

Moon, Paul. *Tohunga: Hohepa Kereopa.* David Ling Publishing, 2003.
Moon, Paul. *A Tohunga's Natural World: Plants, Gardening and Food.* David Ling Publishing, 2005.
Moon, Paul. *The Tohunga Journal: Hohepa Kereopa, Rua Kenana and Maungapohatu.* David Ling Publishing, 2008.
Moon, a professor of history, transcribes the remarkable wisdom of Tuhoi tohunga Hohepa Kereopa.

Nelson, Richard. *Heart and Blood: Living with Deer in America.* Vintage Books, 1997.
Nelson lived periodically among Alaskan Athabaskan and Iñupiat peoples.

Osorio, Jonathan Kay Kamakawiwo'ole. *Dismembering Lahui: A History of the Hawaiian Nation to 1887.* 2002
Osorio, Jonathan Kay Kamakawiwo'ole. 'Gazing Back: Communing With Our Ancestors', published in *Educational Perspectives*, v37 n1 p14–17, 2004.
Osorio is a professor at the Hawai'inuiākea School of Hawaiian Knowledge. He has done much to identify and build alternative indigenous methodologies for academic work.

Reid, Anna. *The Shaman's Coat: a Native History of Siberia.* First published by Weidenfeld & Nicolson, 2002. This edition, Phoenix Publishing, 2002.
Anna Reid investigates indigenous Siberian history, travelling from Mongolia to the Bering Strait.

Reischek, Andreas. *Yesterday in Maori Land.* First published Jonathan Cape, 1926, facsimile edition published by Wilson and Horton ltd, 1952.
Rieschek was an Austrian botanist, taxidermist and explorer. *Yesterday in Maori Land* is an account of his travels in New Zealand.

Robinson, Samuel Timoti. *Tohunga.* Reed, 2005.
Robinson's work draws from his own tribal upbringing as well as secondary research

Rutherford, Leo. *The View Through The Medicine Wheel: Shamanic Maps of How the Universe Works.* O Books, 2008.
Rutherford runs the Eagle's Wing Centre for Contemporary Shamanism. His interpretation and use of indigenous knowledge is controversial.

Somè, Sobonfu. *Women's Wisdom from the Heart of Africa.* Sounds True, 2004.

Somè, recently deceased, was a Burkina Faso philosopher and activist. Born into Dagara culture, Somè has been influential in bringing Dagara spiritual knowledge to the world.

Storm, Hyemeyohsts. *Seven Arrows*. Ballantine Books, 1973.
Storm, of mixed tribal identity, is credited as being the first writer to bring the concept of the medicine wheel to the reading public. Estcheemah is a female elder, chief and the principal source of Storm's knowledge. Unsurprisingly, Storm's interpretation of North American spiritual practices remains controversial.

Van der Post, Laurens. *The Lost World of the Kalahari*. First published Hogarth Press, 1958. This edition Penguin, 1973.
Van der Post was an Afrikaner explorer, journalist, author and soldier.

Alchemy, Religion, Theology, and Occult

Atkinson, William Walker. *The Kybalion*. First published by the Yogi Publication Society, 1908. This edition published by Penguin Group, 2009.
The Kybalion, anonymously authored though generally credited to Atkinson, is a seminal work of spiritual, occult philosophy. Existing in the public domain it has been extensively used by others, most notably by Doreen Virtue.

Blum, Ralph H. *The Book of Runes*. Angus and Robertson, 1984.

Chittick, William C. (edt) *The Inner Journey: Views from the Islamic Tradition*. Morning Light Press, 2007.

Deren, Maya. *Divine Horsemen: The Voodoo Gods of Haiti*. Vanguard Press, 1953.
Deren (1917–1961) was a Ukranian born experimental and avant-garde filmmaker. She first visited Haiti in 1947 after which she became steadily more immersed in Vodou practices and rituals. She shot many hours of documentary film in Haiti, mostly of ritual dance, the work was released posthumously under the same name as her book. *Divine Horsemen* was edited by Joseph Campbell. It remains one of the most authoritative works of Haitian Vodou.

Fortune, Dion. *Applied Magic*. First published Society of Inner Light, 1962. This edition Weiser Books, 2000.
Fortune developed her practice out of the Occultist Meleu of early 19th century London. She was a ceremonial magician and co-founded the occult society, The Fraternity of Inner Light.

Greer, Mary. *Women of the Golden Dawn: Rebels and Priestesses: Maud Gonne, Moina Bergson Mathers, Annie Horniman, Florence Farr*. Park Street Press, 1996.

Helminski, Kabir. *The Knowing Heart: A Path of Sufi Transformation*. Shambhala, 1999.
As well as being a translator of Sufi wisdom, Helminski is a strong advocate of modern Sufism. He is a member of the Mevlevi order of Sufism and together with his wife he directs the Threshold Society.

Pollack, Rachel. *Seventy Eight Degrees of Wisdom: A Book of Tarot*. Element Books, 1993.

Scholem, Gershom. *On the Mystical Shape of the Godhead: Basic Concepts in the Kabbalah*. Schocken Books, 1991.
Scholem (1897–1982), a German-Israeli scholar, is considered the father of modern kabbalistic scholarship.

Telushkan, Joseph. *Rebbe: The Life and Teachings of Menachem M. Schneerson, the Most Influential Rabbi in Modern History*. HarperCollins, 2014.

Psychology and Science

Ackerman, Diane. *A Natural History of the Senses.* Vintage Books, 1991.

Campbell, Joseph. *Myths to Live By.* First published by Viking Press, 1972. This edition Souvenir Press, 1992,
Campbell is notable for pioneering the concept of the literary archetype.

Erikson, Joan M. *Wisdom and the Senses, the Way of Creativity.* Norton and Company, 1988.

Hillman, James. *The Soul's Code: in Search of Character and Calling.* Random House, 1996.
Hillman, James. *Dream Animals.* Chronicle Books, 1997.
Hillman was an American psychologist in the Jungian tradition.

Jaynes, Julian. *The Origin of Consciousness in the Breakdown of the Bicameral Mind.* First published by Houghton Mifflin, 1976. This edition Pelican Books, 1982.
Jaynes' 1976 thesis, radical for its time, was a pioneering and influential work in the development of consciousness studies. Nevertheless, it has been criticized as anthropocentric with a very exclusionary definition of consciousness.

Jung, Carl. *Man and his Symbols.* First published by Doubleday, 1964. This edition Picador, 1978.
Jung (1875–1961) is considered, along with his friend Sigmund Freud, to be one of the founding fathers of psychology and psychoanalysis. Jung is generally considered to be the more mystical of the pair, pioneering concepts such as, synchronicity, the archetype and the collective unconscious. *Man and his Symbols* was Jung's last work, published posthumously.

Kaku, Michio. *Parallel Worlds: A Journey Through Creation, Higher Dimensions, and the Future of the Cosmos.* Penguin, 2005.
Kaku is an American theoretical physicist.

Sheldrake, Rupert. *The Presence of the Past: Morphic Resonance and the Habits of Nature.* First Published by Collins, 1988. This edition Icon Books, 2011.
Sheldrake's Morphic resonance hypothesis is controversial and is not supported by the scientific mainstream. On the other hand, Sheldrake does have academic defenders and certainly nobody has been able to disprove the hypothesis.

Smith, Howard Alan. *Let There Be Light: Modern Cosmology and Kabbalah, a New Conversation Between Science and Religion.* New World Library, 2006.
Smith is an internationally respected astrophysicist, and the author of hundreds of scholarly articles. He is also a practicing Orthodox Jew. While *Let There Be Light* draws parallels between the Kabbalah and modern cosmology, its science is uncontroversial.

Natural History and Nature Writing

Brown, Tom. *Tom Brown's Field Guide: Nature Observation and Tracking.* Berkley, 1983.
Brown is a tracker in the Lipan Apache tradition. He runs the Tom Brown Jr. Tracker School in New Jersey.

Crowe, Andrew. *A Field Guide to the Native Edible Plants of New Zealand.* Penguin, 1981.
This book is recommended reading if you live in New Zealand and wish to get to know the plants in your area better. If you live outside New Zealand you may wish to get an equivalent book for your local environment.

Dawson, Bee. *A History of Gardening in New Zealand.* Godwit Books, 2010.

Deakin, Roger. *Wildwood, A Journey Through Trees.* Penguin Books, 2007.

Dillard, Anni. *Pilgrim at Tinker Creek.* First published by Jonathan Cape, 1975. This edition Picador, 1980.
Dillard makes a strong connection between spirituality and nature observation.

Durrell, Gerald. *The Stationary Ark.* First published by William Collins and Sons Ltd, 1976. This edition Fontana, 1977.

Kinsky, F. C., and C. J. R. Robertson. *The Reed Handbook of Common New Zealand Birds.* 1999.

Jamie, Kathleen. *Sightlines: A Conversation With The Natural World.* Sort of Books, 2012.
Kathleen Jamie is a poet and essayist. *Sightlines* is a collection of essays, brilliantly written and insightful.

Mabey, Richard. *Nature Cure.* Pimlico Publishing, 2006.
A memoir of recovering from depression through rediscovering a love of nature.

Morrison, Crosbie. *Nature Talks to New Zealanders.* Whitcombe & Tombs Ltd, 1961.

Mortimer, John and Bunny. *Trees and their Bark.* Taitua Books, 2004.

Spirn, Anne Whiston. *The Language of Landscape.* Yale University Press, 1998.

Wilson, Hugh. *Stewart Island Plants.* Field Guide Publications, 1982.

Young, Jon. *Coyote's Guide to Connecting with Nature.* 2nd edition, 2010.
Young is a tracker, mentored by Tom Brown, and founder of Eight Shields and Wilderness Awareness School.

Antaeus on Nature. Edited by Daniel Halpern. Collins Harvill, 1989.

The Alphabet of the Trees – A guide to Nature Writing. Edited by Christian McEwen and Mark Statman. Teachers and Writers Collaborative, 2000.

Folk Tales and Mythology

Alpers, Antony. *Maori Myths and Tribal Legends.* Longman Paul, 1964.

Andersen, Hans Christian. *Faery Tales from Hans Anderson.* Dent and Co, (undated)

East of the Sun & West of the Moon, 1914, translated by G. W. Dasent, 1910.

Mosel, Arlene. *The Funny Little Woman.* Longman Young Books, 1973.

O'Faolan, Eileen. *Irish Sagas and Folk Tales.* Oxford University Press, 1954.

Porras, Tomas Herrera. *Cuna Cosmology.* Translated by Anita McAndrews. Three Continents Press, 1978.
At the time of this book's publication the preferred term for this Central American language group was 'Cuna'. This spelling is now obsolete and the preferred usage is 'Guna,' hence the inconsistencies between quoted and unquoted passages in the text.

Werner, Marina. *Stranger Magic: Charmed States and the Arabian Nights.* Chatto and Windus, 2011.
Werner's work is a scholarly analysis of the Arabian Nights.

Art

Busby, John. *Drawing Birds*, 1st ed. Royal Society for the Protection of Birds, 1986.

Edwards, Betty. *Drawing on the Right Side of the Brain*. Fontana/Collins, 1979.

Frost, Seena B. *Soul Collage*. Hanford Mead Publishers, 2001. Frost's book is recommended reading for those wishing to create their own tarot deck through collage.

Gregory, Danny. *The Creative License: Giving Yourself Permission to Be the Artist You Truly Are.* Hachette Books, 2005.
Gregory, Danny, *An Illustrated Life: Drawing Inspiration from the Private Sketchbooks of Artists, Illustrators and Designers.* How Books, 2008.

Hinchman, Hannah. *A Trail Through Leaves: The Journal as a Path to Place*, W. W. Norton & Company, 1997.

New, Jennifer. *Drawing From Life: The Journal as Art*. Princeton Architectural Press, 2005.

Simblet, Sarah. *Botany for the Artist: An Inspirational Guide to Drawing Plants*. DK, 2010.

Philosophy

de Botton, Alain. *The Consolations of Philosophy*. First published Penguin 2000. This edition Penguin, 2008.
de Botton, Alain. *Status Anxiety*. First published by Hamish Hamilton 2004. This edition Penguin, 2005.

Heinberg, Richard. *The End of Growth: Adapting to Our New Economic Reality*. New Society Publishers, 2011.

Schama, Simon. *Landscape and Memory*. Vintage, 1996.

Schopenhauer, Arthur. *The World as Will and Presentation*. First published 1818, this edition translated by Richard E. Aguila, Routledge, 2007.
  Schopenhauer was a notoriously pessimistic German philosopher. His views on the inherent suffering of existence closely reflected Buddhist teachings from which he was probably influenced.

Schweitzer, Albert. *Reverence For Life: The Ethics of Albert Schweitzer*. Editors Marvin Meyer and Kurt Bergel, Syracuse University, 2002.
Schweitzer, a French-German thinker, wrote on a wide range of topics, *Reverence For Life*, has a specifically theological focus.

Taylor, Kylea. *Ethics of Caring: Honoring the Web of Life in Our Professional Healing Relationships*. Hanford Mead Publishers, 1995.
Taylor is a registered psychotherapist. She was a director of the Association for Holotropic Breathwork International.

Woolf, Virginia. *Professions for Women*. Abbreviated version of the speech delivered before a branch of the National Society for Women's Service, January 21, 1931, published posthumously in, *The Death of the Moth and Other Essays*, First published by Hogarth Press, 1942. This edition Penguin Books, 1961.
Woolf, most famous as a novelist, was also a prolific essayist and feminist scholar.

Travel Writing and Biography

Angelou, Maya. *I Know Why the Caged Bird Sings: The Collected Autobiographies of Maya Angelou*. New York: Modern Library, 2004.

Angelou was an American poet, singer and civil rights campaigner. Her autobiographies are more literary than classically autobiographical.

Bell, Gertrude. *A Woman in Arabia: The Writings of the Queen of the Desert*. London: Penguin, 2015.
Bell (1868–1926) was an extraordinary woman. At a time when women had relatively little chance to pursue a career, Bell established herself as successful archaeologist. During World War 1 she worked as an intelligence agent in the middle east and was influential in the creation of British imperial policy and the creation of modern Iraq.

Raine, Kathleen. *William Blake*. Praeger Publications, 1974.

Modern Spiritual Thought

Crombie, R. Ogilvie. *The Gentleman and the Faun*. Findhorn Press, 2009.
Crombie had powerful first hand experience with elementals.

Hawken, Paul. *The Magic of Findhorn*. Souvenir Press, 1975.

Kaushik, Dr R. P. *Towards a New Consciousness*. Darshan Yoga, 1974.
Kaushik, Dr R. P. *Light of Exploration*. Darshan Yoga, 1974.
Kaushik was a lesser known spiritual teacher during a period when eastern spiritual understandings were becoming popular in the west. Most of his thought is original and he had a small following.

Klocek, Dennis. *The Seers Handbook: a Guide to Higher Perception*. Steiner Books, 2004.

O'Sullivan, Natalia. *Ancestral Continuum: Unlocking the Secrets of Who You Really Are*. Simon & Schuster UK Ltd, 2012.

Wright, Machaelle Small. *Behaving As If God in All Things Mattered*. Perelandra Press, 1997.
Wright has written a number of books on flower essences, nature connection and spirituality.

Yogananda, Paramahansa. *Autobiography of a Yogi*. First published Rider and Company, 1950. This edition 1974.

Poetry and Literature

Blake, William.*A Selection of Poems and Letters*. Edited by J Bronowski. Penguin Books, 1958. This edition, 1971.

Goethe, Johann. *Aus Meinem Leben: Dichtung und Wahrheit*. 1833.
Goethe, Johann. *Maximen und Reflexionen*. 1833.

Pullman, Philip. *The Northern Lights*. Scholastic Ltd, 1995.

Rilke, Rainer Maria. *Duino Elegies*, 1923. Translated by Stephen Garmey and Jay Wilson, Harper Colophon Books, 1972.

Remedies and Herbalism

Barnard, Julian. *Bach Flower: Remedies Form and Function*. The Flower Remedy Programme, 2002.

Culpeper, Nicholas. *The Complete Herbal*. First published 1653, W Foulsham & Co Ltd.
Culpeper pioneered modern herbalism and botany, cataloguing thousands of herbs. From a modern point of view one of the more interesting elements of his work is the way in which he blends astrology with herbalism.

de Baïracli Levy, Juliette. *The Complete Herbal*. Faber & Faber Ltd, 1974. This edition 1991.
de Baïracli Levy was more than just a herbalist. She spent years travelling around the world studying plants. She

notably lived for years among nomadic Romani People of Europe, whose traditional knowledge of plants she also transcribed.

Fischer-Rizzi, Susanne. *Medicine of the Earth: Recipes, Remedies, and Cultivation of Healing Plants.* Rudra Press, 1996.

Grieves, Mrs M. *A Modern Herbal*. International London revised edition, Tiger Books, 1973.

Hoffmann, David. *The Holistic Herbal*. Element Books, 1983.

White, Ian. *Bush Flower Essences.* Bantam Books, 1991. This edition Bantam Books, 1998.

Index

the above 34, 38
    see also the upper world
acknowledgement 61, 64, 172
adoption 229
air, element of, 39, 129, 138
Alexander technique 77
allantoin 156
altars 108, 111, 232
alpha state of relaxation 91
alignment 43, 54, 61, 64, 79, 114, 119-20, 126, 168, 190
aloneness 190, 247
ancestors 37, 61, 134, 145, 177, 186, 204-5, 222-33, 241-5
    see also spiritual ancestors
    see also place of the ancestors
ancestral ally 228
ancestral patterning 134,
Angelou, Maya 54, 259
anger, 186, 189
animals 24, 50, 241, 250, 59, 70, 74-5, 80, 103-5, 153, 214
    essence of 101
    human separation from 98-9
    See also power animal
    See also specific species
anterior commissure 129
anxiety 50, 117, 137, 187
archetypes 109, 140, 188, 233, 256
art 77, 212, 229, 238
auditory hallucinations 129
Aurelius, Marcus 43, 253

auric fields 125, 145, 251
Australia 79, 156, 224, 243
Australian Aboriginal people 249
authenticity 50, 114
awe 81, 209, 239, 241, 215
Bach, Edward 249, 251
Bach Flowers, 249
bees 186, 211
belief 24, 119-20, 162, 175, 186-7, 190, 239
belief systems 119, 175, 190
Bell, Gertrude 24, 259
beings 64, 91, 160, 170, 209, 211, 228, 237
    See also earth beings
the below 34, 38
    See also the underworld
Bighorn Medicine Wheel 40
birds 34, 43, 59, 64, 74-5, 102, 211. 214, 237
birth 190, 212, 227
bittercress 181, 252
black cats 150
Blake, William 101, 161
blame 186-8
blockages 60, 65, 230
blueprint 43, 170, 173, 200
body dreaming 144-5
Boscawen-Un Circle 40
boxthorn 68, 78
the brain 129

breathing, 84, 91
brokenness 190
Brown, Joseph Epes 91, 253
bumble bees 198
burdens 190
burial grounds 68
    See also urupa
Busby, John 74
Campbell, Joseph 255, 256
cardinal directions 40, 188
    See also north, south, east, west
Castaneda, Carlos 187, 253
chakras 87, 138
chickweed 86-7
childhood 30, 109, 225, 233, 245
the centre 34, 38, 42, 54, 210, 232
cicadas 34, 51, 82
cleansing. *See* clearing
clearing 60, 110, 119, 125, 134-40
cleavers 120, 124-6, 138, 251
cloak-of-energy-from-other-lifetimes 190
Coastlands 67
the co-creative circle 47-55, 108, 232
co-creatively 29, 50
colonisation 30, 68, 225, 231, 253
Coleridge, Samuel, 90, 148
comfrey 156-7, 252
community 28, 50-4, 68, 78, 14, 117-8, 163, 184-

261

5, 209, 212, 231-2
compulsion to serve 114-5
Cowan, Tom 90
the creator 38, 49, 204
crisis 119
Crombie, Robert 169, 259
Crow Nation 41
crystals 80, 153, 244
Culpepper, Nicholas 86, 157,124, 198, 200
cultural conditioning 51, 177
cultural patterning 50, 116
cults 29
curiosity, 54, 74-5, 125, 153, 168, 238
Dagara people 53
Davis, Wade 25, 254
daemon. *See* gift
dandelion 129, 198-201, 209, 211, 251-2
death 37, 87, 131, 190, 200, 212, 225
deathing 37, 87, 131, 190, 200, 212, 225
dedication 22-3, 61, 187
depression 65, 219
deer 77, 98
denial 19, 69
Deren, Maya 236, 255
the destroyer 49
discomfort 25, 68-9, 78-9, 118, 138, 205, 244
disharmony 61, 40
discipline 22, 37-8, 117, 168, 174, 181, 184, 187, 213
the divine 37-8, 49, 125, 149
divine energy 193
divining 68
domination 68, 168, 189
dream body 145
dreams 24, 149-51, 164
dream world 37, 68, 91-2, 96-8, 164, 176, 229, 245

druids 92, 108, 206
drumming 91
Durer, Albrecht 126
Durrell, Gerald 75, 103
the earth 59, 61, 63, 81, 92, 96, 116, 126, 138, 198-9, 205, 209-12, 228, 246
    as a planet 39, 53, 69, 80-1, 175, 200, 239
    etheric body of 65
    as element, 138, 198-9
    going into 42, 97
    talking to 213
earth beings 209-10
earth energies 209
earth lines 70, 210
east 34-45, 82, 168, 188, 190
elders 40, 53, 205
    circle of 245
eldership 231
elementals 64, 134, 259
elements 61, 63, 70, 139-40, 170, 225, 247, 250
    See also individual elements
empathy 29
emotional imprinting 64
emotions 60, 63, 68, 70, 117, 134, 136-7, 140, 150, 157, 188, 190
    See also specific emotions
the energy beyond thought 38, 44, 120, 178
energy centres 65
energy fields 144
energy healing 19, 69
    See also body dreaming
    See also clearing
energy lines 65, 173, 209
    See also earth lines
the energy plane 64
entities 108, 134-6, 138, 206, 208
environmental despair 69

environmental destruction 59, 64-9
equinox 39, 111, 213
essence
    divine 38, 109,173, 246
    of animals 38, 101-3, 105
    of land 59, 60, 63-4, 225
    of people 53, 229
    of plants 131, 181, 192, 199, 219
    See also remedy
ethics 28-31, 145
etheric world 61, 189
    See also dream world
etheric pathways 64
etheric body of the earth 59, 65
etheric body of water, 67
ethnic group 222, 225, 242-3
ethnicity. *See* ethnic group
Evenki languages 92
everyday world. *See* ordinary world
fairy-boy of Leith 90
faith 49, 239
family 28, 51, 55, 61, 78, 92, 114, 118, 137, 170, 209, 224-5, 229-31, 245
farming 67-8
fear 22, 29, 49, 78-9, 91, 116, 118-9, 131, 135, 137, 140, 152, 163, 175, 184, 187-9, 205, 208-9, 245, 251
Feldenkrais 77
the ferment 187
the fighter 188
Finn McCool 206
flicking-out 118
food 48, 86, 109-10, 116, 225, 245
forests 49, 67, 69, 77, 82, 152-3, 170, 224-5
form 37-8, 44, 101, 117, 134, 173
gallbladder 199
gateways 37, 63, 223, 249
gatha 84
gardens 39, 63, 86, 115, 156-7, 162, 164, 181, 198, 212, 215, 219, 251

gender roles 50
genealogy. 222
   See also whakapapa
Germany 78, 150, 226, 242, 249
gesture 19, 35, 51, 63, 79, 86-7, 101, 119,
   131, 156-7, 174, 181, 251
ghosts 101, 134
gift 18, 53, 114, 118, 174, 200-1
giraffes 105
Goethe, Johann 53, 148
God 18, 149, 173, 247
gods and goddesses 109, 115
grace 58, 70, 105, 157, 184, 232, 252
gratitude 34, 44-5, 79-81, 126, 187, 233
Great Spirit 128
greed 76, 116, 128, 186
greeting 58, 64, 79
grief 69, 87, 190, 251, 108
grounding 199
guardian of the land. *See* spirit guardian
guardianship 19, 59, 61, 76, 99
Guna people 115-6, 257
gurus 18
hallucination 129, 188
hallucinogenic drugs 93
harmony 28, 37, 39, 50, 61, 75, 139
hazards 78-9, 84
heart 18, 28,54, 61, 63, 87, 91-2, 104, 108, 121, 126,
   145, 174, 181,191, 213, 332-3, 251-2
   disconnection from 137, 186
   lightness of 120
   pain in 131
heart-mind 191
healing 19, 51, 119, 126, 136,144-5, 150, 157, 199 229, 232-3, 251
   See also body dreaming
   See also clearing
   See also land healing
the heavens 40, 43, 160, 170
   See also upper world
heirlooms 230
Helminski, Kabir 28
Hercules 98
Hillman, James 98, 256
history 30, 37, 67, 70, 80, 98, 103, 186, 204, 227, 231, 243
Horohoro Forest 69
house clearing 125, 134, 252
humans
   impact on environment 58-9, 64-5, 68, 76,, 98-9
   origin of 241
humility 37, 50, 98, 188, 229
illnesses 82, 134, 140, 144, 233, 251
illusion 39, 58, 93, 110, 188-9, 191, 212
imaginal mind 34, 93, 144
imagination 61, 74, 90-1, 138, 148, 152, 237, 241
imaginative journeying. *See* shamanic journeying
imprint 41, 59, 61, 64, 157, 225, 230, 243
in-between directions 34, 37, 42
indigenous peoples 18, 30, 34, 41, 54, 138, 253-5
   See also specific tribal groups
individuality 49, 98, 200
initiation 51, 190
insects 75, 80, 212
inspiration 74, 149, 187-8, 236
the intellect 90
intention 23, 49, 60-1, 64, 68, 70, 91, 97, 108, 111, 125, 131, 138-9, 160, 185, 204, 228, 230
intrinsic value 48, 50
invocation 44, 48-9, 108, 125
Islam 28, 109, 238
Jaynes, Julian 129, 256
journaling 24-5, 30, 42, 70, 75, 91, 93, 105, 121, 140, 169, 210, 227, 230
journeying. *See* shamanic journeying
joy 174, 199, 210, 219
judgement 50, 137-8, 157, 187, 242, 252
the Kabbalah 173, 255-6
the Kaipara Harbour 69, 224
kaitiaki 76, 170
   See also guardianship
Kaku, Michio 238, 256
Kalahari Bushmen 186
kanuka 58, 67, 82, 238, 249
kapuka tree 150
karakia 170, 236
kidneys 119, 145, 199, 244
Kaushik, R P 131, 178, 259
kingfishers 23, 58, 101
kinship 39, 70, 80, 96, 98-9, 104
knowledge 19, 37, 39, 78-9, 92 150, 168-9, 172-6, 188, 206, 223
Koyukon people 98
the Kybalion 255
land healing 58-71, 125, 209, 252
Laguna Pueblo people 253
Lasavia Remedies 249-52
   See also Wild Weed Collection
latihan 149
leadership 18, 54
letting go 45, 125, 131, 225
Levy, Juliette de Baïracli 156, 259
leylines. *See* earth lines
lighting a candle 23, 48, 108, 110-1, 138, 232

lightness of heart 118
lineage 184, 224, 228-9, 231, 239, 241, 243
   See also whakapapa
listening 29, 34, 37, 59, 64, 68, 91, 129
liver 199, 244
love 22, 37, 76, 105, 131, 186, 229
lower world. *See* underworld
lymphatic system 138
magic 48, 64, 109, 209
mana 38, 49, 188, 230, 232, 243
manifestation 61, 101, 111, 172
Māori people 30, 36, 76, 110, 61, 101, 111, 172, 225, 227, 243
Maori Marsden 172, 254
marijuana 92
master guardian 101
massage 139
Maui 174
mauri 38, 171
medicine sphere 34-45, 48, 53, 64, 139, 160, 168, 188, 190, 205, 232
medicine wheels 30, 34, 41, 44-5, 108, 164
meditation
   general 169, 233, 234
   moving 149
   observational 179
   sensory 77, 92, 199
   standing 192
   walking 84
Medlock River 224
memory 114, 152, 157, 218, 225, 244, 252
merging 92, 137, 140, 192, 205, 225
meridian lines 65, 173
metanoia 190
middle world 39- 184-5
mind 45, 91, 96, 99, 114, 134, 168-9, 174, 188, 191, 247, 251
minerals 42, 51, 59, 74, 80, 86, 116, 129, 157, 214, 249-50
the moon 24, 38, 41, 43, 65, 75, 81-2, 84, 86, 204, 208, 214, 236, 239
morality 28, 187
morepork. *See* ruru
morphic resonance 244, 256
mountains 35, 43, 63, 204, 214, 225, 228, 236
the mystery 44
myths 115, 148, 205-6, 222, 236, 257
mudras 138, 173-4
nature 18, 24, 44-5, 48, 69, 74, 83, 92, 98, 111, 152, 222, 34, 237, 241, 256-7
nervousness 111
noa 110
nomadic peoples 226, 260
north 34-45, 58, 168, 188-90, 205
nourishment 34, 37, 80-1, 86-7, 99, 111, 115-7, 199, 232, 251
observation 23-4, 51, 59, 63-4, 68, 74-5, 118, 140, 144-5, 160, 172, 178, 189, 213, 237
   See also sensory meditation
obsidian 63, 210
objects 23, 59, 61, 110-1, 134, 138, 148, 151, 230-2, 245
the ocean 45, 45, 64-5, 70, 78, 80-2, 136, 200, 224-5, 239
Oldham 224
ordinariness 93, 110
the ordinary 19, 22, 37, 41, 48, 110, 119, 212
open form improvisation 98
Opihi 226
Osorio, Jonathan Kay Kamakawiwo'ole 204, 243, 251
overwhelm 23, 65, 67, 111, 137, 206
Ovid 236-7
owl eyes 74
oysters 76
pain 29, 64, 69, 131, 185, 187-9, 232
paper wasp 51
Paracelsus 249
peripheral vision 77
personal medicine. *See* gift
personality 24, 53, 68, 173, 176, 251
petty tyrants 187-9
physical world. 39, 41, 43,-4, 64, 91, 116, 140, 172, 174
   See also ordinary world
pineal gland 61, 65
pipe ceremony 108, 210, 225
Piripai 67-8, 78, 225, 249
pituitary gland 65
place names 227
place of complete darkness 211
place of the ancestors 204, 228
places of learning 164
plant spirit medicine, 18, 51, 131, 169, 229
   See also wild weed collection
plants 24, 34, 40, 50-1, 59, 68, 70, 74-5, 78-81, 86-7, 124, 129, 131, 153, 156-7, 162, 168, 181, 198-9, 210, 212, 218-9, 226, 249-52, 259-60
   See also specific species
Plato 53
postural muscles 192
posture 35, 77, 105, 185, 192
pounamu 210
power
   illusion of 58, 110
   misuse of 29, 186-7
   of animals 101
   of manifestation 61

of nature 68, 80, 192
of spirit beings 164, 205
of symbols 150
of words 54
personal 37, 41, 49, 91, 111, 120, 137, 163, 174, 188-9
power animal 92, 96-105, 144-5, 160, 185, 204-5, 228
power place 70, 228, 230
power source 98, 114
power with 49-50
prayer 35, 48-9, 79-81, 103, 109, 125-6, 128, 134, 138, 187, 204, 213, 215, 223, 232, 243
prayer of gratitude 79-81, 187
praying mantis 36
presence of action 193
procrastination 181, 252
projection 50, 68, 114, 120, 136, 140, 186-7, 188, 243
protocol 58-9, 145, 209, 228
psychotherapy 136
puha 150
qi 126
racism 242
rakau. *See* talking stick
reactions 29
receiving 49, 108, 116, 145, 150, 232-3
See also revelatory receiving
Reischek, Andrea 230-1, 254
relationships 22, 28, 42, 116, 137, 145, 157, 170, 184, 188
revelatory receiving 149
Rehua 172
reflection 24-5, 28-30, 34-5, 41-2, 50, 59, 64, 93, 114, 124, 150, 188
relaxation 91, 111, 199, 252
rigidity 108, 181
righteousness 28

Rilke, Rainer Maria 148
Ring of Andvari 148
rituals 19, 23, 37, 41, 53, 61, 108-11, 136, 138-9, 172, 177, 189, 232, 255
rivers 63-4, 67-8, 70, 78, 136, 184, 224-6, 228, 241
the rope of mankind 241
ruru 34, 131
the sacred 19, 22, 40, 54, 110
See also tapu
sacred places 48, 111, 226-7
sacred work 45, 110
the sacrum 61
samurai 194-5
sand dunes 67, 198, 225-6, 249
Saturn 157
saunas 136, 139
scapegoating 140
Schopenhauer, Arthur 175, 258
Schweitzer, Albert 28, 258
scotch thistle 218-9, 251-2
Scotland 90, 218
seeds 37, 86, 124, 129, 168, 181, 198-201, 211-2, 218, 247
seeing with the heart 76
the seer 208
self-esteem 50-87
self-importance 152, 184, 187-9
senses 45, 51, 74, 90, 92, 96, 105, 129, 144, 191
sensory body 63, 90
sensory meditation. *See* meditation
separation 44, 69, 98, 137
service 19, 35, 45, 64, 79, 109, 187, 204
skeletal system 144
sketching 74, 105

shadows 25, 29, 37,-8, 44, 51, 93, 109, 118, 131, 140, 163, 173, 189-90, 209, 243
the shadow magician 188
shadow projection 136, 140
the shaman 37-8, 92, 176
shamanic journeying 30, 40, 90-3, 98, 148, 150, 169, 224, 229-30
to death and the unknown 190
to find ancestral ally 228
to find our spiritual ancestors 204-5
to find power animal 96-7
to find spiritual teacher 160-1
to find warrior spirit guide 185
to find wise one 205
to places of learning 164
to the circle of elders 245
to the underworld 208-11
shamanism 18, 92
shame 118-9, 128, 187, 211, 229-30, 232, 242
sharing 54, 93, 145, 148, 150, 188, 205, 225, 232, 243
shields 185
Sheldrake, Rupert 244, 256
shock 67, 126, 135, 199, 252
skin 51, 77, 86, 125, 140, 145, 156, 211, 245, 250
singing 48, 64, 126, 138, 184, 213
slothfulness 181, 252
smell 34, 51, 59, 74, 77, 126, 212
smudging 138
socialization. *See* cultural conditioning
society 50, 69, 99, 115, 117-18, 186
solstices 39, 11, 213
Somè, Sobonfu, 50, 53, 223, 254
song lines. *See* earth lines

the soul 53, 148, 204, 223, 251
soul loss 140
soul retrieval 19, 199, 252
sounding 64, 126
south 34-45, 188-90, 205
spirals 35, 43
spirit, element of, 22, 37, 44, 49, 140, 176
spirit that moves through all things 44, 48
spirit guardians 64, 80
spirit world 19, 92
    See also dream world
spirits 49, 61, 91, 108, 223, 232
    See also entities
spiritual ancestors 204-5
spiritual teacher 156, 160-3
stagnation 65
standing meditation. *See* meditation
stars 34-5, 38, 43, 65, 81, 86, 214, 237, 239
stinging nettles 78-9
stoicism 253
stone circle. *See* medicine wheel
stones 34-5, 42, 45, 80, 138, 150, 152, 170, 211, 214
the subconscious 38, 116, 157
Subud 149
Sufism 28, 255
Sumohadiwidjojo, Muhammad 149
the sun 34, 38-40, 43, 81, 156, 174, 188, 198-200, 209, 211-13, 236-7, 239, 249-50
superstitions 150
surrender 34, 38, 44, 131, 149, 190-1, 193
sustained focus without will 144
symbolic language 148-153
symbols 35, 59, 111, 140, 145, 148-53, 160, 168, 185, 205, 211, 229

symbolism
    of a dandelion flower 200
    of a ring 148
    of a shell 54
    of a spiral 43
    of a wasp 51
    of an owl 131
    of the co-creative circle 48
    of power animals 98
    of turquoise 150
    of shoes 153
synchronicity, 41, 69, 256
Tagore, Rabindranath 46
Tainui 152
talismans 245
talking stick 54. 232
talking to the earth 213
Tane 170-2
taniwha 64
taste 51, 59, 61, 74, 75-7, 86, 90, 124, 157, 198, 251
Tawhirimatea 170
tapu 38, 110, 134, 172, 226
    See also the sacred
tarot 119, 153, 176
te kore 38
theology 92, 255
the third eye 61, 65
the Three Baskets of Knowledge 170-2
the three wisdoms 173-4
tohunga 92, 252
toroa 76
touch 34, 77, 126, 149, 168
transformation 37, 70, 119, 131, 187, 189
trauma 22, 49, 118, 134-5, 140, 224, 233, 243
trees 23, 59, 67, 78, 153, 160, 179, 192, 204, 226, 256-7

apple 179
cabbage 153
coprosma 131
ginko
hazel 206
kaikawaka 152
kapuka 152
macrocarpa 68
oak 224, 244
puriri, 58
totara 49
willow 114
trust 22, 37, 49, 92, 116, 143, 163, 168, 173, 181, 205, 210, 228
truth 28, 118, 163, 168, 174, 184, 191, 209, 226
the underworld 42, 92, 208-10
the universe 35, 38, 42, 48, 50, 90, 126-7, 239, 244
the upper world 40, 160, 164, 228
urupa 225-6, 230
Van der Post, Laurens 186, 255
vibrational memory 225
Virgil 208
visioning. *See* shamanic journeying
visions 24, 37, 61,65, 68,90-1, 93, 97, 149, 151, 173, 219, 225, 230,
the void 38, 190
vodou 236, 255
voodoo. *See* vodou
vulnerability 29, 168, 188, 191
Waiheke Island 69, 75, 149, 249
walking 22, 44, 75, 77, 82-4, 121, 152-3, 224
warrior spirit guide 184-95
warriorship 187, 190
water
    as an element 81, 116, 139
    as part of landscape 75, 78, 186, 210-1, 225

    energy of 131, 176, 224

    memory of 67

    use in clearing 45, 108, 111, 134, 138-9, 179

waterways 58-9, 70, 81

weka 102

west 34-45, 82, 149, 188-9

whakapapa 222

Whakatane 67, 134, 227

whales 65, 74, 144

white sage 138

whenua 135

the whole 28, 38, 43, 59, 76, 78, 212

the will 39, 49, 184, 188, 190, 193, 233

wild pigs 78-9

Wild Weed Collection 19, 86-7, 124-31, 156-7, 183, 198-200, 218-9

wisdom 18, 34, 37-8, 49, 54, 99, 148, 163, 168, 175, 205-6, 223-4, 230, 241

the Wise Jew and the Three Rings 148

the Wise One 205

Woolf, Virginia 48, 114-5, 258

Wordsworth, Dorothy and William 82

wounds 29, 50, 59, 69, 119, 188, 219, 237-8

zoos 103-5

www.ingramcontent.com/pod-product-compliance
Lightning Source LLC
Chambersburg PA
CBHW061153010526
44118CB00027B/2954